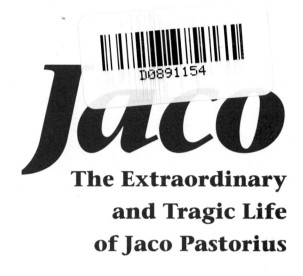

Jaco

The Extraordinary
and Tragic Life
of Jaco Pastorius

"The World's Greatest Bass Player"

BY BILL MILKOWSKI

Miller
Freeman
Books

San Francisco

Published by Miller Freeman Books
600 Harrison Street, San Francisco, CA 94107
Publishers of GPI Books, *Bass Player,* and *Guitar Player* magazines
A member of the United Newspapers Group

Distributed to the book trade in the U.S. and Canada by
Publishers Group West, P.O. Box 8843, Emeryville, CA 94662

Distributed to the music trade in the U.S. and Canada by
Hal Leonard Publishing, P.O. Box 13819, Milwaukee, WI 53213

Library of Congress Cataloging in Publication Data
Milkowski, Bill, 1954-
    Jaco : the extraordinary and tragic life of Jaco Pastorius, "the world's
greatest bass player" / Bill Milkowski
        p.   cm.
    Discography: p.
    ISBN 0-87930-426-X (paperback)
    1. Pastorius, Jaco. 2. Jazz musicians—United States—Biography.
I. Title.
ML419.P43M55   1995
787.5'092—dc20
[B]   95-13947

Editor: Jim Roberts
Cover Design: Deborah Chusid
Cover Photograph: © Norman Seeff

Printed in the United States of America
    98 99 00   7 6 5 4 3 2

CONTENTS

Dedicated to my daughter
Sophia Vincenza Milkowski
(born April 1, 1995)

ACKNOWLEDGMENTS

Everybody in the music business and on the scene has a Jaco story. I tried to collect as many of them as I could during the years of my work on this book while adding in a few of my own. I am grateful for the cooperation of the Jaco Pastorius estate and would like to extend a special thanks to Jaco's parents, Stephanie and Jack Pastorius, as well as his two younger brothers, Gregory and Rory Pastorius, and his oldest son, John Pastorius.

Thanks to Jim Roberts of *Bass Player* magazine for a keen eye in editing this book. Other people whose input was invaluable on this project: Bob Bobbing, Charlie Brent, Peter Erskine, Delmar Brown, Kenwood Dennard, Alex Foster, Don Alias, Michael Brecker, Joe Zawinul, Mark Egan, Ricky Schultz, Ricky Sebastian, Peter Yianilos, Mike and Leni Stern, John Scofield, Miles Evans, Hiram Bullock, Billy Burke, Allyn Robinson, Bobby Economou, Bobby Colomby, Ira Sullivan, Paul Bley, James Cannings, Melton Mustafa, Scott Kirkpatrick, Geri Palladino, Kevin Kaufman, Bob Mintzer, Othello Molineaux, Bob Moses, Jeff Andrews, Charles Norkus, Randy Bernsen, Brian Melvin, Neil Weiss, Dave Bargeron, and Gil Goldstein.

I would also like to acknowledge the help and encouragement along the way of Matt Resnicoff, Jean-Jacques Magalas, Christine Martin, Lee Mergner, Donna Russo, Michael Bloom, Laszlo Gardony, Big Ed Maguire, Jedi, Lenny Charles, David Dunton, Will Lee, Marcus Miller, Victor Bailey, Jeff Berlin, Joe Ferry, Mike Kermisch and Mark Tessier, Tom Moon, Neil Tesser, Matt Pierson, Marvin Williams, Garland Hogan, Keiko Yuasa, Koichi Sakaue, Koichiro Kuno, Albert Elegino, Yuko Denbo, Izumi Sato, Aldo Mauro, Mark Levine, Ebet Roberts, and Don Hunstein.

And a special thanks to Angela "The Mommy" Bartolone for her stubborn persistence and helpful feedback throughout this project.

"He who is a legend in his own time is ruled by that legend. It may begin in absolute innocence but to cover up flaws and maintain the myth of Divine Power, one has to employ desperate measures."

—Arthur Rimbaud

"The more famous you are, the more fearful you get of falling off the pedestal, letting people down."

—Marilyn Monroe

Foreword

I THINK OF JACO A LOT TODAY, especially in my teaching of music. I come across students who play well and have good taste, who have good time and know the language—but somehow it's not *flying*.

I have a body of study devoted to students who fall into that category, and I have a name for this syndrome: I call it "id lock." A lot of the problem is that the emotional center, the id, is locked for these people. They know music but they're not screaming it from their heart, as Jaco did. He did not suffer from id lock at all. His id was wide open. He was fearless. And fear is really the biggest enemy of creativity.

I'll tell you a story about this cat. I used to live in upstate New York, and my house was in a valley between two mountain ranges. The woods dropped down to a stream that was fed by two waterfalls that came off the mountains. The approach to the stream sloped down about 15 feet to the water, and it was rocky all the way down. You could slip and trip on the rocks, so people would walk down there slowly and even use their hands to make sure they didn't fall. The stream itself was icy cold. In the springtime, after the snow melted, it could be up to your chest at the deepest part, but in other places it was only a foot or two deep, so you couldn't really swim in it.

I took Jaco to this place. And when he got to the spot where he spied the stream, he just went nuts. "Oh, man! A mountain stream! I love this, man! This is the greatest!"

He was standing at the edge, which was about 15 feet from the stream but not directly above it, because the ridge sloped away from the water. In one motion, he just ripped off all of his clothes and jumped off the ledge. He didn't know how deep the water was. The water was maybe three feet deep, Jaco was about 15 feet up— and it was all rocks on the bottom. He was already in the air as I was yelling, "*Jaco! Nooooooooooo!*" And he was halfway down by the time I got "no" out.

It flashed in my mind that in a split second I was going to see him die in front of me. And I felt all this sadness. But he made a miraculous move—as soon as his body hit the water, he kind of *glided*. He somehow managed to turn all of that downward energy into forward energy. And Jaco was big. But somehow he straightened out, and he came up laughing, screaming hysterically. I'd never seen anything like that. Nobody got into the stream that way; everybody would put in one toe and gradually sit down, trying not to trip on the rocks. But this guy was like Tarzan or Indiana Jones. It was like a movie stunt. I saw it, and I still don't believe it.

Jaco was just fearless. His id was wide open, and he experienced life on that level on a daily basis. To me, he was just the highest cat to be around.

—*Bob Moses*

Jaco: Man and Myth

*"My name is John Francis Pastorius III
and I'm the greatest electric bass player in the world."*

THE LIFE AND MUSIC of Jaco Pastorius are legendary. A potent force in modern American music, he has been
hailed as a genius and dismissed as a madman. Of course, there is a
fine line between artistry and autism, as the eminent Swiss psychol-
ogist Carl Gustav Jung once theorized—and in Jaco's case, the
tightrope he walked was tenuous at best.

Like his heroes Charlie Parker, Jimi Hendrix, and Jesus Christ, Jaco
didn't make it to 40. Yet, in the relatively short time he spent on the
planet, he totally revolutionized his instrument and left behind an
incredibly rich body of work that will stand the test of time. In jazz
schools and music conservatories all over the world, his name is spoken by students in the same reverential tones reserved for such gods
as Bird and Mozart. As one aspiring bassist put it, "Jaco opened the
door and we walked through."

In New York, they still talk about his legendary gigs, his marathon
hangs, his outrageous antics onstage and off. Stop in some night at
the Village Vanguard, the Blue Note, Sweet Basil, the Lone Star—all
showcase clubs where Jaco headlined in his heyday. Or drop in at
any of the marginal joints he played during his dark years. Talk to
the clubowner, the doorman, a bartender, or any of the regulars on

1

the scene. Talk to musicians or their managers or the employees in record stores around town. Talk to jazz critics from the daily papers or correspondents from *Down Beat, Musician,* or *Billboard.* Talk to the homeless cats panhandling outside the clubs or hanging on the West Fourth Street basketball courts. Everybody, it seems, has a tale to tell. It's all become part of the ever-growing body of folklore that fuels the Jaco myth and goes hand-in-hand with his musical legacy.

Jaco was to the electric bass what Paul Bunyan was to the lumber industry, what Muhammed Ali was to boxing. Like Babe Ruth and Jimi Hendrix, like Charlie Parker and John Belushi, he was a larger-than-life figure who lived to excess and was worshipped by multitudes. Throughout the international music community, those two syllables—Jaco—still resound with authority, a testament to his musical genius and the power of his charisma.

The rise and fall of Jaco Pastorius, the self-proclaimed "World's Greatest Bass Player," is not just a tragic tale of genius gone awry. It is also an indictment of a callous, uncaring industry that often turns its back on those who helped to build it. It is an indictment of a musicians' union that buries its head in the sand, ignoring its own. And it is an indictment of a political system that offers no safety net of health care for those who need it most.

Jaco rode fame like a skyrocket to oblivion. His rise to the top with Weather Report, the premier fusion band of the '70s, was followed by a tragic fall from grace in the mid-'80s that left him spiritually broken, physically beaten, homeless, penniless, and hopelessly out of touch with reality. In the end, his bizarre behavior on the streets of Greenwich Village and Fort Lauderdale was a cry for help, an expression of his inner torment. He was raging out of control, and there was no support system, no network of agencies that could counsel him or offer aid. Even his own family and friends were powerless to change Jaco's perception of his condition or the world around him.

"He had people in awe of him trying to help," said Bobby

Colomby, the drummer and A&R man who "discovered" Jaco and produced his stunning self-titled debut album in 1976. "But something in his psyche, something inside of him, wouldn't let him be happy. This man was suffering from a mental illness, and his refusal to be helped was just another manifestation of that illness. We do not have a system in this country that deals with this very well. Unfortunately, in our society, if a guy sneezes or coughs, he's got a cold and we all feel bad for him. We relate to it. If a guy has a tumor, we sympathize. But if a guy has a mental illness, he's a 'nut case.' We don't respond well to that. We don't fully understand that it's an illness. And that leads to tragic results."

In the end, "The World's Greatest Bass Player" began to express a macabre death wish. He'd drink himself into a stupor and fall asleep on the railroad tracks. He'd walk into a bar and pick a fight with the largest, meanest-looking dude in the joint, and then stand at attention with his arms at his side and let the guy wail on him. It was as if he were searching for his own executioner. And eventually he found him in the person of a 25-year-old nightclub bouncer trained in the martial arts, a brute who had no idea who Jaco was, what he had created in his lifetime, or what his music meant to thousands of fans all over the world.

By the summer of 1986, Jaco had burned nearly all of his bridges. Plagued by wild mood swings and the emotional difficulties brought on by manic depression, a condition only exacerbated by alcohol, he drove fellow musicians from his inner circle. They simply found it too exhausting and heartbreaking to hang with him. Word of Jaco's erratic and unpredictable behavior on the streets reached the industry's movers and shakers, who came to regard him as poison. And nothing, it seemed, could slow Jaco's downward spiral. As drummer Peter Erskine so harshly but accurately put it, "It's tough when a guy sets out to join the ranks of the jazz legends who completely fucked up their lives."

Once a giant in the industry and the talk of the jazz world, Jaco had been reduced to *persona non grata*, a bum panhandling on the streets of New York City for beer money. Banned from most of the nightclubs around town—just as Charlie Parker and Bud Powell had been in the twilight of their careers—he often pawned his bass. His closest companions were the hustlers and street types who congregated at the West Fourth Street basketball courts and in Washington Square Park. He seemed to have what Graham Greene once called a "Cophetua complex": an emotional need for low-class people.

For every old friend who offered Jaco a helping hand to lift him out of his doldrums, there was one who turned his back on him. Some would sidestep him when they spied him disheveled and red-eyed, begging for money on the street. Others would simply avoid eye contact in the cold-blooded manner that has become second nature to New Yorkers. As one colleague admitted, "It was just too painful to have to stare that shit in the face. And besides, I'd done my share of baby-sitting."

What caused this deterioration? How could a brilliant artist, a loving father, a loyal friend, a spiritual person, turn into such a deranged denizen of the streets? The long answer is as complex as the human brain itself. The short answer is simple: drugs, alcohol, and fast living—the same catalysts that hastened the deaths of such other geniuses as Charlie Parker, Charlie Christian, Jimi Hendrix, and Billie Holiday.

But dig beneath the surface, get beyond the stereotypes, and you'll discover a myriad of reasons for Jaco's downfall: unresolved anger about his parents' early breakup, guilt about his own failed marriages, and the sadness of being estranged from his children—all coupled with an innate need to pay penance for those "sins."

He also felt the constant pressure of maintaining his self-declared status as "The World's Greatest Bassist" and had a deep-seated fear of running out of new ideas. He harbored a lot of inner rage toward the hordes of "Jaco clones" who latched onto his technique, copped his personal voice, and got gigs at a time when record-company executives and clubowners were turning their backs on him. (But as Jaco would say, with a tone of righteous indignation, "I know what I invented.") He had problems with alcohol and cocaine, but the heaviest cross to bear was his illness, a manic-depressive condition coupled with a chemical imbalance in his brain that caused him to involuntarily flare up and lose control.

It was probably inevitable that Jaco would meet a violent end. Those close to him had seen the signs for years. They had witnessed his gradual decline from the glory days with Weather Report to a sad state of homelessness on the streets of New York. They had seen him panhandling, sleeping on park benches, stalking around the streets

of Greenwich Village dazed and confused, muttering incoherently and confronting pedestrians with bizarre, provocative behavior.

Those who didn't witness it first-hand heard all the unsettling gossip through the grapevine. Every week there was some new horror story, some tale of Jaco showing up drunk for a gig with warpaint on his face or mud splattered across his body, falling off a balcony in Italy, riding naked through Tokyo on a motorcycle, hurling his bass into the sea, trashing a stage, getting his teeth knocked out in some ugly barroom brawl. And the whispering spread like wildfire from one musical community to the next, helping to fuel the Jaco myth.

"Unfortunately, whenever you heard about Jaco, it was always in connection to some bizarre thing he had done," says Victor Bailey, the bassist who replaced Pastorius in the Weather Report lineup in

1982. "And it seemed like people just delighted in telling these Jaco stories. They would come up to you with big smiles on their faces and say, 'Did you hear what Jaco did?' But I think those people were ignoring the fact that he was sick and needed help."

Drummer Brian Melvin lived with Jaco for four months at the end of 1986, a particularly dark period in Jaco's life. "Everyone was saying that Jaco was crazy," remembers Melvin. "They would talk about how he shaved his eyebrows and walked naked down the street, how he did this and that. His reputation was that he was capable of doing anything at any time. That became the norm for Jaco. The people around him helped to create this reputation through all their gossip, but I think he perpetuated it himself. After a while, he had this 'bad boy of jazz' image that he had to live up to."

Guitarist Pat Metheny believes that Jaco ultimately got caught up in his own myth. At one point during my 1984 interview with Metheny, we found ourselves trading Jaco gossip. Suddenly, Pat stopped the conversation and said, "See, this is exactly what Jaco loves. He gets off on the idea that people are sitting around talking about him all the time. And that's part of his problem."

Many fans outside of New York were naïvely unaware of Jaco's painful final years. And when the sad details finally became known, they could only shake their heads in disbelief and wonder: "How could this terrible thing have happened to someone so gifted, so famous?"

How indeed. In 1978, at the age of 27, Jaco was sitting on top of the world, riding the crest of his international notoriety. As Peter Erskine put it, "At one point, he was like *the* biggest thing in the music business, like the Michael Jackson of jazz or something. He made such an incredible impression. For a creative instrumental musician to have that kind of impact is really unheard of. Here was someone who had what seemed to be the most unbelievable potential. He really had the world by the tail."

With his large hands, long fingers, and double-jointed thumbs,

Jaco seemed to be born to play the bass guitar. In his prime, he had the speed and dexterity to create solos that matched the explosive genius of Dizzy Gillespie and Charlie Parker. His revolutionary approach to the instrument—playing melodies, chords, harmonics, and percussive effects all at once—was wholly unprecedented. And his theatrical stage presence—doing flips off his amplifier, throwing his bass up in the air and then whipping it savagely with his strap—was a direct nod to the rock performance ethic.

For me and for thousands of other fans around the world, Jaco was a beacon, an educator, a great unifier who single-handedly bridged the gaps between R&B, rock, jazz, classical, and Caribbean music. He was the personification of fusion music, turning on rock crowds to new music by providing the links between Bird's blazing bebop ("Donna Lee"), Duke Ellington's classic jazz elegance ("Sophisticated Lady"), John Coltrane's explorations ("Giant Steps"), and Johann Sebastian Bach's contrapuntal brilliance ("Chromatic Fantasy"), while blending in Jimi Hendrix's cathartic feedback squalls ("Purple Haze," "Third Stone from the Sun"), James Brown's infectious good-foot grooves ("The Chicken"), Bob Marley's reggae lilt ("I Shot the Sheriff"), and the Beatles' harmonically sophisticated pop ("Black-bird," "Dear Prudence").

No one before Jaco had transcended so many idioms. No one had so expertly woven together the essence of those disparate worlds into such a seamless package. And he presented it with a demeanor that was decidedly punk—an unprecedented stance in the jazz world. He even named one of his songs "Punk Jazz," an apt description of his music. As he told Damon Roerich in a 1980 *Musician* interview: "I'm a punk from Florida, a street kid. In the streets where I come from, a punk is someone who's a wiseguy. And I'm sort of a wiseguy, inasmuch as I don't give a shit!"

In that interview, Jaco went on to say: "Punk is not a bad word. It's sort of someone you respect because he's got enough balls to stick up for himself. It has nothing to do with the punk music movement

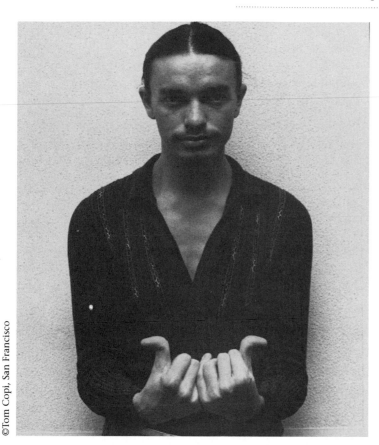

©Tom Copi, San Francisco

that's coming out of England now, where people are sticking needles through their noses. I've been calling my music Punk Jazz for ten years, since long before this English music came along." (Ironically, fellow bass innovator Stanley Clarke once referred to Jaco as the "Sid Vicious of jazz," a reference to the doomed bassist of the Sex Pistols, the band that spearheaded the punk movement in the U.K.)

As Jaco rocketed into the consciousness of the international music community, he quickly attained a larger-than-life status. Stories of him walking up to the likes of Ron Carter and Rufus Reid and introducing himself as "The World's Greatest Bass Player" are the stuff that legends are made of. In a relatively short period of time, Jaco had gone from complete obscurity as a self-described Florida beach bum to worldwide renown, winning critics' polls in Italy, Germany, France, Japan, and the United States. Full of a gunslinger's swagger, he was always quick to point out that "it ain't braggin' if you can back it up." And he could.

The brash, cocky manner in which he strutted around onstage, the way his energetic presence filled a room, the way he played his instrument with such force and invention—all of this fed the Jaco myth. As one fan said, "I always thought of Jaco as being invincible, as someone who could bounce back from anything. That's why, when I heard he was in a coma, I just figured he would pull out of it and go back to being Jaco again."

But what did it mean to be Jaco? Was it merely a persona he created, a role he assumed like some theatrical professional wrestler stepping into the ring? Where did John Francis Pastorius III end and Jaco begin? And, one could ask, would he still be alive today if he had been content to be simply John Francis Pastorius III rather than Jaco?

"Maybe he couldn't deal with the pressure of having to be Jaco every day, of having to take the next step musically," speculates Peter Erskine. "There was always the question of 'What's Jaco going to do next?' and all the pressure that went along with that. To me, that's what destroyed him."

Drummer Ricky Sebastian offers another take on that theory. "One day I saw him lying on the sidewalk and said, 'What are you doing, man? Get up from there.' And he said, 'No, it's all over, man. I'm never gonna top what I've done already. I'm just living on my past.' In hindsight, I really understand what he was saying. I mean, can you imagine the pressure? Fame is something you dream of for so long and work so hard to attain, and then all of a sudden— *boom!*—you get it, and everybody is talking about you and you're winning all the polls and stuff. For that not to go to your head takes a really strong personality, and Jaco had a big ego to begin with. So you can imagine the effect all the sudden fame had on him."

In his glory years, Jaco had tribes of followers in cities all over the world. All he had to do was step off the plane—they were always waiting for him, like disciples waiting to touch the hem of His garment.

But what lay beneath the myth was a complex, tormented individual. Jaco was an utter enigma, easily misunderstood and often maligned by those who observed his unpredictable behavior from a safe distance. As one friend sadly commented, "I wish people would have had more sympathy and compassion for him. I mean, the cat suffered toward the end. They called him crazy, but they didn't have to walk in his shoes. Some people never got a chance to see the real person, before he became the sideshow that was 'Jaco.' A lot of people saw only the asshole—the rude, obnoxious person they'd rather forget. It's a shame, because he really was a good guy and a loyal friend."

Like a lot of people, I still harbor mixed feelings about Jaco's passing. Sadness for the torment he endured. Anger for leaving us. I grieve over the talent wasted, the promise unfulfilled. If he were alive and healthy and living a productive life right now, what kind of music would Jaco be creating? Would Jaco, who was acutely attuned to the concept of groove, be turned on by the current fusion of jazz and hip-hop? Jaco loved funky James Brown tunes, often pointing to saxophonist Maceo Parker's early work on *All the King's Men* as "the real deal." Those same grooving bass lines and funk rhythms are the basis (via sampling) for much of contemporary hip-hop music. Might Jaco be collaborating with Public Enemy or A Tribe Called Quest today? Or would he have gotten into some new conceptual cross-fertilization of hip-hop and jazz on his own, something like the direction that such young jazz composers as Steve Coleman and Greg Osby have taken? Or would he have put his bass aside to concentrate on orchestral works?

We'll never know. We've lost our chance to discover what he might have achieved as an artist. And those of us who knew Jaco also feel the loss on a more personal level. We miss the wise-cracking prankster who seemed to embrace life with such a passion, enriching our lives in the process.

Jaco once confided, "I'm not a star. I'll never be a Frank Sinatra or Elvis Presley or Ray Charles." Then—in a rare, revealing moment—he added, "I'm really not even Jaco." Peter Erskine seemed to pick up on that sentiment when he said to me in a 1986 interview, while Jaco was confined to the psychiatric ward of Bellevue Hospital, "I just hope he does whatever it takes for him to come back and be happy and use that beautiful mind of his to make music again. And he doesn't even have to be Jaco again, as far as I'm concerned. He doesn't need to be anything but himself, which is John Francis Pastorius III, a pretty remarkable human being and a great guy."

When word of Jaco's demise came down, those in the know back in New York sighed a deep sigh for the inevitable. Perhaps guitarist Hiram Bullock expressed it for everyone when he said, "I'm shocked, but I'm not surprised."

"The World's Greatest Bass Player" slipped off to that big jam session in the sky on September 21, 1987—ten weeks short of his 36th birthday. John Francis Pastorius III is gone, but his spirit prevails. It's in the music. Just listen.

ONE

Star-Spangled Jaco

"Me and Jimi Hendrix built the World Trade Center Towers
by ourselves—with our bare hands!"

J ULY 4, 1986: I'm rudely awakened by that most hateful
of sounds, a relentless *rrrrring-rrrrring-rrrrring* in the middle of a posi-
tively delicious dream. I roll over and spy the clock. It's 7 AM, an
ungodly hour for any civilized Manhattanite, especially us jazz writers. We're nocturnal beasts by nature, making the scene, doing the
late-night hang—the Village Gate, the Vanguard, the Blue Note,
Sweet Basil, Visiones, Bradley's, the Dump—often seeing the sunrise,
always sleeping 'til noon.

"Who the fuck could that be?" I mutter to my wife as I fumble for
the phone in a state of grumpy delirium.

"Who else?" she shoots back, her voice dripping with contempt.

Her hunch proves prophetic as an all-too-familiar raspy voice on
the other end barks out, "Yo! Milkowski! It's J.P. How you doin'
baby?"

"Jaco, it's seven in the morning. What the hell you doin'!"

"Hey man, I'm ready to burn, baby. It's the Fourth of July and your
boy is gonna play 'America the Beautiful' on the court. You gotta be
there, man. I'm bringing out my amp, I'm gonna hook it up to a
generator, and I'm doin' it—*period*! You know what I'm talkin'

15

about. Get dressed and come on down. I really need you there, man."

"Yeah, yeah, Jaco. I'll be there. What time?"

"Right now! We can get in a couple games of two-on-two before I start. You gotta come, man."

"Well, I ain't comin' now—but I'll be down there."

"You gotta come *now*, man. It's the Fourth of July and I'm good to go. You know what I'm talkin' about. This is gonna be my greatest performance yet. You gotta cover it for *Down Beat.*"

"Yeah, all right, Jaco. Just let me wake up first."

"You know where to find me. The court." (*Click.*)

I hang up the phone, turn off the ringer, and roll over, trying desperately to get back to that dream. A few hours later I'm up, pounding down black coffee and shaking the cobwebs out of my head.

"Jaco said something about a concert," I tell Angela, who looks none too amused. "He's going to celebrate the Fourth by playing 'America the Beautiful' on the basketball court down on West Fourth Street. This I've got to see. Let's go down and check it out."

During his glory years with Weather Report and later with his own Word Of Mouth band, "America the Beautiful" had been one of Jaco's signature pieces. At the peak of his powers, he would galvanize audiences with his deconstruction of that patriotic song, thrashing about the stage, leaping onto his bass from high atop his amplifier, whipping the strings with his strap until the speakers spewed waves of white-hot feedback and howled like wounded animals in agony. It was his nod to Jimi Hendrix's tumultuous version of "The Star-Spangled Banner" at Woodstock.

But those days were behind Jaco now. There were no more grand stages awaiting him, no more overflow crowds at the Beacon Theatre or Lincoln Center. He had long since been banned from the Bottom Line and had taken to performing in Washington Square Park before an unsavory assemblage of winos, homeless Vietnam vets, and assorted street people. And yet, there was always the possibility

that on this day Jaco would be "on." Anyone who knew what that meant would be wise to go check him out.

By 10:30, we're heading downtown from our place on 29th Street and Second Avenue, strolling toward the Village on a steamy Independence Day in New York City. As we cross over to Sixth Avenue on the Fourth Street side, I notice the usual crowd of spectators lining the fence alongside the basketball court. Homeboys are running and gunning, jamming and profiling for girlfriends, and impressing the tourists. I scan the ranks. No sign of Jaco.

Dismissing it as yet another of Jaco's "total wipes" (his term for an elaborately engineered, mischievous prank), I begin to head back uptown—and then I spy a rumpled figure on the ground, over in one corner of the court. One of Jaco's street pals is hovering over him like a disheveled guardian angel. Nearby, propped against the fence, are Jaco's Fender Jazz Bass and Acoustic 360 amplifier.

Goddamn—he really did it! I think to myself as I approach "The World's Greatest Bass Player," who is curled up in a fetal position and fast asleep.

"What happened?" I ask the Puerto Rican guardian—whose name just happens to be Angel.

"He just fell asleep. He's been runnin' wild, man. Been up for three days."

"Did he actually play?"

"Yeah, man. He plugged in and let it rip. He played for about an hour. Dig it, man. Jaco was killin'!"

Jaco is barefoot and has on his usual basketball attire—bright red sweat pants, tie-dyed T-shirt, orange high-tops, Seminole Indian headband. Pinned to his shirt is a round metal button bearing Jaco's image with "#1" scribbled next his face in Magic Marker, a gift presented by an admirer from Sweden. Upon closer inspection, I notice that Jaco's clothes are dripping wet.

"What's the deal? Why is he wet?" I ask Angel.

"Oh, after he played he went for a swim."

"A swim? Where?"

"Hudson River. He swam out to the Statue of Liberty, touched it, and swam back. At least that's what he said."

"What else did he say?"

"He was saying this shit about 'Me and Jimi Hendrix built the World Trade Center towers by ourselves—with our bare hands!' Man, he was really *out*! And then he went to sleep right here on the court."

"Is he all right?"

"Yeah, he's all right. He's just tired. He's been at it for three days, man. You know what I'm sayin'?"

I knew all too well.

TWO

The Early Years

"Rory, man, I'm the best bass player on earth."

J ACO CAME INTO THE WORLD on December 1, 1951. The firstborn son of Stephanie Haapala, of Swedish and Finnish descent, and Jack Pastorius, of German and Irish blood, he was christened John Francis Pastorius III, the third link in the Pastorius clan, whose name comes from the Latin for "shepherd."

John Francis Pastorius Sr., Jaco's grandfather, was a drum sergeant in the local drum and bugle corps of Bridgeport, a small town outside of Philadelphia in the area of Pennsylvania known as King of Prussia. His firstborn son, John Francis Pastorius Jr.—Jack —followed in his father's footsteps by taking up drums at an early age. Young Jack also exhibited early signs of possessing a natural gift for drawing, but music became his real passion.

"It was just a hobby in the beginning," says Jack, who has had a lengthy career as a drummer and singer on the lounge circuit. "I never expected to be a musician. But as it turned out, it's what I've done all my life."

During his hitch as a navy flier, Jack had an opportunity to meet other music-minded servicemen at jam sessions held aboard the aircraft carriers. One of the guys he met and became good friends with was a saxophone player named Teo Macero, who would later come into his own as a producer at Columbia Records, where he presided over historically important sessions by the likes of Miles Davis and Thelonious Monk. After their stint in the service, Jack and Teo played together around California in a jazz quartet before going their separate ways. Teo went on to New York; Jack returned to Philadelphia, got married, and moved to suburban Norristown to raise a family.

By this time Jack had formed a vocal ensemble called the Casuals, patterned after such slick four-part harmony groups as the Four Freshmen and the Hi-Los. In the summer months, the Casuals would perform at nightclubs along the New Jersey shore. During the winter, they headed down to Florida in search of gigs at the beachfront clubs in Fort Lauderdale. Because Jack was constantly on the road as a working musician, his family saw very little of him while his children were growing up.

Jaco recalled those days in his DCI instructional video, *Modern Electric Bass*, which was made in 1986: "My father said to me, 'Jaco, look, I'm gonna come back in a year'—he was on the road a lot— 'and when I come back, I want you to know where every note is on the neck. If I say I want a C# on the G string, you better know where it is.' And when he came back the next year, I knew it."

Jack's long stretches away from home, plus his heavy drinking habit, put a serious strain on his marriage to Stephanie. Meanwhile, a second son, Gregory, had come along on February 6, 1953, and a third son, Rory, arrived on December 27, 1955. The three boys grew up in a household where music was a priority. When he was home, Jack often practiced his drums, playing along with records by Frank Sinatra, Tony Bennett, and Nat King Cole, and instructing his sons on the proper way to hold the sticks. (One of the most cherished items in Stephanie's family scrapbook is a picture of Jaco at the age of three, playing on a toy drum while holding the sticks with a traditional grip.)

Jack would occasionally take the two older boys along with him to his gigs in Philadelphia, often encouraging them to get up onstage and sing along with the band. Gregory, shy and sensitive, always refused. But Jaco jumped at the chance to get up in front of people and perform. Gregory has vivid memories of a six-year-old Jaco singing Sinatra's "Come Fly with Me" with his father's band. Even at that young age, he was already a showman in the making—the proverbial chip off the old block.

The similarities between father and son went well beyond the obvious physical resemblance. Jack's sons grew up calling him "Mr. Personality," and Jaco would later aspire to that title. Like his father, Jaco had an outgoing, gregarious personality and was seemingly always "on." Like his father, Jaco was a great kidder given to puns, pranks, and off-color jokes. (As Jaco put it, "We start telling jokes, and we tell them the way the musicians tell them. It doesn't offend us, but sometimes we offend other people.") And after meeting Jack, I discovered where Jaco had gotten some of his stock lines, including one oft-quoted remark: "You know what I always say—on a sinking ship, it's women and the rhythm section first."

Both father and son prided themselves in their remarkable endurance, their ability to "hang with the cats," talking trash and drinking mash until dawn, night after night. They fancied themselves as consummate jazzbos, bon vivants with an insatiable appetite for excess, inhabitants of a hip underworld with its own code of ethics, its own customs, and its own secret language. Their braggadocio was informed as much by jazz lore as it was fueled by an inner confidence, a charismatic all-knowing cool. Each in his own way elevated "the hang" to high art. And it is somehow telling that when pressed to put Jaco's untimely death into perspective, Jack reportedly told one intimate, "Jaco just couldn't hang, man."

Besides inheriting his father's party-animal endurance and his obvious flair for showmanship, Jaco also inherited his father's weakness for alcohol. As Pat Jordan pointed out in an article in the April '88 issue of *Gentleman's Quarterly*: "On those rare occasions when Jack Pastorius had a gig near Fort Lauderdale, he often took his eldest son with him to the club. Jaco would watch while his father entertained the audience with his drums, a piano, and a steady stream of humorous, hip patter. The audience repaid him by buying him round after round of drinks that Jack threw back, seemingly without effect." That whole scenario would be played out again years later, with Jaco's constituency.

Near the end of the summer of 1959, the Pastorius clan moved to Fort Lauderdale. It was a smooth transition for the boys, who had no qualms about leaving friends behind in Norristown. In fact, they thrived in the exotic environment of their new home. Compared to Pennsylvania, Florida was like an explorer's dream—it was all sunshine and beaches, swamps and mango trees. Jaco and Gregory, being only 14 months apart, hung out together like best pals, soaking up the tropical climate as they explored their new playground.

To burn off his seemingly endless supply of energy, Jaco would race wildly through the woods and along the spotless white-sand beaches, swim for hours in the ocean, or climb the palmetto and mango trees that grew around their home. His animal-like athleticism and manic energy earned him a second nickname from Rory, who began calling his brother "Mowgli" after the wild-boy character in Rudyard Kipling's *The Jungle Book*. (Years later, during his Word Of Mouth phase, Jaco would establish Mowgli Publishing and have his business affairs handled by Mowgli Management).

During the week, Gregory and Jaco would wake up each morning at 3 AM to deliver newspapers on their bicycles, finishing just in time to serve morning mass as altar boys at St. Clement's Church before school began. On weekends, Stephanie would take the boys to the beach, where Caribbean bands played for afternoon limbo contests. Jaco was captivated by the sound of the steel pans in the Trinidadian bands, and he was particularly impressed by Fish Ray, a colorful character who hung out on the beach and played washtub bass in one of the bands. At least on a subliminal level, Fish Ray could have been Jaco's first bass influence.

But while the Pastorius boys were adjusting nicely to their new

surroundings, the marriage between Jack and Stephanie was disinte-
grating. "That's when things were starting to break up with Mom
and Dad," recalls Gregory. "For the most part, he was on the road.
He was gone a lot. He would show up, be home for a couple of
weeks, then go back out on the road again. And a lot of times when
he came home drunk they would have these terrible fights, which
always upset Jaco. We'd hide in the closet whenever they fought.
Right then and there, we made a pact that we would never drink—
but we both became alcoholics later in life."

As one family friend commented, "Jaco had a very confusing
upbringing. He was raised by this fairly strict Finnish woman, and
every once in a while this loose, funny, Showtime guy would breeze
in and entertain him." Eventually, Jack and Stephanie separated. She
remained in Fort Lauderdale with the three boys; he returned to his
birthplace in Bridgeport, Pennsylvania. But Jack's periodic visits to
Fort Lauderdale allowed him to watch his boys grow up.

Jaco attended elementary school at St. Clement's. At his confirmation, he chose Anthony as his confirmation name, becoming
John Francis Anthony Pastorius. But he was always known to friends
and family alike as simply Jaco. "I didn't even know his real name
was John until I was seven years old," says Rory. "I remember my
mother and I were in the kitchen doing the dishes and talking about
family history, and she told me what Jaco's real name was. When I
heard it, I couldn't stop laughing. At that point, Jaco walked into the
kitchen, and I ran up behind him and started teasing him. 'Your
name is John! Your name is John!' It just sounded so funny to me."

There is some dispute as to who came up with the nickname of
Jaco. Jack claims he came up with it, while Stephanie says it was her
idea. But both agree that the name was derived from Jocko Conlon,
a well-known umpire in baseball's National League. In fact, Jaco
even spelled it that way for several years; at the top of all his home-
work and test papers and book reports, he would print: Jocko Pastorius.

Apparently, it wasn't until years later that he began spelling it J-a-c-o. As Gregory explains, "It was when he met Alex Darqui [the pianist who would later play on Jaco's 'Continuum']. Being French, Alex figured it was spelled like 'Paco.' One day he left a note with the name spelled J-a-c-o; Jaco must've liked it, because from that point on he started spelling it that way himself."

One of Jack's favorite pastimes on his visits to Florida was watching Jaco play in Little League baseball games. Proud Papa Jack would occasionally get involved as announcer, manning the microphone and entertaining the crowd with his colorful play-by-play, which was blasted over a makeshift PA system. Jaco, who loved the limelight, thrived on this kind of attention. "There were always a lot of people at the Little League games, and he liked that," says Gregory. "I was just the opposite. As soon as I heard my name announced over the loudspeaker when I came up to bat, I froze. But when Jaco heard his name announced, he would look around to see who was watching him."

Jaco wore number 11 on his uniform and played both shortstop and centerfield. An excellent athlete, he made the all-star team at age 11 and dominated the league the next year. When he went on to the Senior League, for ages 13 to 15, he became known as one of the best players in the league. "Jaco wasn't big, but he knew how to use his muscles properly to swing the bat," says Rory, who was perhaps Jaco's biggest fan. "Plus, he had excellent hand-eye coordination. He was just so far ahead of anyone his age. He always led his team in homers and had one of the highest batting averages in the league."

Gregory recalls that Jaco was a fierce competitor in everything he attempted, whether it was baseball, football, or basketball. "He played to win all the time. He approached sports with the same kind of intensity that he would apply to music later in his life." Flamboyance was also part of Jaco's persona from an early age. He was boastful about his accomplishments in school and on the playing field, often calling himself "the best" at whatever task he undertook.

Gregory has one of Jaco's elementary-school essays, a work that reveals the boy's rock-solid confidence in his own abilities. It reads: "People think I'm a hothead, but I'm doing what I'm doing, and I do it good. So I can see it's not going to be easy being me."

Although there was the customary sibling rivalry between them, Gregory nevertheless idolized his accomplished older brother. As he told *GQ*: "One day, a kid told me that my brother was an egomaniac because he was always saying he was the greatest. I didn't know what 'egomaniac' meant, but I said, 'But Jaco *is* the greatest.' I worshipped him. He was the best big brother any boy could ever have."

Rory recalls a boyhood incident when Jaco's boastful nature got him in trouble at a baseball game. "He had hit a grand slam and was maybe bragging about it a little bit, so when he came up to bat again the pitcher decided to try to intimidate him by throwing at his head. Jaco ducked, but he couldn't get out of the way in time. The ball beaned him and he fell down. Dad was watching from the grandstand, and when he saw this happen he got all excited and charged the mound. He wanted to kill that pitcher! It was a wild scene. Here was this grown man chasing after a scared little 13-year-old kid, and my Mom was pretty embarrassed by the whole thing. Dad was just being protective of Jaco, but he lost his cool."

While Jaco was a bold, athletic daredevil, frequently putting his body in harm's way, Gregory was bashful and slightly overweight. "Greg was definitely chubby as a kid," says Rory, "and Jaco would always tease him about that. He used to say, 'Well, there's Chubby Checker and there's Fats Domino, so Greg must be Massive Monopoly.' And of course Greg would get upset."

Observing this, a very judicious Stephanie decided that if Jaco was going to be the star athlete, then Gregory would be the musician of the family. She enrolled Gregory in the Fort Lauderdale Boy's Choir, hoping that he might take an interest in singing. She also bought him an acoustic guitar and signed him up for lessons. But progress came slowly, and Gregory became discouraged.

"I went to the music store every Saturday for four months, struggling with these stupid songs that I didn't want to play. I wanted to learn Beatles songs, but the teacher had me playing corny beginners' songs. I just hated it. Then one day Jaco picked up my guitar and started fooling around. He had it all figured out in about 20 minutes. He was actually playing a Beatles tune. This really made me jealous—I had been struggling for months and couldn't play a single song, and here Jaco picks it up and starts playing so naturally, right away. At that point, I marched into my mother's bedroom and announced, 'That's it. The guitar lessons are over. I quit.' Jaco was always beating me, whether it was baseball or basketball or running races, and here was yet another thing he could do better than me, so I didn't want any part of it. I just couldn't deal with it."

Jaco was 12 when he began dabbling on Gregory's guitar, and he had already been playing drums on a small kit his parents bought him. At age 13, he formed his first band with two friends from school; there was Marco Pangello on keyboards, Johnny Caputo on bass, and Jaco on drums. They called themselves the Sonics and had a theme song called "Sonic Boom," which Gregory recalls sounding a lot like the Yardbirds' "For Your Love" (although that song had not yet been released).

Rory remembers seeing the Sonics perform: "They would wear Beatle wigs throughout their set, and for their big finale they would take the wigs off and throw them into the audience. It was funny. We've got some home movies of those gigs. Jaco's big feature was 'Wipe Out,' where he would do this long drum solo. And I remember hearing people around me saying, 'Wow, not only is Jaco the best athlete in school, he's the best drummer too!' And he was. He had impeccable time. In fact, he probably would've ended up being a great drummer if he hadn't broken his wrist."

That injury occurred in the late fall of 1964, when Jaco was attending Northeast High School and playing on a youth-league football team. According to Rory, Jaco had made a good showing in practice and was threatening to take over the position of first-string quarterback. The regular quarterback, feeling threatened by Jaco's ascent, devised a scheme with some teammates to ruin Jaco's chances for a spot in the starting lineup.

As Jack recalls, "These thugs just ganged up on him during a practice game. There was a pileup after a play, and Jaco was on the bottom. It was really a cheap shot. I can remember hearing the sound of that bone cracking. When they got off him, he was lying there with a broken left wrist. I carried him off the field in my arms and took him to a hospital."

Complications arose. "The problem was that the wrist broke in a growth center," Gregory explains. "Jaco started developing calcium deposits that built up and pinched a nerve. That made his left arm numb all the time. He had limited movement in that arm, and eventually he had to have an operation to correct the situation. They had to break off all the calcium. It was fine after that, but there was a loss of strength in his left wrist. He was never able to play drums properly after that injury. For playing funk, a left-handed snare hit is very important—and Jaco just didn't have the same power in his left hand after that injury."

Jaco explained the problem in a 1983 interview: "I was playing legit snare with a traditional grip, not a matched grip. And after I broke my left wrist, I couldn't hit a snare drum anymore. From the age of 13 to 17, I couldn't really get a pop on the snare drum. I would hit it and my wrist would almost shatter. It was like glass after that injury."

At age 15, Jaco began playing drums in Las Olas Brass, a nine-piece horn band that did cover versions of popular tunes by such artists as Aretha Franklin, Wilson Pickett, James Brown, and the Tijuana Brass. Eventually he was replaced by another drummer, Rich Franks. As Jaco put it, "He was older and a much better player than me, technically. So the band wanted him instead of me." Around the same time, the bass player, Kenny Neubauer, was preparing to leave the band. "He played a Hofner bass and was the best bass player in

Florida at the time," Jaco recalled. "He was really a phenomenon. But he got an offer to go to Europe for the summer. So when he left, I just switched over from drums to bass."

Jaco took some money he had earned from working his paper route and bought an electric bass in the local pawn shop for $15. Though he had no experience playing bass, he seemed to adapt to the instrument quite naturally. Gregory recalls seeing Jaco practicing relentlessly. "I can remember hours and hours and hours where we would sit watching TV shows like *Hawaii Five-O*, *The Dick Van Dyke Show*, and *Jeopardy*, which were our favorites, and the entire time Jaco would be playing the bass, constantly moving his fingers up and down the neck and working out patterns. Eventually, he made himself a mini-amplifier in shop class at school. It had headphones, so Jaco could sit there on the couch watching TV with the headphones on, practicing his bass and hearing what it sounded like through an amplifier without disturbing anyone else in the room."

When Jaco became determined he was indeed going to become a bass player, his dedication and cunning helped him to escape some of the household chores. "My mother was very big on making sure we all had chores to do," says Gregory. "There was no way around it. She actually built a stool in the kitchen so we could reach the sink to do the dishes. But when Jaco started getting serious about bass, he told her, 'Mom, this is what I do now. I can't do these dishes anymore because the dishwater softens my calluses. I need to keep these calluses hard to play the bass.' And she went along with it.

"She was always very supportive of Jaco's interest in music. She let his bands practice at our house all the time. We had a full set of drums, a Hammond B-3 organ, and all these amplifiers in our living room. She basically gave up her living room for Jaco's band—for years, it functioned as a rehearsal hall. And when the police would come by after getting noise complaints from the neighbors, she would go outside to run interference for Jaco. She was incredibly supportive."

High school friends like drummer Scott Kirkpatrick, guitarist Jim Godwynn, and bassist Bob Bobbing all remember the broken-wrist incident. They also recall with amazement how smoothly Jaco made the transition from drums to bass. "We used to hang out a lot when we were 15 and 16 years old," says Kirkpatrick. "He was a drummer when I met him. In fact, he had the same set of silver-sparkle Ludwig drums that I had. But when he started playing bass, he progressed so rapidly it was incredible. Jaco had a gift. He was one of those guys who can pick up an instrument and learn it in three days. I remember him picking up a saxophone, and in just a few days he was blowing really incredible sax lines. He was just a phenomenon that way."

Rory also has vivid memories of Jaco's rapid progress on bass. "By the time he was 16, he was probably the best bass player in South Florida. By the time he was 17, he was *definitely* the best bass player in the entire state. In fact, I'll never forget something he said one day when he was 17 going on 18; he looked me in the eye and said, real seriously, 'Rory, man, I'm the best bass player on earth.' I looked back at him and said, 'I know.' It may have been a case of brotherly pride, but Jaco was playing stuff then that nobody else was even thinking of. I remember him playing me the basic seeds of what later became 'Continuum.' He already had all that together when he was 18."

Bob Bobbing was Jaco's biggest fan and supporter at a time when no one else paid him much attention. "Jaco was actually very unpopular around Fort Lauderdale before he became famous. Back in the early years, no one would even hang with the guy. Everyone would say he was a nervous wreck and an egomaniac. They didn't like the way he looked, they didn't like his clothes, they didn't like the fact that he was the only white guy playing in all-black neighborhoods like Liberty City. It was partly a racist thing, but jealousy also played into it. Jaco was really an outcast until his first album came out. After that, everybody wanted to know him."

Bobbing first saw Jaco playing with Las Olas Brass on Fort Lauderdale Beach during Spring Break in 1967. "I remember thinking he was a weird-looking kid. I mean, he was intriguing to watch. He was really skinny, and he had these long arms and long fingers and this really big head. I swear, he looked just like E.T."

He eventually met Jaco later that year at an audition for Kane's Cousins, a popular South Florida band led by Terry Kane. "Jaco came in with his bass already strapped on—no case—and said he had walked eight miles to the audition. We were both competing for the spot in this band. Jaco went first and played the Jimi Hendrix tune 'Fire.' They wanted him to play just the bass part, but he did all these busy fills and things. Needless to say, he didn't get the gig. They ended up hiring me, because Jaco overplayed. But we exchanged numbers and became good friends."

In the summer of 1968, Jaco made a discovery that greatly affected his entire approach to the bass. As Bobbing recalls, "One night Jaco and I went to this nightclub in Fort Lauderdale called the She Lounge to check out a band called Nemo Spliff. The bass player was Carlos Garcia, and he was using this really cool left-hand muting technique. I remember when we walked in they were playing 'I'm Tired,' a song by Savoy Brown that was popular at the time. Jaco really got off on how funky the bass sounded. He was checking out Carlos to see how he was able to get those staccato notes happening in his bass lines. After that gig, Jaco went home and started experimenting with it himself. He would borrow Nemo Spliff tapes that I had, and he'd check out Carlos to get that muted thing down." That technique became the basis for Jaco's signature 16th-note funk style, which would later crop up on such tunes as "Come On, Come Over" and "Opus Pocus" from his debut album, *Jaco Pastorius*, and "Barbary Coast" from Weather Report's *Black Market*.

Jaco was also impressed by Garcia's amplifier, an Acoustic 360. As Bobbing points out, "Before that, Jaco mainly used a Sunn amp, which was a good amp for that time, but this Acoustic amp went far beyond anything on the market. It was the first of its kind. It had an 18-inch speaker in a horn-loaded cabinet. The next day, we went down to Modern Music in Fort Lauderdale and ordered two of them—one for each of us. That amp gave Jaco the power and clarity he needed to play fast lines and chords on the bass without the speaker breaking up and causing distortion. The Acoustic amp, combined with the sound of his Fender Jazz Bass, the muting technique he got from Carlos Garcia, and Rotosound roundwound strings, all helped to give Jaco his sound. It was a brighter, punchier sound with longer notes. That became Jaco's voice on the instrument."

Jaco had gotten his first Jazz Bass from Bobbing, in exchange for an upright bass. A 1960 model, it was fitted with two stack-knob pots for volume and tone, one for each of the single-coil pickups. Soon after Jaco got the bass, he replaced the stack-knob pots with the controls used on Jazz Basses made after 1961: two pickup volumes and a single tone control. As he told me later in an interview, "The circuit with the concentric knobs just didn't seem to have enough punch. In a studio or a nightclub setting where you're playing straightahead jazz with just a piano player and a drummer, it sounds great. But when you're playing in a larger musical environment with a loud band, the bass just doesn't cut through. You end up having to turn your amp up too loud, and you wear out the amp that way."

A little later, when he was 19, Jaco acquired another Jazz Bass, a '62, that he converted into a fretless by pulling out the frets and filling in the slots with Duratite wood putty. To protect the fingerboard from the abrasive roundwound strings, he coated it with about ten layers of a marine epoxy called Petitt's Poly-Poxy. This provided a harder surface that gave the bass a unique "singing" quality.

The next significant step in the evolution of Jaco's style was his discovery of artificial harmonics, also known as false harmonics. "He already knew about open harmonics," says Bobbing. (Natural, or open, harmonics are produced by placing a finger lightly on a string without depressing it and then plucking the string. This produces a "chiming" sound that is derived from the overtone series for that string. The pitch produced depends upon the subdivision of the string.) "To get false harmonics, you use one extended finger like a capo and then pick behind it. A guy named Clay Cropper had shown me the technique, and I passed it on to Jaco. His initial comment was something like, 'Oh, I've seen guitar players do that. I ain't got time for that. I'm too busy learning this other stuff.' But he eventually picked up on it in a big way." Probably the most familiar example of Jaco's use of false harmonics is in the intro to the Weather Report hit "Birdland."

In 1969, Jaco began making an impact on the South Florida scene with a hot trio called Woodchuck, which featured Billy Burke on Hammond B-3 organ, Bob Herzog on drums and vocals, and Jaco on bass. They worked a lot at the Button and the Four O'Clock Club, and all the local musicians came by to check them out. Burke, who was like the Jimmy Smith of South Florida, was the main draw of the band, and his superior musicianship challenged Jaco to rise to a new level in his own playing.

"That was the band that put Jaco on the map, as far as South Florida was concerned," says Bobbing. "They had so much soul and feeling. Las Olas Brass was basically just a Top 40 cover band. But Woodchuck was it, man. That's where Jaco's Jerry Jemmott-style funk lines started coming together. [*Jemmott was a top session bassist at the time.*] And that's when he really started becoming a performer. He was singing, and he had a lot of stage presence. That's when people really started taking notice of Jaco."

As Burke recalls, "Woodchuck was a real funky group. We were doing Major Lance tunes, 'Cleanup Woman' by Betty Wright, all kinds of obscure, hip R&B tunes that hadn't crossed over to the white neighborhood yet. It was a real rebel-type band. It was basically R&B, but it was really jazz in the sense of stretching out and improvising on the bandstand. It was very daring for the time."

Burke was also a regular jammer at the Downbeat Lounge, a night-club located in a predominantly black section of Fort Lauderdale. Jaco would occasionally drop by and sit in with the soul bands. "I had already been playing in several bands around South Florida when I met Jaco," says Burke. "He was just a punk kid in the audience at my gigs. Later I'd see him at these jams at the Downbeat Lounge, but never on bass. He'd come in with a baritone sax or sometimes an alto sax and just play parts in the horn section. We actually had a ten-piece band there backing up this crazy singer who called himself the Mona Lisa. The cat had pink hair, and he sold bad reefer on the side. It was a hysterical scene."

Bobbing recalls accompanying Jaco to the Downbeat on more than a few occasions. "The place was just a wooden shack in the funkiest section of town. It had a real Deep South juke-joint vibe and was populated by a wild bunch of characters, from female impersonators to all kinds of pimps and players mixed in with hard-core blues fans. And one of the characters we'd see there was Billy Burke."

Another regular at the Downbeat Lounge was a tenor saxophonist named Tyrone Weston. "Tyrone was a monster player," says Steve Finn, a close friend of Jaco's who was a roadie for Woodchuck. "Jaco got a lot of his sax ideas from Tyrone—but none of us were completely convinced that Tyrone was even human. I mean, he was that strange. I don't know where he came from, but I do know that he was a mystic. You'd never know how he got anywhere. You'd turn around, and he'd be there sitting in a chair, smiling, as if he had just materialized. He hung with this strange, pasty-faced white guy who said he was a witch. I'm sure Tyrone had some sort of strange influence on Jaco."

Billy Burke confirms that Weston was indeed a phenomenal horn player and mentions that he also had a bad heroin habit. "Great player, but a real nut case. We'd have to start looking for the guy on Friday morning if we wanted him for a gig that night, 'cause you never knew where he'd be. Sometimes we'd find him down by the sea wall in Middle River—he'd practice his horn by the water because he liked the acoustics there. Sometimes we'd find him out by the city dump. He was a real trip, that guy."

After Woodchuck broke up, Jaco played briefly with the Uptown Funk All-Stars, a pickup group that included Burke, drummer Rich Franks, trumpeter Melton Mustafa, and guitarist Gary Carter. They gigged at the Windjammer Lounge on the beach in Fort Lauderdale.

To supplement his club work, Jaco took a day job at Pirates World, an amusement park in Dania, just south of Fort Lauderdale. (Years later, Jaco would name a hard-swinging composition after this town.) One of the musicians Jaco befriended on that gig was drummer Bobby Economou, who would later appear on Jaco's debut album.

"We were playing in the pit band of this musical theater," recalls Economou. "We did shows all day for the people at the park, and each show lasted about 40 minutes. I remember the day I met Jaco. We were sitting there having a hamburger before the first show started. The Blood, Sweat & Tears tune 'Spinning Wheel' was on the radio—it was the #1 song at the time—and Jaco was telling me he had just locked his mother in the closet because she was bugging him. He was a pretty edgy cat, a few years older than me and incredibly confident. He was always bragging that he was the best this and the best that. Regardless of whether he could do something or not, he would always profess to be the best at it. And I was kind of taken aback by this kind of behavior. I didn't know what to believe at that age. I really didn't know what was good and what was bad."

Meanwhile, Bobbing continued to follow Jaco's progress from band to band, bringing his Sony reel-to-reel recorder to the gigs. Today he is one of the most knowledgeable Pastorius scholars around, with an impressive collection of early Jaco material. Perhaps the rarest tape of all in the Bobbing archives is a 1968 sound-on-sound recording of Pee Wee Ellis's "The Chicken," with Jaco playing all the instruments: bass, drums, guitar, alto sax, and recorder. Soon after making it, Jaco sent a copy to Alice Coltrane, the widow of the great saxophonist John Coltrane and an accomplished musician in her own right. He got back a letter of encouragement, which inspired him to forge ahead on his musical mission.

Throughout his career, from his early days with Woodchuck to his years with Weather Report and his own Word Of Mouth ensembles and his final gigs with Florida pickup bands, Jaco would continue to play "The Chicken." For him, it was a proud reaffirmation of his "white trash" R&B roots—but his first wife, Tracy, confides that "in later years, after Weather Report, that song was a red flag to us that he was over the edge."

Tracy Lee was a pretty, vivacious blonde who had caught Jaco's eye at Northeast High in 1967. As one friend put it, "Jaco sort of made up his mind that he wanted her. He just walked up to her one day and said, 'You and me belong together.' He just claimed her, like a caveman or something."

While Tracy was demure, Jaco was domineering. And while Tracy had lived a somewhat sheltered life up to that point, Jaco already exuded a kind of worldly confidence. Through the sheer force of his overbearing personality, he exerted a heavy influence over the introverted Tracy. As she puts it, "From the time I was 15 until I was 27, he was my father, my brother, my one and only."

The two sweethearts became inseparable in high school and eventually moved in together before finally getting married in the summer of 1970. "They had committed themselves to each other in high school," says Gregory, "and Jaco's attitude was, 'Hey, we don't need to get married.' You know, it was part of that whole '60s hippie aesthetic. He didn't believe in the convention of marriage. But they ended up getting married when Tracy was pregnant, more to please my Mom, I think, than for themselves." ("I don't remember the exact date," says Tracy, "because we weren't into that sort of thing then. But we were both 18 at the time.")

In late 1970, Jaco hooked up with a slick, well-rehearsed white soul band called Tommy Strand & the Upper Hand. (Economou went on to join Sassafras, a band led by Bobbing. But he and Jaco were destined to meet again.) Scott Kirkpatrick, the drummer who played in the Upper Hand, recalls Jaco as "the ultimate groove player." Kirkpatrick, who went on to become a studio drummer in Los Angeles, says, "I have never played with anybody since who could groove like Jaco could in that band. I don't think there will ever be anybody to come along who has that kind of groove power. He played so funky, but he wasn't into the kind of slap-thumb style of bass that's so popular today. He was just playing with two fingers on his right hand, and he was laying down the funkiest, most innovative lines I've ever heard in my life."

On a typical night, the band would open their set with an arrangement of Willie Dixon's "I Just Want to Make Love to You" before moving into their Sly Stone medley of "Thank You (Falettinme Be Mice Elf Agin)" and "I Want to Take You Higher." Then it would be something like Buddy Miles's "Them Changes," Chicago's "More and More," and a Beatles medley, followed by the obligatory "Proud Mary." They did faithful renditions of Aretha Franklin's "Rock Steady," the Ides of March's "Vehicle," James Taylor's "Fire and Rain," and Herbie Hancock's "Watermelon Man." And, of course, "The Chicken."

In the context of these commercial pop and soul tunes, Jaco unleashed a torrential downpour of ideas. On Bobbing's tapes of the band, you can hear the seeds of what would later become "Barbary Coast," "Liberty City," and "Kuru." Guitarist Randy Bernsen remembers marveling at Jaco's abilities back then. "Someone had told me about this guy named Jaco, a great bass player. I finally met him one night when I was playing a gig at a place in Dania called the Sandpiper. I was sitting on the stage during the break, and he walked up and started staring at me, like I was in his place or something. Then he introduced himself and said, 'Man, we got to play together some-

Courtesy Bob Bobbing

Jaco circa 1970, surf-fishing at the beach

time.' This was just after he had joined Tommy Strand & the Upper Hand, and I started to hang around with him a lot at that point."

Tommy Strand & the Upper Hand had a steady gig at the Seven Seas Lounge on Collins Avenue in Miami Beach. During this period, Jaco and Tracy took up residency on Southwest Third Avenue in Fort Lauderdale. "It was a piece of shit house, just a box," recalls Scott Kirkpatrick. "I couldn't believe they could live like that. Jaco was constantly listening to Ray Charles and other black music, and I remember thinking, 'God, what a lifestyle. This guy eats and sleeps and drinks music.' How Tracy put up with that, I don't know."

Mary Pastorius was born on December 9, 1970, just eight days after Jaco's 19th birthday. The prospect of suddenly having to provide for a family made the skinny man-child take stock of himself.

"After Mary was born, we were in the hospital looking at her through the glass in the maternity ward," says Gregory. "Jaco turned to me with a real serious expression on his face and said, 'Well, this is it. Now I *gotta* be the greatest bass player that ever hit the planet. I gotta go out and do something so I can make a real living at this. I can't keep playing in stupid bars for no money. I've got a family to take care of.'"

Armed with enormous talent and an ego to match, Jaco became a man on a mission, ready to take on the world.

THREE

On the Road

"He lived on McDonald's fish sandwiches,
had that one set of clothes, and
carried his bass with him all the time."

JACO CONTINUED PLAYING with Tommy Strand & the Upper Hand through 1971. (Because of the leader's penchant for snorting coke on and off the gig, the vehemently anti-drug Jaco sometimes referred to the band as Tommy Toot & the Lower Root.) To supplement his income, Jaco began picking up work aboard luxury liners embarking from the Port of Miami bound for the Caribbean. Though these cruise-ship gigs were generally lounge-music situations, the voyages gave Jaco an opportunity to soak up the sounds of calypso and reggae. (Jaco later told *Down Beat*: "When we were docked, I'd just hang out, hit the streets. I got close to some guys in the Wailers.")

Gregory remembers skipping his high school graduation in June 1971 to go on one of these cruises with his older brother. He also recalls spending the rest of that summer with Jaco and Tracy and their newborn daughter in Ocean City, Maryland, where Tommy Strand & the Upper Hand had a rare extended engagement.

Around this time, a golden opportunity was about to present itself to Jaco. Wayne Cochran, the great white soul singer from Georgia, was searching for a new bassist to join his fabled and funky

C.C. (Chitlin' Circuit) Riders band. A kind of missing link between James Brown and David Clayton-Thomas, Cochran was an earth-shaking soul shouter with a slick 14-piece horn band geared strictly for Showtime. A sanctified chick-chaser, booze-taster, and money-waster, the pompadoured singer delivered his between-songs banter with the zeal of an evangelist minister addressing his flock.

In a non-stop grind of one-nighters, Cochran and his C.C. Riders traveled up and down the East Coast in a cramped band bus. It was hardly an ideal situation—Cochran was a demanding bandleader and the pay was merely adequate—but for a young man yearning for professional experience and adventures on the road, it was a dream gig. Bob Bobbing had been approached about filling the bass chair in the C.C. Riders, but he immediately steered the band to Jaco. As he recalls, "I got a call from Bob Gable, the baritone saxist in Cochran's band. My band, Sassafras, had opened for them at a club in Atlanta sometime around May of 1972. I guess he was impressed by my playing—enough to ask me if I wanted the gig. At the time, I was busy booking bands through my production company as well as playing in Sassafras. So I told them to go check out Jaco. I made a comment to the effect that 'this guy is beyond your wildest dreams.' I kept telling Bob Gable, 'This guy Jaco will kill you. Don't even think about anybody else for the gig.'"

Gable and Charlie Brent, Cochran's musical director, went down to Miami to check out Jaco at Shula's, where he was playing with Tommy Strand & the Upper Hand. After the first set, Brent and Jaco talked. "I remember my first words to him were, 'You're a wonderful fucking bass player, man.' He had everything we were looking for—groove, soul, and a hunger to play all night long, which you needed in this band. We did five sets a night, six nights a week. You really had to have drive and stamina to keep up. And this skinny little kid had it."

Brent arranged for an audition at Bachelors III, a nightclub jointly owned by actor Bobby Van, New York Jets football star Joe Namath, and some behind-the-scenes investors reputedly connected to the

Florida rackets. "I didn't want to rehearse him with the whole band, so I just whipped out the book of charts, put it in front of him, and counted off the show. We went from one tune straight to the next, and he just burned it to pieces! I mean fucking *burned* it—played every note I had written."

The next day, Brent had yet another revelation about Jaco's unique talents. "I had the whole band come in, and I put out a chart I had written especially for that rehearsal. Jaco looked at it and then came over and told me he couldn't read. I said, 'Then how the fuck did you play all those tunes yesterday?' And he says, 'I caught the show a couple of weeks ago,' which just simply fried me. The kid had total fucking recall!"

Jaco was immediately offered the gig—but, incredibly, he turned it down. Rather than jumping at the chance, he held out for more money and also asked to be exempt from one of Cochran's unwritten rules: No women or children allowed on the band bus. A few weeks later, thanks to Brent's persistent lobbying on Jaco's behalf, Cochran finally agreed to the terms. Jaco joined the C.C. Riders at $250 a week and headed out on the road with Tracy, daughter Mary (still in diapers), and a busload of scruffy R&B hounds.

Jaco was a high-strung 20-year-old when he joined the C.C. Riders in the summer of 1972. Eager to learn more about music, he found a mentor in Brent. "He was real green when he joined the band," says Charlie. "I used to tell him he was young, dumb, and full of cum." Only two years older than Jaco, Brent was already a seasoned touring veteran as well as an accomplished arranger and composer. And he knew he had found his dream bassist.

"Jaco came along just in time," Brent recalls. "I was losing a bass player named Artie Goleniak, a real pro who had played with Joey Dee & the Starlighters in New York during the early '60s. Artie had been on Cochran's gig for years, much longer than I had. Anyway, the guy was leaving because he had a wife and children and his wife was gettin' on his case by that time. Artie had developed a great rapport with the horns—the band was four trumpets, three trombones, four saxophones, and a three-piece rhythm section, so you needed a pretty good bass player for the band to work. I was the musical director, and to have this guy leave was like having a woman leave you. It was that kind of thing. There was nobody who could take his place."

Goleniak had promised to stay in the band until Brent found a replacement, so Charlie cagily put on the big stall. "I just kept putting it off and putting it off until finally his wife got too crazy. So I started going out to clubs to check out different bass players. And that's how I ran into Jaco."

Soon after Brent found him Jaco was onboard the bus, where one of his closest friends on the long rides between gigs was tenor saxophonist Randy Emerick. "It was a rough grind, but we were living the R&B life. And to us, that was just about the best life you could possibly have," says Emerick, who ten years later would play baritone sax in Jaco's Word Of Mouth big band.

On the band's trips through the Midwest, Randy and Jaco would pay regular visits to a friend in Cincinnati who had an impressive record collection. "We'd go a hundred miles out of the way just to swing by his place. Jaco and I would go over to his house and stay up all night, taping as many R&B records as we could in the few hours we were there. And we'd listen to those tapes over and over in the back of the bus, checking out the bass parts from one record, the drum parts from another, the horn lines from another, and so on. We were constantly researching all that music. We were totally into R&B, on and off stage."

During this period, Jaco was checking out the work of Charles Sherrell and Bernard Odum, two great bassists who worked with James Brown in the '60s. He paid especially close attention to Jerry Jemmott's 16th-note work on the great B.B. King album *Live & Well*. And he learned the Tommy Cogbill bass line on Wilson Pickett's "Funky Broadway," the Duck Dunn bass line on Sam & Dave's "Soul Man," and the bass lines from many other R&B songs that had been cut for the Stax and Atlantic labels. (Jaco's funky bass line on "Come On, Come Over" from *Jaco Pastorius* can be traced to Dunn's work on the 1967 Carla Thomas single, "I Like It.")

But Brent says that Jaco's two favorite tunes during his tenure with the C.C. Riders were Betty Wright's "Cleanup Woman" and David Rose's "Holiday for Strings," better known as the theme to *The Red Skelton Show*, a popular television program. (Jaco would later do an incredible steel-pans orchestra arrangement of this tune).

As Charlie recalls, "He liked 'Cleanup Woman' because of the groove, and he liked 'I Love Lucy' because of that dominant augmented-11th chord with a 13th on it. He just loved the sound of that chord." Brent eventually worked "Cleanup Woman" into the act. "We had this routine with 'Cleanup Woman' where Wayne would send all 11 horns out into the audience while the rhythm section stayed up onstage—just me on guitar, Allyn Robinson on drums, and Jaco on bass. We would be holding down the groove while Wayne and the horns were marching around the club. Sometimes they'd follow Wayne out the door and down the street with half of the audience falling into a second line behind them."

Brent paints a vivid picture of the wild frontman's manic energy. "Cochran would climb up a telephone pole and start barking at the moon, with the horns still playing the riff to 'Cleanup Woman.' I mean, this was some seriously crazy motherfucker. Meanwhile, the three of us would be back in the club, just holding that groove together. And Jaco would be throwing in all kinds of harmonics over the changes. If I wanted to take a guitar solo, he would cover the bass and rhythm guitar parts at the same time. And he could keep up that groove all night long. He had incredible stamina, that kid."

The C.C. Riders' "home office," strangely enough, was in Calumet City, Illinois, where the band's managers owned a bowling alley called the Castaways Lanes. "So we were in and out of the Chicago area all the time," says Brent. "As a matter of fact, we held band rehearsals at that bowling alley. On one occasion [the well-known Chicago tenor saxophonist] Eddie Harris came by. Now, Jaco knew who he was and I knew who he was. We were both hip to 'Freedom Jazz Dance' and 'Listen Here' and things like that, but the rest of the guys in the band were like, 'Who's Eddie Harris?' So we blew off rehearsal for a while and started jamming. Eddie whipped into a dangerous 7/4 thing on the organ, and Jaco just grabbed the groove and killed it. I mean fuckin' killed it! We just smoked that fuckin' bowling alley."

Jaco's ten-month stay with the C.C. Riders was the most intensive period of woodshedding in his career. Besides playing the demanding five-hour shows every night, he practiced on the bus as the band traveled from town to town. "He had that bass in his hands constantly," recalls Brent. "And he had this little practice amp with headphones, so he could sit there and work out new ideas without disturbing anybody. When he came up with something, he'd say, 'Hey, man, check this out,' and put the headphones on you while he played some new lick.

"Sometimes, as a prank, he would slip those headphones on guys who were asleep and blast them out of their seats with all these ringing harmonics in their ears. He did that to me once at a hotel, when I was crashed out after being up for three days straight. I thought it was a fuckin' fire alarm going off. I jumped to my feet and ran out of the room in a panic before I figured out what the hell was going on."

Tracy was a quiet presence in the background whenever she rode the bus. She remembers being at once intimidated and fascinated by the rowdy C.C. Riders atmosphere. "I never talked to anyone on that bus, but I listened a lot. I hadn't been too well educated and hadn't been around that much. And I remember learning a lot from just listening to Randy Emerick."

She also remembers a lot of pot smoking on the bus. "Jaco and I were the only ones who didn't smoke pot, so it was kind of shocking for me to sit there with Mary on my lap and watch these guys doing shotgun hits on each other. It was really a pretty wild scene." Emerick confirms Jaco's adamant anti-drug stance. "He had an attitude about alcohol and drugs. Basically, his attitude was, 'I just wanna play music and later for the rest of that shit.' If anybody else was drinking a lot or smoking, he would avoid it. He never indulged."

According to Emerick, Jaco could barely read music when he

joined the band. But he also remembers how quickly he adapted to Charlie Brent's demanding charts, particularly on such Brent originals as "Rice Pudding," "Ming of Mings," and "Three Views of a Secret," a title that Jaco would later cop for one of his own compositions. "Charlie worked out some pretty sophisticated arrangements over difficult chord changes, but Jaco always picked it up quickly, mostly by ear," says Emerick. "Eventually he did learn how to read and how to voice chords while he was in that band, and Charlie was his main teacher. They'd sit in the back of the bus and Charlie would quiz Jaco about chords and intervals. He would say things like, 'Jaco, what's the fifth of this chord?' 'What's the fourth of B-flat?' And Jaco just treated it like another competitive game, like he was playing Jeopardy or something."

Drummer Allyn Robinson was a key part of the rhythm section that powered the Cochran juggernaut. He established a solid link with Jaco's groove-oriented style, and together they drove the band to frenzied heights. Robinson recalls that Jaco's entire wardrobe in those days consisted of tennis shoes, a pair of corduroy pants, and three T-shirts. "That's all he ever wore. He was an odd bird but highly motivated. He lived on McDonald's fish sandwiches, had that one set of clothes, and carried his bass with him all the time. He checked into hotels as little as possible. He would sleep on the beach instead of checking into a hotel, just to save money to send back to his wife. We weren't making all that much, but Jaco was sending Tracy $50 a week."

Because Jaco's high energy level and eccentricities were just too much for some of the C.C. Riders, few of the musicians were willing to share a room with him. But Charlie Brent, a hellraiser himself, seemed attracted to Jaco's manic energy. They ended up rooming together on the road and establishing a close rapport.

"Basically, nobody wanted to room with a guy who was running around saying, 'Hey, I'm the greatest fucking bass player in the world.' Jaco had a monstrous ego, and some people in the band couldn't deal with that. He clashed with everybody, even the bus driver. I liked his cocky attitude, because I have the same attitude myself, but I used to tell him, 'Man, you can't talk this shit to other people, telling them "I'm the greatest fucking bass player in the world," unless you can back up that crap.' I mean, he would walk up to people like Ron Carter and say that shit, which made everybody else crazy. But I just laughed. Because to me, he *was* the greatest bass player in the world."

One rule of the Cochran band that Jaco violated with impunity concerned the wearing of tuxedoes on certain prestigious gigs. "Jaco was a rebel," says Brent. "He wouldn't wear the band uniform. He just didn't believe in that kind of discipline. I ended up buying him a 50-foot cord so he could play behind the stage and not be seen. He did lots of gigs like that—off camera, so to speak."

Jaco's defiant streak and constant bragging did not sit well with Cochran, notes Brent. "I had to fight with Wayne all the time about Jaco. He'd want to fire him, and I'd keep trying to tell him, 'He's too fucking good! He's worth the aggravation.' Wayne had a big ego too, and you can't have two stars on the same bandstand."

During their ten months on tour together with the C.C. Riders, Brent and Jaco engaged in a kind of macho one-upsmanship (the same type of competitive relationship he would later develop with his Weather Report mentor, Joe Zawinul). "We had the kind of relationship where it was a 'you-got-no-fuckin'-balls-unless-you-do-this' kind of thing," says Charlie. "We were constantly daring each other to do crazy things. I remember once we pulled into a hotel in Calumet City in the dead of winter, and Jaco says to me, 'You got no fuckin' balls unless you hit the pool before me.' Now, I was coming off a fucking stupor after being up for two days and then sleeping for 24 hours, so I just went to the pool and walked out on the diving board and dove in. When my head hit the ice, I remember hearing Jaco laughing his ass off. Man, I wanted to kill that skinny asshole from Lauderdale."

But as much as Brent wanted to murder him that day, he came to regard Jaco with awe, particularly after one incident on the road.

"We were in the Midwest somewhere, and Jaco decides he wants a fretless bass. So he goes down to the hardware store and buys a pair of pliers and some wood compound. He comes back to the hotel and starts tearing the frets out of this green Fender bass I had bought in New Orleans. For some reason he didn't have his own bass on this particular road trip, so he was playing mine.

"Anyway, he's ripping the frets out, and I'm screaming, 'Don't do that, man! We got a gig tonight! You won't be able to play that bass the same way without frets.' But I swear, that night he played better than he ever played before. He was sliding up to notes and doing all these things he couldn't do on a fretted bass. It was amazing to me that he did that." (Of course, Jaco had already defretted his own '62 Jazz Bass some years before, so he wasn't a stranger to fretless technique—but Brent didn't know that.)

"Then there was this other night in Texas when he started hitting harmonics on the first and second and third frets, doing changes way down at the fucking bottom of the neck. *Nobody* does that! But this guy was getting a real touch down, and he could play harmonics below the fifth fret. Now, I played some bass myself, and this was fuckin' news to me. That's when I knew he was the fucking messiah."

Brent was equally impressed by Jaco's budding talent as a composer and arranger. "He kept bugging me, always asking me about how I did this arrangement or why I wrote something a certain way. He was curious about how I dealt with harmonies and chords. He was always picking my brain for information. So one night I told him, 'Man, you want to know how the fuck I do this? Well, sit down and shut up and I'll tell you everything.' Which I did. We stayed up all night in that hotel room in Lexington, Kentucky, talking about arranging and theory and writing. I was eating a bunch of speed at that time, so I sat down and just rapped to him 'til sunrise, told him everything I knew. When I finished, I told him, 'That's what's happening, that's what I'm doing, that's how it's done.'"

Three days later, Jaco came to rehearsal with a chart he had written for the band. He called it "Amelia," after Amelia High School in

Chicago, where the Cochran band had played a particularly memorable gig. As Brent recalls, "That was the first thing he orchestrated for a big group, and it was fucking gorgeous—full of these wonderful horn voicings. And to think that he came up with this chart in just three days is amazing to me. I couldn't believe that all this flowing, moving, meaningful music was coming out of this skinny little kid who didn't know shit about nothing except playing the bass. But the truth was, he was just way ahead of everybody. He was this raw talent evolving before our eyes."

When Brent saw that Jaco was developing into an accomplished arranger, he decided to leave the C.C. Riders. "I showed him everything I knew and split," he says. "I figured they had somebody better than me to do the job, and they did. So I went out to Los Angeles to work on movie scores. I left Jaco running that band. And if it wasn't for his personality, he might still be running that band."

Jaco took over the role of musical director of the C.C. Riders, but his tenure was short. Without Brent there to run interference for him, Jaco soon clashed with Cochran. He found himself out of the group only a few weeks later.

Allyn Robinson looks back at that period as a magical time in his life. "It was inspiring to be around Jaco then. He was so motivated and so gifted—he was just a natural. And he had so much ambition. He had a zest for life that you just couldn't help admiring. It was just full-tilt with this guy all the time. When we hit the stage, his attitude was, 'Let's do it!' He had such a desire and a need to be just that one step ahead of the pack. It was a God-given thing."

Robinson maintains that no one else was playing bass back then with the kind of confidence and invention that Jaco was demonstrating on a nightly basis. "This was something totally new and different. Everything you heard him doing years later with Weather Report and on his solo records—the harmonics, the chords, the percussive effects he got by rubbing his hands on the strings—he was doing all of that stuff in Cochran's band back in 1972. And for me, it was exciting to hear all this fresh stuff night after night."

Courtesy Charlie Brent

Robinson contends that the most amazing aspect of Jaco's impressive talent was that his virtuosic chops never got in the way of the groove. "His playing was so emotional and so creative, but it wasn't cluttered. As busy as it often was, it always flowed. It was like a living, breathing thing; it had that yin and yang. The beauty in Jaco's playing was not in the obvious things. It wasn't that he could play fast; it was in his phrasing."

Wayne Cochran and the C.C. Riders circa 1972; Jaco is in the middle row, second from left

Robinson had grown so attached to Jaco's groove-conscious, interactive style of playing that it was hard for him to hook up with other bassists after Jaco left the C.C. Riders in the early part of 1973. "I don't know where it came from or how it happened, but when we got together, man, it was sheer magic. Jaco just made me sound so good. I've never had a musical hookup with another bass player like that, before or since. There'll never be another to come along like

Jaco. To me, there's bass before Jaco and there's bass after Jaco. That's just the way it is. I mean, this guy was touched by God."

Bob Bobbing points to the C.C. Riders phase as the time when everything came together for Jaco in a dramatic way. "That gig was like the oven for Jaco Pastorius. It was a big horn band with no keyboards, so Jaco was able to experiment with chords, harmonics, and that whole soloistic approach to the bass, which he became so famous for years later. I like to call it 'creative overplaying.' And when he wasn't playing gigs, he was practicing all the time. So by the time he came out of that band, Jaco's chops were at a peak, better than they were when he was in Weather Report. His playing with Wayne Cochran was the best bass playing I've ever heard in my life."

Jaco returned to Florida in early 1973 to spend time with Tracy and his daughter. It was around this time that Jaco got involved with Bakers Dozen, a 13-piece laboratory band formed by pianist Vince Maggio. One charter member of that ensemble was Peter Graves, a trombonist and musical contractor in the South Florida area who also ran the house band at Bachelors III in Fort Lauderdale. Graves eventually hired Jaco for a steady gig at Bachelors III, where he would back visiting acts like the Temptations, the Four Tops, and the Supremes, along with such singers and celebrities as Nancy Wilson, Mel Tormé, Bobby Rydell, Frankie Avalon, Phyllis Diller, and Charo.

As Graves recalls, "I had heard about Jaco for years. I was even told by some people, 'Don't hire this guy, because he's too brash.' But I liked guys who played with attitude, and Jaco definitely had plenty of that. So I got him on the gig. And the things that he didn't do as well, like reading charts, were more than made up for by his raw musical talent. If he missed something one time, he would never miss it again. He had an incredible memory and an amazing capacity to pick up things by ear."

Graves encouraged Jaco to write charts for the band to help support his family, which now included a son, John, who had been born on October 20, 1973. "They were going through a pretty tough time then," Graves remembers. "They lived in a small apartment above a laundry and didn't have much money, so I would give him these extra gigs just to keep him and the kids alive. Because of Jaco's reputation for having a cocky attitude, a lot of other people wouldn't hire him. And it was because of this trust between us that we became close friends. He sensed that I wasn't going to abandon him."

Some of the other players who were in and out of the group at the time included drummer Danny Gottlieb, guitarist Pat Metheny, trumpeter Ron Tooley (who would later work with Jaco in the Word Of Mouth septet), and bassist Mark Egan, who would occasionally sub for Jaco. During this period, Jaco also had a part-time teaching gig at the University of Miami under jazz department head Bill Lee (father of bassist Will Lee).

Egan took lessons with Jaco during the summer of 1973 and remembers them as being especially inspiring. "His energy level was so infectious. I never met anyone who was as motivating as Jaco. He used to tell me, 'You can do anything. If you want to walk through a wall, you can walk through a wall.' And I believed him. We would get together to play, and after being with him for a couple of hours I would be buzzing for days."

It was at Bachelors III that Jaco met percussionist Don Alias, who would become a close friend and important collaborator throughout Jaco's career. As Alias recalls, "I was playing with Lou Rawls at the time, and we were in Fort Lauderdale to do a TV show and a gig at Bachelors III. I remember walking into the first rehearsal with the house band, and the only person I heard was the bass player. It wasn't that he was playing too loud—it was just that I had never heard anybody play like that before. So I introduced myself to Jaco. He had heard of me from *Bitches Brew* [the groundbreaking 1969 Miles Davis fusion album that Alias played on], and we just hit it off from there."

Alias eventually got Jaco into the Lou Rawls band, though that gig was short-lived. They toured together for a period of six months before Rawls gave Jaco his walking papers. As Alias recalls, "Jaco was playing so good and so musical—any singer with any kind of ego would get intimidated by that. I happened to think it was wonderful, but Lou just thought he was playing too much."

Soon after parting company with Rawls, Jaco hooked up with saxophonist Ira Sullivan, a Chicago native who had migrated to South Florida, where he was regarded as something of a legend by the jazz students at the University of Miami. "Jaco used to come and see me play when he was in the Cochran band," says Sullivan. "He'd bring some of the cats from the C.C. Riders to check me out. I was working at a club called the Rancher Motel Lounge in Miami, where I had been playing a steady gig for seven years. So we struck up an acquaintance there."

At Jaco's suggestion, they got a jam session together at pianist Alex Darqui's pad. The chemistry clicked so well that they began getting together on a regular basis just to run through standards and Sullivan originals. On one occasion, Jaco brought along his drummer pal Bobby Economou (from the Pirates World gig), just to hang out and dig the scene. "Ken Katz was on drums," Economou recalls, "but at some point Jaco asked me to sit in on a tune. It happened to be Herbie Hancock's 'Maiden Voyage,' and apparently they liked the way I played it, because after the rehearsal they asked me to join the band. But I was already making good money with Bob Bobbing's band, Sassafras, and wasn't too eager to leave."

Whenever Sassafras would come off the road, Economou would participate in wild jams with Jaco at Criteria Studios, where studio engineer Alex Sadkin gave them free time after hours. Sadkin, who had played with Jaco in Las Olas Brass back in 1967, would go on to become a successful producer of big-name pop acts like Duran Duran, but at the time he was just getting his feet wet at Criteria.

"We would jam and just roll tape, documenting whatever we played," says Economou. "After a while, we began working tunes into these jams. It was very hip. I remember bringing tapes of these jam sessions with me when I was on the road. I would sit in my hotel room and listen to these jams with Jaco and wonder if maybe I should quit Sassafras and join Ira's band."

Jaco kept badgering Economou. "I thought about quitting Sassafras, but it was a very hard thing for me to do. I come from a middle-class background, and my parents had always stressed financial security and that sort of thing. I was pretty conservative, and I wasn't willing to take risks like Jaco did. But he came down hard on me, accusing me of being greedy, saying that all I cared about was money. He attacked my philosophy of life and said that music was the only thing that mattered. I was torn. I didn't know whether to stay on the road and make some good money with Sassafras or go after the idealistic jazz thing with Jaco."

Economou eventually quit Bobbing's band to join the Sullivan quartet. By this time, Ira had secured a four-night-a-week gig at the Lion's Share, a Miami jazz club with a young clientele, many of whom were music students at the University of Miami. Sullivan says the group was on the cutting edge of fusion at the time. "The kids loved it because Economou was able to play that funk beat underneath while still giving me the jazz line on top. He sounded like a young Tony Williams. And of course Jaco was killing everybody. I used to refuse to play with Fender bass players until he came along. Now there's bassists all over the world who play like Jaco—grabbing that handful of harmonics, playing chords, and soloing like a horn player. He had that sound and that incredible speed. He made the bass a solo instrument, which was something people hadn't heard before. It was really like the shot heard 'round the world."

The young crowds that flocked to the Lion's Share were hard-pressed to put a tag on the music the Sullivan band was making. As Ira remembers, "They'd sit there during the first set and say, 'Man, it sounds like Miles.' Second set they'd say, 'No, it sounds more like what Herbie's doing with the Head Hunters.' Then, after the third set, they'd tell us, 'Man, we never heard no music like this before.' And that's why I decided not to record it. I figured anything that good, just let it lay."

In addition to standards and Sullivan originals, the band played some of Jaco's compositions. These included the beautiful ballad

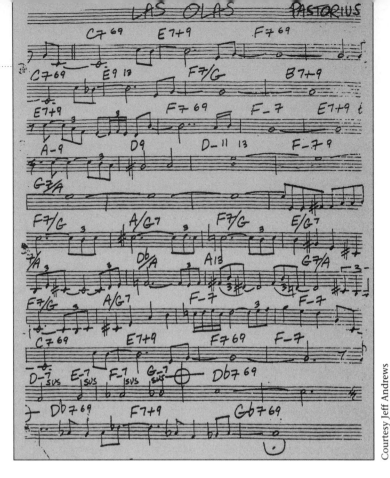

Jaco's handwritten scores for "Las Olas" and "71+"

"Las Olas," a 71-bar bossa nova he called "71+," and "(Used to Be a) Cha Cha," which later appeared on Jaco's debut album.

Sullivan remembers Jaco being "straight as an arrow" during their stint together at the Lion's Share. "He was a nice young man, a family man. He didn't smoke, didn't drink. All he wanted to do was play the bass, and play baseball or basketball or racquetball. He was always full of energy. All he was looking to do at the time was create music and play his instrument better than anybody else in the world. And he did."

Economou recalls the period with Jaco and Ira Sullivan at the Lion's Share as a time of both musical and spiritual growth. He remembers engaging in many lengthy, thought-provoking, late-night conversations with Jaco about the nature of music, the meaning of life, the experience of death and the afterlife.

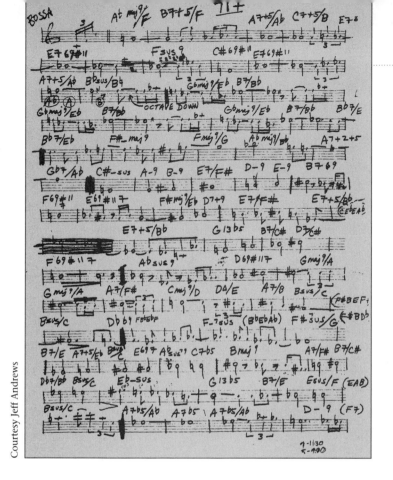

Courtesy Jeff Andrews

"Jaco was a really religious guy at the time. He and I used to read the Bible and talk about it. We had a routine of sitting up on his roof on Hollywood Boulevard, reading the Bible and discussing it for hours. And I remember Jaco telling me once how he was actually at the crucifixion of Jesus Christ. He said one time when he had a really high fever he was so delirious that he entered this vivid dream state. And he was there, right in front of Christ hanging on the cross. He explained this dream in great detail. And you have to remember, Jaco was completely straight at this time. He didn't drink and he never tried drugs. He was seriously straight when he had this dream."

Jaco also told Economou he thought he was going to die young. "Jaco always talked about dying at the age of Jesus Christ [33] or Charlie Parker [34]." Steve Finn confirms that Jaco had predicted an early death. "He used to say that shit when he was 17. Actually, none of us in that group believed we would see 35, so it wasn't an out-of-the-ordinary thought at that time and place. But Jaco really hung with it. He got more and more obsessed with it, and it was somehow tied to a sense of greatness. In Jaco's mind, he was tied in with Christ and Bird and everybody important who had died before 35."

At some point during Jaco's period of intensive Bible study, Randy Bernsen came along with more food for thought. "One day Randy brought by this thing called *The Urantia Book*," recalls Economou. "This book is about 2,000 pages long and contains some really wild stuff. The first quarter of it describes the dimensions of the universe and goes into how many universes there are, how many planets there are, and the level of consciousness on our planet compared to the rest of the universe. The second quarter of the book talks about the rank of the angels in the universe. The rest of the book talks about Jesus Christ and his mission on the planet.

"*The Urantia Book* also talks about a universal music—the music the angels are listening to. I remember Jaco being amazed by the possibility of music in other realms. This book also has a very noble description of the musician; it praises musicians as having something like a sacred duty on the planet, which is a notion Jaco really related to.

"I was a devout Christian and really into the Bible," Economou continues, "but Jaco talked me into checking out *The Urantia Book*. After I did, I became almost obsessed with it. Every day for the next three years, I read that book. It just turned my whole life around. And Jaco got deeply into it too. It got to a point where we would sit on the roof of his place with *The Urantia Book* and meditate and wait for UFOs to come and pick us up. We were both totally convinced it was a real possibility. And Jaco believed that he was such a special person the aliens would want to check him out."

It was during this period that Jaco got his first serious taste of alcohol. "I remember getting really drunk with Jaco at the Lion's Share a few times," says Economou. "But every time it happened back then,

©John Stix

it just seemed to be a lot of fun. It wasn't the self-abusive thing it became for him later in his life."

In the winter of 1973, Jaco made an important connection with Paul Bley, the jazz pianist who had worked with such great bassists as Charlie Haden, Gary Peacock, and Steve Swallow in his adventurous trios of the late '50s and early '60s. Bley, who lived in New York City at the time, had made it an annual custom to spend several weeks during the winter at the Miami-area home of his wife's parents. On one such occasion, he performed a solo-piano concert at the Planetarium in Miami, and Jaco was in attendance. They talked after the performance and struck up an immediate rapport.

In the summer of 1974, Bley invited Jaco up to New York for a month-long engagement at a now-defunct jazz club on McDougal Street in the heart of Greenwich Village. As Bley recalls, Ross Traut was the original guitarist on the gig but Pat Metheny ended up completing the engagement. "Pat came as Ross's guest on opening night and asked to sit in. He ended up playing the rest of the month while the other guy just sat in the wings. So I guess Pat's aggressiveness belied that baby face."

Bley, Metheny, Pastorius, and drummer Bruce Ditmas established a tight rapport. "That band never left the bandstand," says Bley. "We were very horny to play. We'd play continuous hour-long suites, which gave us a chance to incorporate some of the written material while inventing transitions from one piece to the other. Conceptually, it was just a simple translation of the acoustic music to an electric setting. But to electric musicians at the time, it was earth-shattering."

Bley decided to document the music by taking the quartet into Blue Rock Studio on June 16, 1974. The resulting album, titled simply *Pastorius/Metheny/Ditmas/Bley*, was released on Bley's Improvising Artists label. "That album turned out to be too successful," he says. "I got frightened off by its success. I thought, 'Now they're gonna have to get me a truck and a roadie and a light show and smoke bombs to tour with this band.' So I never did another electric album like that again, even though it outsold all the other records in the Improvising Artists catalog."

Around the same time, Jaco appeared on *Party Down*, a gritty R&B album by Miami guitarist Willie "Little Beaver" Hale, one of his old jamming buddies from the days at the Downbeat Lounge. The bassist listed in the credits is one "Nelson (Jocko) Padron," but the funky 16th-note bass lines are unmistakable.

In 1975, Jaco also played on a session for Ira Sullivan's self-titled album for the A&M/Horizon label. He appears on only one track, "Portrait of Sal La Rosa," playing a custom-made acoustic bass guitar. His name is misspelled in the credits as "Joco Pastorious."

Toward the end of summer, Jaco met Bobby Colomby, the drummer for Blood, Sweat & Tears and a budding A&R man. Colomby was in Fort Lauderdale with BS&T to play at Bachelors III. "I was strolling along the beach in the afternoon when I spotted this vivacious blonde," recalls Colomby. "I was really knocked out by her, so I walked up, introduced myself, and started talking to her, trying to pick her up. She told me she was working as a waitress at Bachelors III, and my next question was, 'Are you married?' And she tells me, 'Yes, my husband is the best bass player in the world.'

"Well, at first I thought she was being a typically supportive wife. I figured the guy was probably a mediocre bass player, but I decided to humor her anyway, mainly because she was so cute. So I said to her, 'Well, I'm a musician and a producer, and I would really like to hear this husband of yours.'"

The following afternoon, Jaco met Colomby at Bachelors III. "This guy walks into the club and says, 'I'm Jaco, Tracy's husband.' He was barefoot. He was carrying his bass, and he had a basketball tucked under one arm. I looked at him and said, 'Oh, so you're the best bass player in the world, right? Nice to meet you.' I asked the roadies to set up a bass amp so we could see just how good this guy really was. I was fully expecting to get a good laugh out of it.

"So Jaco plugs in his bass and starts playing. As I sat there listening, my eyes started bugging out and my hair was standing on end. I couldn't believe it. He wasn't kidding—he *was* the greatest bass player in the world! I had heard hundreds of bassists in my time, but none of them even approached the facility that Jaco showed that afternoon. I was absolutely stunned by what he was doing on the bass. He was definitely coming out of the James Jamerson and Jerry Jemmott style of playing, but he went well beyond their scope. He was doing things on the bass that I had never heard anybody do before—harmonics, chording, impossibly fast lines. He was playing stuff like 'Donna Lee' and 'Portrait of Tracy.' It was all there. It was all in his hands and in his mind. He was truly a phenomenon."

Riding on the massive success of Blood, Sweat & Tears, Colomby had been offered a production deal by Steve Popovich, head of A&R at Epic Records. "He basically told me, 'Anything you find that you want to produce, we'll put out.' I'm sure he was expecting me to come up with some pop band like BS&T—but I found Jaco instead."

Despite Colomby's enthusiasm and sincerity, Jaco was skeptical. He had been approached before by would-be entrepreneurs who promised record deals, but nothing had ever come of it. Undaunted, Colomby returned to New York, where he began putting the pieces together to orchestrate a record deal for his discovery. "I called up Steve Popovich and told him I was ready to produce my first record. I said I had found someone very special. I told him this guy was a unique player, a revolutionary talent. I explained that it wasn't a pop act, but that the guy was a serious genius who deserved a showcase."

Popovich's response was predictable: "Bass? You want to produce a guy who plays bass? What kind of record can you make with a bass player?" But the Epic honcho finally agreed to give Jaco a listen.

"We flew Jaco to New York and held the audition in the back of a restaurant," Colomby recalls. "We set up a bass amp, and Jaco came in to play for Popovich and Jim Tyrell, who was the head of marketing at Epic. I used to play in a band with Tyrell, who was also a bass player, so you can imagine his reaction upon hearing Jaco for the first time. At one point he turned to me and said, 'Oh my God!' Needless to say, they gave me the go-ahead to do the record."

Jaco was signed to an Epic deal on September 15, 1975. Nearly a year before, he had put together a demo of some original tunes at Criteria Studios in Miami—with Bobby Economou on drums, Alex Darqui on piano, Don Alias on congas, and Othello Molineaux on steel pans—so he was ready to move ahead with the album. A month after signing, Jaco was in New York at Colomby's home studio, laying down tracks for his revolutionary debut.

Colomby's idea was to showcase Jaco in every setting that he loved—R&B, jazz, Latin, and symphonic. For the funky R&B number, "Come On, Come Over," he contracted David Sanborn and the Brecker brothers for the horn section and brought in Sam & Dave to

Courtesy Sony Music Entertainment

Portrait of Jaco taken by Don Hunstein for the cover of his debut album

do the vocals. The latter proved to be a controversial move that greatly upset Jaco and created tension in the studio. Jaco wanted the co-writer of "Come On, Come Over," his old Woodchuck bandmate Bob Herzog, to sing the lead vocal. But Colomby insisted on some kind of name recognition for Jaco's coming-out party.

The prelude to "Come On, Come Over" was a bass/conga duet with Don Alias on "Donna Lee," highlighting Jaco's uncanny ability to blow through a demanding bebop tune with ease. With that stunning two-and-a-half-minute showcase, Jaco single-handedly ushered in a new era of electric bass. (Historical note: On the album, the composer credit is given to Charlie Parker, although Miles Davis claimed to have written the tune. In his autobiography, *Miles*, Davis stated that "Donna Lee" was first recorded on a 1947 Parker date and mistakenly credited to Bird at that time.)

Discussing "Donna Lee" with Neil Tesser in a 1977 *Down Beat* interview, Jaco said: "I felt that I had never heard anyone clearly outline a tune on the bass. Maybe someone has done it before, I don't know because I don't listen to that many records, but I had never heard it before. I had never heard someone take a tune like 'Donna Lee' and play it on the bass without a piano player so that you always could hear the changes as well as the melody. It's a question of learning to reflect the original chord in just the line. Players like Wayne Shorter, Sonny Rollins, Herbie Hancock, Ira Sullivan can do that. I wanted to be able to do it too."

Alias says that the idea for a conga/bass duet was strictly Jaco's. "Talk about uniqueness! That was the secret to Jaco. Besides his musical talent, he had the ability to conceptualize and recognize certain musical combinations that were totally unique. I had thought about conga and drums, conga and trumpet, conga and piano, but never conga and bass. It was really an inspired notion, and what ended up on the record was a first take. And, of course, that started the avalanche—every bass player I know now can cut 'Donna Lee,' thanks to Jaco."

Colomby secured Herbie Hancock for the session and prominently featured his brilliant acoustic piano playing on "Kuru/Speak Like a Child" and "(Used to Be a) Cha-Cha." In the liner notes, Hancock wrote: "Jaco is a phenomenon. He is able to make sounds on the bass that are a total surprise to the sensibilities. Not only single notes, but chords, harmonics, and all sorts of nuances with the color of the instrument that when combined and translated through Jaco make for some of the best music that I've heard in a long time."

The drumming was top-notch throughout, with Return To Forever's Lenny White on three tracks, Narada Michael Walden on "Come On, Come Over," and Jaco's old pal Bobby Economou on "Kuru/Speak Like a Child." As Bobby recalls, "I remember being in the studio with Jaco, Herbie, and Don Alias. At the other end of the studio were all these string players. It was a long piece of music, and there was some real magic on that track. We just barreled through it. We recorded it live in the studio, almost as if on a dare. Jaco's attitude was, 'Fuck this overdub shit! Let's do it live!' He was always doing daredevil stuff like that, just to be different. But Jaco really kicked my ass on that tune. That session was one of the highlights of my career."

More than anything, *Jaco Pastorius* established its creator as one of the rare talents who can be credited as a "sound innovator" on an instrument. "He changed the sound of, and the approach to, the electric bass," says Rich Appleman, chairman of the Bass Department at Berklee College. "The electric bass became Jaco's voice, much as the trumpet did for Miles Davis and the tenor saxophone for John Coltrane. The greatest jazz musicians do this.

"Jaco also created a repertoire for his instrument, both through his interpretation of such tunes as 'Donna Lee' and with his own compositions. His use of harmonics was revolutionary. 'Continuum' is a great example of the way Jaco used harmonics to compose on the bass—just listen to the chord at the beginning, where he plays B, F#, and C# harmonics over the open E string to create a major 6/9 chord that sets the mood for the piece. The head of this tune is something that all contemporary bassists should learn, to gain insight into composing on bass. And the bass solo is equally inspiring. Jaco's phrasing is beautiful; he plays 16th-notes in various groupings and intertwines them with quarter-note triplets, doublestops, octaves, and a smashing low E that caps one long phrase—incredible!"

Several months prior to his signing with Epic, Jaco had been playing around the Boston area with Pat Metheny, whom he had met at the University of Miami. Metheny had recruited Jaco to complete a trio that included drummer Bob Moses, who had worked with Metheny in Gary Burton's quartet. Moses fondly recalls his first meeting with the phenom from Fort Lauderdale. "We used to play a

lot at a joint called Pooh's Pub. That was where I met Jaco, back in '74. He really hadn't done much of anything yet outside of Florida. He had played and recorded with Paul Bley, and there was a buzz about him like, 'This cat is bad. He's playing the bass like nobody else plays the bass.'

"My first impression of Jaco was that he seemed very quiet and shy. He was wearing glasses, and he had on his First Baptist T-shirt. I remember him being very respectful towards me, like, 'Oh man, I'm really honored to play with you.' But then something happened that was really unusual. On the first gig, Metheny called 'All the Things You Are.' Now, that's just about the first tune that any aspiring jazz musician learns, because it's the perfect example of the cycle of fifths. But Jaco says, 'Man, I don't know it. You got a sheet on it?'

And I think, Oh my God—we're gonna play a jazz gig with a cat who doesn't know 'All the Things You Are.' Oh fuck! What is that gonna be about?

"So Metheny puts the music in front of him, and Jaco just glances at the thing for half a second and proceeds to play this tune better than I had ever heard it played in my life. I mean, he just tore it up from the first note. We played it super uptempo, and he was throwing in all kinds of arpeggios and harmonics—just roarin', man! He went way up on top of the beat—just flying! By the time we were halfway through the first chorus he didn't look at the music again. And I thought, Well, this cat has it in the genetic code. That's the only explanation. Because some people work 20 years to play that song, and this cat had never played it before and he was already way beyond everybody else."

In December 1975, Jaco traveled to Ludwigsburg, Germany, to record *Bright Size Life*, Metheny's debut album for the ECM label. In the liner notes Metheny's mentor, vibist and Berklee educator Gary Burton, wrote: "Pat's counterpart on bass, Jaco Pastorius, is an equally startling young player and a true innovator on electric bass. Because of the similarity of their respective talents, they are a great match."

And yet, Moses confirms that there was some tension between Jaco and Metheny. "Jaco's shit was too strong, and the truth of it is Metheny did try to suppress it. I actually had to referee between those two cats. I mean, they loved each other but they were also at each other's throats. And I could see both points of view. First of all, it wasn't Jaco's music, it was Metheny's gig. He organized it and flew Jaco up to play his music, so it was definitely his thing. But at the same time, when you have a group like that it kind of has to be an equal thing. If you've got somebody as strong as Jaco, and myself for that matter, it should be an equal thing.

"It didn't happen at first, but after two or three gigs Jaco realized he wasn't getting any room, so he would start bogarting. He'd do stuff like turning a waltz into a reggae in the middle of the tune, and Metheny would get pissed. He didn't want a reggae, but Jaco was so strong with that shit. And whenever he did it, the audience would go completely nuts. And when we'd do some rave-up shit, some killer, loud, crazy Afro-Cream shit, Jaco's spirit would take over. Metheny would always come back afterwards with the lightest, most gentle bossa nova. He'd completely take it back to Jim Hall or Wes Montgomery just to regain control of the band. He'd never let us do two or three in a row like that. There were some funny tensions within that group, but a lot of great music managed to get played in spite of them."

Perhaps because of these tensions, Metheny wondered whether he should use Jaco on *Bright Size Life*. As Moses explains, "Before we made that record, Metheny had already gotten some pressure from ECM not to use Jaco. I don't think [label head] Manfred Eicher even knew who Jaco was, plus he had some biases against electric bass. His attitude was, 'This is jazz. It has to be acoustic bass.' And since Metheny was, at that point, trying to get some credibility as a jazz player, he was considering Manfred's point."

For a brief period, Metheny seriously considered using Dave Holland for the record. "Holland had already played with Miles Davis," says Moses. "He was an acoustic bass virtuoso who fit the ECM pedigree. And Jaco was seen as this crazy rock & roller or something. I didn't know what Jaco was, but he certainly wasn't a pure jazz player. So Metheny was kind of going along with that whole idea, even after we had done all these gigs around Boston with Jaco."

Moses says that Metheny went as far as having a lengthy rehearsal with Holland just prior to the recording of *Bright Size Life*. "We went up to Woodstock and played all the music from that album with Dave at his house. After the rehearsal, Metheny was still vacillating—'I don't know. It's a jazz album. I should probably use Dave— it's acoustic bass, he's more famous, he's got credibility.' And I said to him, 'Man, you are *crazy* if you don't use Jaco. With all due respect to Dave Holland, Jaco blows him away! Your music is twice as alive with this cat. And it's great that it's electric bass. It makes the music 20 times more exciting, more grooving.'

"Dave Holland had a much more intellectual approach. He's fine—he's a great bass player, no doubt. But with him it was just more precious, more of a museum kind of thing. Jaco's thing was thrilling, exciting. It had that fresh kind of vibe like Prince or something. It went beyond a musical thing—it was the energy he brought to it."

Metheny eventually decided to go with Jaco, who played brilliantly throughout the sessions. Even so, Moses maintains that *Bright Size Life* didn't even come close to conveying what the trio had been achieving back in Boston. "I don't listen to that album," he says. "In fact, I never listened to it. I don't think I got past the first tune. A lot of people love it, but for me it just doesn't capture what we were doing, and it makes me really sad that this record is the only representation of that band. Live, it was like a power trio. It was like Cream, but with a lot of 16th-notes and a million chord changes, because Metheny's music was really complex. That shit was loud, and we were funking too. We were playing some Afro-Cuban shit, and Jaco was just tearing it up. But the ECM vibe kind of squelched all that energy. They didn't want it to be too ballsy and grooving. To me, the album is really lightweight compared to what we were doing on the gigs."

Moses has vivid memories of Jaco's athletic, charismatic stage presence in that band. "I remember an entrance he made one time that blew my mind. We were playing a gig at a club where they had a fence all around the stage that was about chest high, and the only entrance to the bandstand was through this corridor down the middle of the room. Jaco would make these amazing entrances where he would strap on his bass and jump straight-leg over fence. So before we even played a note, people were saying, 'Wow!' They were primed.

"Anyway, this one night Jaco starts running towards the stage. Metheny and I are already onstage, and here's Jaco running towards us full tilt, barefooted and barechested, with his bass strapped on. And when he gets like two feet from the stage, he does this incredible flip where he goes feet-over-head. He lands on the bandstand, and then using his head as a pivot he flips his legs up over his body and comes back around so he's standing again. Then, in one motion, he plugs his cord into his amp and hits the first note. As we started playing, he gave me this look like, 'Am I bad or what?' That was a move that James Brown couldn't have made. It really blew my mind."

In late 1975, Bobby Colomby arranged for Jaco to sub for bassist Ron McClure on several gigs with Blood, Sweat & Tears. In the band at the time were such players as Don Alias, pianist Larry Willis, trombonist Dave Bargeron (who would later be a member of Jaco's Word Of Mouth big band), and guitarist Mike Stern, who would become one of Jaco's closest friends as well as a member of his Word Of Mouth sextet.

Although they didn't actually become friends until they played together in BS&T, Stern remembers meeting Jaco in 1973. "The very first time we met was in Florida," he says. "I was living in Washington, D.C., and playing in a rock & roll band. We got a gig down in Miami at a place called the Flying Machine; there were three bands on the bill, and Jaco had a piano/bass/drums trio that played before our band went on. After their set, I went up to Jaco and said, 'Man, you sounded great.' I was really drunk and kind of falling all over myself, but Jaco was totally straight. That was when he was living the clean life.

"I was just getting into jazz at the time and was very impressed by Jaco. He was playing this bebop shit at burning tempos, and you could hear all the Latin and Cuban influences in his music, too. I was an Eric Clapton fanatic then, just a basic rock and blues guitarist, and what Jaco was doing that night was far beyond me. I was really in awe of him."

Two years later, when he was a student at the Berklee College of Music in Boston, Stern saw Jaco playing at Pooh's Pub with Metheny and Moses. "He looked familiar but I didn't say anything. And besides, I had been so drunk on the night when I met him that I didn't really remember it well. But Jaco walked up to me and said, 'Hey, man—I know you. We met in Miami at the Flying Machine about two years ago.' He really had an incredible memory. And he was still totally straight—no booze, no drugs at all."

The next time they met was in BS&T. "We played together for about three months and got to be really close. This was right before he joined Weather Report. I remember Jaco being very health-conscious then. He was really into physical activity like swimming and playing basketball and baseball. The only thing was, he was unusually hyper. He couldn't sleep at night—he would sleep maybe a couple of hours and then get up and start playing sports right away. Some of the guys in the band were doing cocaine, but Jaco refused to do it when they offered it to him. He would say, 'No, man, I don't need that stuff. I'm high all the time just naturally.' And he really was."

Jaco was very supportive of Stern. "It was my first major gig, and I was really scared," says Mike. "Jaco gave me a lot of feedback; sometimes he could be pretty blunt about it, but it was in a humorous way. I remember one time I took this solo that never got off the ground. It sounded terrible, and I was feeling really depressed about it. Some of the guys in the band came up to me afterward and said, 'Man, don't worry about it. You just had an off night.' They were trying to make me feel good and bolster my confidence. But Jaco came up to me and yelled, 'Stern! That solo didn't swing—*at all!*' He was right, of course. But he was also telling me, in a sense, not to take myself so seriously, which was good advice."

Stern remembers another piece of advice that Jaco gave him during their three-month stint with BS&T. "He used to say, 'Forget about playing bebop. Turn it up and play that screaming shit. That's what the guitar was invented for. The guys playing those other instruments only wish they could do that.' And it's interesting, because that's pretty much what Miles told me when I joined his band five years later."

With the release of his debut album only a few months away, Jaco was on the verge of superstardom. Everything was in place for his entry into Weather Report.

FOUR

Weather Report

"Hey kid, do you play electric bass too?"

JACO HAD HIS INITIAL ENCOUNTER with Joe Zawinul sometime in early 1975. It happened in Miami.

Weather Report was in town to play the Gusman Theatre. After the soundcheck, Zawinul was standing on the corner outside the theatre when he was approached by "this skinny kid with long hair and wild clothes." Their exchange went something like this:

Jaco: "I've been following your music since Cannonball Adderley, and I really love it."

Joe: "So, what do you want?"

Jaco: "My name is John Francis Pastorius III, and I'm the greatest electric bass player in the world."

Joe: "Get the fuck out of here!"

But Jaco persisted, and Joe admired him for his ballsy stance. "He kind of reminded me of myself when I was a brash young man. I used to go around saying, 'I'm the baddest' when I was coming up in Cannonball's band."

Joe asked for a demo tape. The next morning Jaco came by his hotel room with a cassette of a typical night at the Lion's Share with Ira Sullivan's group. Although the maestro liked what he heard, he explained that Weather Report already had a great bassist in Alphonso Johnson. Jaco left the hotel somewhat dejected, but he kept in touch with Zawinul over the next several months, sending him letters and more gig tapes.

Joe remembers being particularly impressed by Jaco's handwriting in those letters. "It was really ornate and beautiful, like a Mozart score. And I also liked what he was saying. He seemed like a smart kid who was seriously into the music."

While in New York to record his solo debut, Jaco boldly approached several of his favorite musicians to announce his arrival. "He had a real aggressive personality," remembers guitarist John Abercrombie. "He just went knocking on doors. He went to Keith Jarrett's house and played his bass for him. He went to Tony Williams's house. He went up to Woodstock and met Jack DeJohnette. He just wouldn't be denied. He was always so hungry to jam. He came to my loft and we played for a couple of hours—just sort of screaming at each other through our instruments."

Violinist Michael Urbaniak remembers being introduced to Jaco around this time by Alan Pepper, proprietor of the Bottom Line. "I came by the club one night, and Alan said to me, 'I want you to meet this kid from Florida. He's a really great bass player.' And there was Jaco sitting in the audience with his bass guitar. We talked, and after the show he came back to my apartment on 57th Street. He ended up sleeping on my couch for about a week or so."

During this period, Jaco also made trips down to Philadelphia to visit his father. One of the musicians he sought out in Philly was the great guitarist Pat Martino. They got together for some informal jamming, but none of the music was recorded.

In January 1976, Alphonso Johnson announced he would be leaving Weather Report to start a new band with drummer Billy Cobham and keyboardist George Duke. (The band was the CBS All-Stars, which also included guitarist Steve Khan and saxophonist Tom Scott.) Weather Report was only halfway through the recording of *Black Market* when Johnson split, causing a temporary dilemma for the band.

"At first, I didn't know what to think in terms of replacing him," says Zawinul. "And then I remembered this kid Pastorius. He had just sent me a rough mix of his solo album, and I was really floored by it, particularly the song 'Continuum.' So I called Jaco and the first thing I asked him was, 'Hey kid, do you play electric bass too?' He got such a warm, rich sound on that Fender fretless, I thought he was playing an upright bass."

Zawinul and Wayne Shorter arranged for Jaco to come into the studio and play on "Cannonball," an homage to Cannonball Adderley, who had died on August 8, 1975. "Cannonball was from Florida too, and I wanted that Florida sound on this particular track. Plus, I remembered how much Jaco loved Cannonball's music, so I figured he might be the right guy to use. We brought him in, and that was more or less his audition. Wayne and I talked it over, and we both agreed that this kid could play."

In addition to playing on "Cannonball," Jaco contributed a tune to *Black Market*: "Barbary Coast," a funky, slow-moving vehicle propelled by Jaco's crisp, muted bass figure. "At first, I didn't like that tune so much," Zawinul remembers. "It sounded too much like a Horace Silver line to me. But then we worked a little bit with it and got a nice groove happening. And, of course, that became a kind of signature piece for Jaco."

"Barbary Coast" opens with the sound of a train roaring along a railroad track, its horn blasts fading into the distance. This sound is much more than atmospheric filler; it resonates with deep meaning for anyone who grew up in Fort Lauderdale near the tracks that run alongside Dixie Highway. As a kid, Jaco would often wander along those tracks for miles, dreaming of places he might visit one day. Ironically, those same tracks run past the Kalis Funeral Home in Fort Lauderdale, the site of Jaco's wake on September 24, 1987.

Jaco officially joined Weather Report on April 1, 1976. His earthy R&B feel dramatically altered the character of the band and helped to catapult it to a new level of popularity. As Zawinul puts it,

"Weather Report was a really powerful group with Alphonso on bass. But Jaco was in a space all his own. He was so different from all the other bass players of that time. He had that magical thing about him, the same kind of thing Jimi Hendrix had. He was an electrifying performer and a great musician. And he was really responsible for bringing the white kids to our concerts. Before Jaco came along, we were perceived as a kind of esoteric jazz group. We had been popular on college campuses, but after Jaco joined the band we started selling out big concert halls everywhere. Jaco became some kind of All-American folk hero to these kids."

Part of Jaco's appeal was the sheer visceral strength of his groove-oriented bass playing, which he had honed to perfection during those ten months on the road with Wayne Cochran & the C.C. Riders. You could feel Jaco's powerful 16th-note lines pushing the band, challenging the soloists while still holding down the groove. The clarity of his ideas and the speed of his execution astounded listeners. As Chip Stern noted in a *Musician* article on Weather Report: "Jaco Pastorius, one of the most original and inspired musicians of the decade, is able to take on Miroslav Vitous's rhythmic-harmonic-melodic role and put up the funk as well."

A natural extrovert, Jaco was acutely aware of the concept of Showtime, an awareness he inherited from his gregarious father. With his Florida hippie attire (baggy white beach pants, tie-dyed T-shirts, headband or Phillies baseball cap covering his shoulder-length hair) and wild stage antics, Jaco quickly developed a charismatic stage persona that captivated the curious.

One of his favorite tricks was to spread baby powder on the floor so he could shuffle and slide across the stage with the ease of a young James Brown. "He would never go on without that baby powder," remembers one Weather Report roadie. "And if he ran out of the stuff, he'd send me out to the nearest store and hold up the show until I got back with it."

Peter Erskine vividly recalls his first encounter with Jaco's baby-

On stage with Weather Report at the Berkeley Jazz Festival, 1976

powder routine. "We were in Japan. It was my first concert with Weather Report [in the summer of 1978]. During the soundcheck the road crew was spreading baby powder on the stage, and I asked, 'What's that for?' Jaco indicated *shoosh* to them, like it was some big secret or something. He looked at me sort of smiling and said, 'You'll see.'

"That night we started the concert with 'Elegant People,' a Wayne Shorter tune. Just before it kicked into the funky section, Jaco came over to me and yelled, 'Check it out!' And he started doing these amazing James Brown moves, gliding across the stage on one foot like he was ice-skating. I couldn't believe it. It looked so great, I just started laughing. And all the while, he was playing the funkiest bass so effortlessly and looking back at me and smiling. That was the best welcome into the band I could have imagined."

Throughout his time with Weather Report, Jaco would use his solo feature in concert to pay tribute to his heroes, quoting liberally from Jimi's "Purple Haze" and "Third Stone from the Sun," Bird's "Donna Lee," Wilson Pickett's "Funky Broadway," and the Beatles' "Blackbird." With this pastiche of musical styles, Jaco not only entertained the audience but opened some ears to new sounds, providing a bridge between the rock and jazz camps. Young white rock fans would flock to Weather Report shows to see Jaco throw his bass up in the air like Pete Townshend of the Who and do backflips off his amp, and they'd come away with their first taste of Charlie Parker and John Coltrane.

While some critics dismissed Jaco's stage antics as shameless grandstanding, they could not deny the brilliance of his playing. With the exposure generated by his solo debut album and Weather Report's *Black Market*, both out by the summer of 1976, Jaco was heralded as the big noise in the industry, the guiding light of a new generation, the player who was single-handedly changing the role of the electric bass. The facility with which he played was unprecedented in the short history of his instrument, which had been invented only 25 years before. His time was flawless, his stamina staggering, and his melodic invention went well beyond the accomplishments of such electric bass pioneers as Monk Montgomery, James Jamerson, Duck Dunn, and Jerry Jemmott. And Jaco's creative use of harmonics was nothing less than revolutionary.

As Mark C. Gridley points out in his book *Jazz Styles: History and Analysis*, Jaco could more than cover all of the standard jazz bass-playing styles: "He walks persuasively, as he proved on 'Crazy About Jazz' (contained in Weather Report's eleventh album, which has the same title as their first: *Weather Report*). He plays in the nonrepetitive, interactive way [identified with Scott LaFaro], as evidenced on 'Dara Factor One' (also on the eleventh album) and 'Dream Clock'

(*Night Passage*). And, he is a natural funk player, providing the proper rhythmic feeling in accompanying soul singers Sam & Dave on his own album (*Jaco Pastorius*), as well as the dancing feeling he lent Weather Report's 'Barbary Coast' (*Black Market*), 'Palladium' (*Heavy Weather*), and 'River People' (*Mr. Gone*)."

Playing keyboards at the Automat Recording Studio, San Francisco, December 1977

Bass players everywhere quickly picked up on Jaco's message. At a time when Stanley Clarke represented a new standard on electric bass, one based heavily on the thumb-slapping innovations of Larry Graham and Louis Johnson, along came Jaco with a wholly different concept. He swung open the doors for an entire generation of players, inspiring them to explore new sounds and challenging them to extend their technique on the instrument.

Mark Egan recalls those days: "I had been listening a lot to Stanley Clarke and was very impressed by what he was doing with Return To Forever. But Jaco's approach was much more advanced harmonically, and he played with such frightening intensity and attitude. That's one thing he taught me when I studied with him—just by playing with him, just by being in the same room with him, he taught me to play with a kind of conviction I never knew before."

While Zawinul and Shorter served as his mentors, Jaco was especially close to his rhythm-section mates in Weather Report, drummer Alex Acuña and percussionist Manolo Badrena. "Playing with Jaco was really a treat," says Acuña says of his former comrade. "His grooves were so strong and his tone was so unique, so fresh. It was like being in the desert, all thirsty and hot, and then somebody comes along and offers you a nice cold glass of lemonade. That's basically what Jaco did for me when he joined the band."

Jaco's outside projects during his first year with Weather Report included guest appearances on Al Di Meola's solo debut, *Land of the Midnight Sun,* on rocker Ian Hunter's *All-American Alien Boy,* and on Joni Mitchell's *Hejira,* an album that presented the bass monster as sublime accompanist. Jaco's playing on *Hejira* is marked by thoughtful restraint and tender lyricism on tunes like "Black Crow" and the haunting title track; he also achieves an uncanny vocal quality on "Refuge of the Roads," which must rank with Zawinul's "A Remark You Made" as one of Jaco's most poignant statements on the instrument.

It didn't take long for young Pastorius to assert his presence in Weather Report. On the band's next album, 1977's *Heavy Weather,* he not only contributed two compositions, "Havona" and the classic chops showcase "Teen Town," but was credited as co-producer alongside Zawinul. "That was a matter of his workmanship and his input," says Joe. "Jaco had a lot of input on that album, and I believe in giving credit where credit is due. We all contributed a lot in those days, in different areas. For Wayne, the studio was really not his

©Tom Copi, San Francisco

thing. He was there a lot of the time, but he let us run the board. And Jaco had an especially good working knowledge of the mixing board. I knew the music inside out, that was my strength, but Jaco knew a lot about adding reverb to the instruments and getting a good drum sound. And his work at the board gave such a huge presence to his bass sound.

Tony Williams, Jaco, and Herbie Hancock at the Automat Recording Studio, San Francisco

"He had really keen ears. He could hear all the parts very clearly, and we worked well together, side by side, with all 20 fingers on the board. This was before automation, you understand. Jaco was definitely a hands-on producer. Wayne did other things, like coming up with song titles, but as far as putting the music on tape, it was mostly Jaco and me working together. Long after everybody else had gone home, he would still be at it, sitting there with the engineer and doing the mixes."

Heavy Weather was a phenomenal success, far outdistancing the sales of the more esoteric *Black Market*. Initial sales figures were around the 400,000 mark; the album has since gone gold (500,000 units sold) and been reissued on CD as part of the Columbia Legacy series. The tune that converted many listeners into Weather Report fans was "Birdland," a catchy Zawinul composition inspired by the composer's memory of hearing the Count Basie band in the 1950s at the famous New York jazz club of the same name. That riff-driven tune received tons of radio airplay in 1977 and served as an introduction to jazz for many listeners crossing over from the rock or pop camps. It also received wide exposure in discos and was later covered by the Maynard Ferguson big band and the Manhattan Transfer vocal group, among others.

Another striking number on *Heavy Weather* was "A Remark You Made," an evocative ballad Zawinul had written specifically with Jaco's singing fretless bass in mind. As Joe explains, "That boy had a sound that was so easy to write for, especially ballads. There were many strengths that Alphonso brought to the band, but tone-wise he was in another category. What I wrote for Jaco, I could never have written for Alphonso."

Zawinul often referred to Jaco as "The Catalyst" for his ability to ignite a session or concert with sheer drive. "He was this excitable young kid when he joined the band," says Joe. "Wayne and I were already into our forties, and this kid Jaco kept us young with his energy and charisma on the bandstand. And his stamina was incredible. I have never seen another bass player have such stamina. He could play those 16th-note lines at super-fast tempos over and over and never slow down or stutter. We used to do this one tune called 'Volcano for Hire,' which is just burning 16th-notes, and every night he would nail it. He was always on, always pushing the band. And that really kept all of us on our toes. Every band needs what I call a warhead—the driving force, the motor. And in this band, Jaco was the warhead."

While 1977 was the year that established Weather Report as a force in the marketplace, it was also the year that marked the beginning of Jaco's marital troubles. In their early years together, Jaco had always been extremely possessive of Tracy, often to the point of being a smothering father figure. Now coming into her own at age 26, Tracy was beginning to assert her own place in the relationship. Meanwhile, the relentless touring and constant presence of groupies put a serious strain on the marriage. As one family intimate noted, "It's hard to have a husband who's out of town nine months out of the year, you know?"

Around this time, Jaco began making a play for a Florida woman named Ingrid HornmüOller, an exotic beauty who had been born in Sumatra to an Indonesian mother and a German father. The two were introduced by Geri Palladino, a hairdresser from Florida who had been a close friend of both Jaco and Tracy. "Ingrid's brother Paul was the drummer in a trio that also included my boyfriend at the time, a bassist named Dave Wilkerson," explains Palladino. "So one night I brought Jaco over to Ingrid's apartment, and they ended up hanging out all night. They spent all their time together after that. He was in love with Ingrid, and she was tremendously in love with him."

Ingrid says their first meeting may have been earlier than that. "From 1971 to 1976, I was a stewardess on Eastern Airlines. Jaco used to take Eastern flights back and forth from New York to Miami at that time, and he claimed he met me on a plane. I honestly don't remember it."

Ingrid does remember going to her first Weather Report concert in 1976, though. "There was this big to-do about Weather Report being in town. I think it was their first concert in Fort Lauderdale since Jaco had joined the group. My brother Paul was going with Geri Palladino and some friends. At the time, I was not much involved in that group of people; I had my own life, my own friends. I had been married once before, I worked for an artist, and I was into a whole different lifestyle. But I ended up going with them and saw Jaco for the first time.

"The following day, Geri invited me to a party, which is where I met Jaco and talked to him. After that we used to run into each other at nightclubs around town. Jaco was married, you know? But he was showing interest in me. He'd always come over and talk to me and flirt. And this went on for at least a year. Again, I had my own life. I wasn't investing too much time in it."

Ingrid wasn't Jaco's only indulgence that year. During Weather Report's world tour, he began developing a taste for vodka. Pat Jordan reported this incident in *GQ*: "One night before a gig, Zawinul was drinking vodka in the band's dressing room, as he often did. He offered Jaco some. Jaco refused. Zawinul told him to loosen up a little. Jaco took his first drink that night, then his second. 'He got strange after two drinks,' says Zawinul. 'He started throwing things. I knew right away I had made a mistake.'"

Jaco had actually consumed alcohol before this time. Charlie Brent recalls getting Jaco drunk on Metaxa brandy as far back as 1972. And Bobby Economou remembers drinking with Jaco in 1973 during their engagement at the Lion's Share. But those were isolated, infrequent incidents—drinking didn't become a bad habit with Jaco until after he had achieved fame with Weather Report.

The price of fame is more than just a loss of privacy. There is also the ever-present assault from groupies and other hangers-on, waiting in the wings with tempting offers of free booze, drugs, sex in exchange for that momentary brush with fame. And that's how Jaco got initiated into the cocaine fraternity.

A few of Jaco's old friends from Florida, like Bob Bobbing, were repulsed by Jaco's "extended family" and upset to see these parasites plying him with cocaine in exchange for his company. "After he joined Weather Report and got famous, too many people were trying to sensationalize their relationship with him," says Bobbing. "That's why I stopped hanging out with him. Too many groupies came out of the woodwork after that first album. These phony people would do whatever he wanted just to hang with him—get him drinks, cocaine, whatever—just so they could say, 'Wow, I hung with Jaco!' And these were some of the same people who were putting him down the year before as a showoff. I really hated the whole hypocrisy of that scene, so I went away."

When guitarist John Scofield met Jaco in 1976, he remembers him being straight and healthy. A year later, when they both happened to be staying at the Sunset Marquee Hotel in Los Angeles, Jaco was heavily into cocaine. "It seemed that most every musician I knew at the time was into cocaine," says Scofield. "It was the drug of the day. You would go to a session, and there would be lots of lines of cocaine laid out for the musicians. It was just the thing to do back then."

Bobby Economou was on the road with Blood, Sweat & Tears in 1978. During a break in their heavy touring schedule, he went to visit Jaco while Weather Report was completing the follow-up to *Heavy Weather, Mr. Gone*. "Jaco called and told me to fly out to Los Angeles so I could hang with him while he and Joe mixed the record. He actually tried to get me an audition with Weather Report, but I just wasn't ready for that gig, either emotionally or playing-wise. I was drinking a lot, and I was a mess. So I went out there to hang with Jaco, and at that time the drugs were really happening. We were doing a lot of drinking, too. There were a couple of all-nighters where Jaco and I just stayed up and partied in Los Angeles. I remember wandering around Sunset Strip with a bottle of tequila between us. It was empty before sunrise.

"I also remember Jaco going back to the studio really drunk one time and Zawinul yelling at him about that. We got into all kinds of crazy trouble on that trip, but it was mostly in fun. It wasn't really self-destructive then. We were like two country boys going wild in the big city, having fun and staying high the whole time."

Economou eventually got into an Alcoholics Anonymous program and turned his life around. Jaco never made that move. In retrospect, Economou says, "Jaco's biggest problem was that he had such a powerful personality people wanted to be with him or be a part of his entourage. They fed him cocaine to get on his good side, so they could feel cool. But underneath that powerful personality he was basically very insecure. I remember one night during one of our binges, we were both really drunk and Jaco started crying. He hugged me and was crying like a baby and saying, 'Economou! What am I doing here? All the expectations on me, man—the responsibility! What am I going to do?' He was obviously feeling the pressure of being on top."

By 1978, Jaco was indeed sitting on top of the world. He was named #1 electric bassist in both the critics' and readers' polls of *Down Beat* magazine. *Mr. Gone* came out and instantly went gold. Musicians and fans around the world sang his praises. But even as Jaco became ruler of the bass empire, his family life was crumbling around him. His fights with Tracy became more frequent and more physical, inflicting untold trauma on eight-year-old Mary and five-year-old John. And Jaco began courting Ingrid more aggressively.

As she recalls, "One day in the summer of 1978 he called me out of the blue and said, 'You've got tickets leaving at such-and-such time to arrive in Amsterdam at such-and-such time.' And I told him, 'Well, I'll think about it.' But eventually I went. It was only supposed to be one week, but I wound up staying and finishing the tour with Weather Report in Europe.

"Obviously it wasn't right, what Jaco and I were doing," she continues. "I know it was very traumatic for Tracy. But it felt right in a sort of spiritual way. Jaco's marriage to Tracy was dissolving, and I think he was really broken up about that. He felt strongly about making the marriage work, perhaps because of his frustration about his parents' breakup."

Tracy filed for a divorce at the end of 1978 and eventually got custody of the house and kids, which left Jaco feeling bitter and angry. This led to more drinking

Jaco with his children Mary and John circa 1978

and drugging, which only enhanced his depression, triggering the cyclical process of self-abuse that would soon spin out of control.

And Jaco grew increasingly fatalistic. As Zawinul recalls, "We were in Barcelona playing a gig, and afterwards Jaco and I went back to the hotel. It was late in the evening, and we were sitting on this bench outside the hotel, drinking a little bit and talking about philosophers—Schopenhauer, Spinoza, Nietzsche. All of a sudden he looks at me and says, 'You know what, man? I'm not gonna be 35 years old.' And I said, 'What the fuck are you talking about? You're a young punk, you got everything going for you in life. Just do what you're doing, and you're gonna live to be 105, okay?' And that was it—but it was a weird and kind of scary thing for him to bring something like that up, out of nowhere."

By the summer of 1978, Peter Erskine had replaced Acuña as the drummer in Weather Report. Erskine and Jaco struck up a close friendship and had an especially strong hookup as a rhythm section. "Jaco basically got me into the band," says Peter, "and I will always feel a debt of gratitude to him for that. He had heard me in Miami with Maynard Ferguson's band around 1977 and later recommended me for the gig. He kind of took a chance after hearing me just that one time. But on his recommendation, they hired me sight unseen for a Japanese tour."

Erskine's first encounter with Zawinul, the stern patriarch of Weather Report, came in New York during rehearsals for that summer tour. "I got to the S.I.R. Studios on time and started setting up my drums. I was very eager to meet everyone and start playing. Meanwhile, these guys kept calling in to say they were running late. The rehearsal eventually started about five hours later than it was supposed to. Joe came in first and was very cool. He just kind of sauntered over and shook my hand. Wayne was friendly. Jaco bopped in, said hi, and then ran back out to get a six-pack of beer.

"I was so impatient, having sat around all day waiting for them, that when Joe started noodling on the synth, I jumped up and started playing along with him. Finally, Jaco came back in with a six-pack of Heineken, and he looked up to the stage where we were jamming. He had a big smile on his face. He ran up and grabbed his bass, and we just started jamming before going into 'Gibraltar.' When we finished, it was like we had just done a show or something, the vibe in the room was so high. I remember Joe and Wayne and Jaco were all slapping hands, and they included me in on that, which really made me feel like I was a part of the band. So the next

day I asked Joe, 'Can I tell my friends I'm in the band?' I was really excited and wanted to go public with this. And Joe said in that gruff manner of his, 'You can tell your friends you're going to Japan.'"

Weather Report circa 1979: Jaco, Peter Erskine, Joe Zawinul, and Wayne Shorter

During his first tour with Weather Report, Erskine noticed that Jaco was no longer the straight-laced family man he remembered from their first encounter the year before. "He was partying pretty hard all the time. Jaco and Joe had this ultra-macho competitive thing going on—bragging a lot and drinking a lot and trying to see who could out-hang who. And it was at that point that Jaco started to pursue some other muse. He started to change."

In the early part of 1979, Weather Report made a trip to Havana, where they took part in the historic Havana Jam, the first concerts held in Cuba by American artists in 20 years. The three-night festival, sponsored by Columbia Records, was held at the Karl Marx Theatre and featured a stellar cast of CBS recording artists, including Billy Joel, Stephen Stills, Kris Kristofferson, and an all-star jazz group with Stan Getz, Bobby Hutcherson, Dexter Gordon, Tony Williams, and Woody Shaw.

Besides appearing with Weather Report, Jaco also performed a set with guitarist John McLaughlin and drummer Tony Williams, who had played on some tracks from *Mr. Gone*. Billed as the Trio Of Doom, they played music that was fast, frenzied, and full of energy. This lineup promised to be the ultimate fusion power trio, but Jaco's erratic behavior on and off the bandstand virtually sabotaged the gig.

As McLaughlin recalls: "It was such a shame. Tony and Jaco and I had rehearsed in New York, and what a trio that was! What a pleasure it was to play with them! After one rehearsal, we actually went in to record with Joni Mitchell [for her *Mingus* album]. We did one tune; later they wiped Tony and me off the track, which I also thought was a shame. But the rehearsals for our Trio Of Doom gig were happening, and we went down to Havana with high expectations.

"We started off our set with my tune 'Dark Prince,' which is an uptempo C-minor blues with altered changes. It was really a chance to stretch, but Jaco just threw down the music, walked back to his amp, turned it up to 11, and started playing in A major really loud against it. I was looking at Tony like, 'What's going on here?' It was nothing like the rehearsals. He did the same kind of thing to Tony's tune. And then he went out and did his whole audience routine. It was a fiasco."

To this day, McLaughlin jokingly refers to that ugly episode as the Bay of Gigs. "I was so mad at Jaco. He came offstage saying, 'Yeah, man, that was the shit!' And I told him, 'I have never been more ashamed in my life to be onstage with somebody. That was the worst shit I ever heard in my life. I don't want to see your face for at least a week.' I really was mad at him. Tony was mad, too, but he wouldn't say anything. He got mad later. We went into the studio to try and do something, but there was a big fight between them. Jaco was acting crazy and being very obnoxious, and Tony just got fed up with it. He flipped out and smashed his drums and walked out of the studio. And that really tore Jaco to strips.

"It was evident to me during this period that something was going on with Jaco that didn't have too much to do with music. There was something happening in his mind. I don't know what it was—it was some kind of idea or image of himself, of what he had to do or what he felt he was supposed to do. It was really crazy. It certainly had nothing to do with what we were playing. It was strictly Showtime, and it was sad."

Erskine says the trip to Havana was the first time he remembers Jaco as being out of control. "The Trio Of Doom set was a disaster, to everyone's embarrassment and disappointment. After the set, Tony and John were both disgusted. And Jaco's response was to jump into the ocean from a backstage balcony of the theater, amidst plenty of dangerous rocks. There was a lot of drinking going on during these concerts, especially of a Cuban drink called *mojito*, which was some kind of rum-and-lime-juice concoction. At one point, Joe had to rescue Jaco from trouble when he stated taunting one of the guys from the Fania All-Stars, a group of Puerto Rican and New York musicians. Jaco got into some kind of a racial name-calling situation, and Joe stepped in to prevent a fight. Joe had to do that on several occasions during the time when we were all in the group together."

On July 26, 1979, Jaco and Ingrid were married in the ruins of a Mayan temple in Tikal, Guatemala. The newlyweds moved into a house that Jaco had purchased in Deerfield Beach, not far from the home in Pompano Beach that Jaco had shared with Tracy.

Later that year, Weather Report released *8:30*, a live double-album documenting their recent world tour. Jaco also went out that year with Joni Mitchell on her Shadows and Light tour; the band included Pat Metheny on guitar, Michael Brecker on saxophone,

Lyle Mays on keyboards, and Don Alias on drums. Originally the group was supposed to include Wayne Shorter, but there was a provision in Weather Report's contract that no two members of the band could appear together in any side project, so Brecker was hired instead.

Jaco was supposed to be the musical director of the group, but he failed to show up for the first week of rehearsals, so the job fell to Metheny. As Don Alias recalls, "Joni appointed Jaco musical director, and his original idea was to go out with a small band—just me and him and Metheny with Joni. She wanted to do something else; she hired Mike Brecker and got Lyle Mays on keyboards and the Persuasions for backup vocals. Jaco's attitude was sort of negative in the beginning. When he finally showed up for rehearsals and saw all the extra musicians, he was kind of indignant, like, 'Oh, man, what's going on?' And we all tried to explain to him, 'Jaco, this is what the deal is. You gotta try this out, because this is what she wants.' In other words, we had to spank him a little bit. But when we started playing together, he realized it was a great combination."

Brecker has fond memories of that tour and says that Jaco's playing was in peak form at the time. But he adds that off the bandstand the tour was "pretty much a drug blowout," referring to the seemingly endless supply of cocaine that kept both Jaco and himself on the edge the whole time.

"The first time I met Jaco was back in 1975 on his solo record date," says Brecker. "I played in the horn section for 'Come On, Come Over,' the funk tune with Sam & Dave. My brother Randy was on trumpet and Dave Sanborn played alto. It was a brief encounter, but I enjoyed playing with him. I remember being totally knocked out by what he did with 'Donna Lee,' and I also remember that Jaco was totally straight then. But by the time we got together for this Joni Mitchell tour, he was definitely drugging a lot. There was a lot of partying going on. It was just a symptom of the times—everybody was doing cocaine then."

Ingrid recalls driving with Jaco to a Joni Mitchell gig at the Greek Theatre in Berkeley, California. On the way there, they got stuck in a traffic jam. Some guy in the car next to them recognized Jaco, rolled down his window, and offered him some blow. "Jaco didn't want to disappoint this guy, so he did it. People were always coming up to Jaco when he was on tour and offering him cocaine, just to get next to him."

While they might've been using cocaine at night before and after the gigs, by day the Mitchell band spent their time playing basketball at the YMCA gyms along the way. "We had a good team," says Brecker. "Everybody had played either high school or college ball.

Joni's manager, Elliot Roberts, was an especially good player. Don Alias and myself were the tallest guys on the team—and Jaco was a real hustler. What he may have lacked in form he more than made up for in pure hustling. He liked to compare himself to [Boston Celtics star] John Havlicek. He was very competitive, very intense on the court. And he always played to win."

During Joni's road show, Jaco was featured in a solo bass spot every night. Using the repeat function of an MXR digital delay, he would lay down an ostinato, loop it, and then play solo lines on top of the repeating riff. As he played, he would—of course—slide around the stage on the baby powder sprinkled beneath his feet, and he would often get the crowd to clap along with the beat while he danced and strutted his James Brown moves. As the solo gathered speed, Jaco would turn up the built-in fuzz tone of his Acoustic 360 amplifier full blast and launch into an explosion of feedback, quoting from Jimi Hendrix's "Third Stone from the Sun" and "The Star-Spangled Banner" along the way. He would then climax his showcase by laying his bass down on the stage (pickups still howling), climbing on top of his amp, and jumping onto his instrument. Sometimes he would mockingly whip the bass into submission with his guitar strap, like some sort of a comical Marquis de Sade. (One good example of Jaco's solo showcase can be heard on the track "Slang" from Weather Report's *8:30*. And you can see him in action on the video from the Shadows and Light tour, released on Warner Video.)

The audience was often driven to a frenzy by Jaco's cathartic ritual, just as the crowds at the 1967 Monterey Pop Festival went wild when Jimi Hendrix set his guitar on fire. Like Jimi, Jaco knew how to engage and excite a crowd. And there was no one else in jazz, with the possible exception of Sun Ra, who had such a theatrical streak—and such a desire to entertain. As Jaco once confided to me with a knowing wink, "This ain't nothing but a show. It's just show business, that's all."

In early 1980, Weather Report released *Night Passage*, which contains the enigmatically titled "Three Views of a Secret," a moving, dramatic ballad that Zawinul regards as Jaco's finest composition. Jaco may have copped the title from a tune Charlie Brent had written in 1971, but this piece is strikingly original and a crowning achievement in his career.

"'Three Views of a Secret' shows that Jaco was extending the legacy of Mingus as a bassist with serious compositional skills," says Ken Pullig of the Jazz Composition department at Berklee College. "Appropriately, it has three main phrases—'A,' 'B,' and 'C'—and is in 3/4 time. 'A' is a bluesy 16-measure melody that presents the three pitches that provide the fundamental motivic resources for the whole piece: B, E, and G. This melody makes use of octave displacement and contains some very creative reharmonization choices for the key center of E. 'B' is a more complicated 24-measure section that modulates to D-flat and then B before returning to E. 'C' is a 16-measure section made up of an eight-measure melody that is repeated. The fundamental melody pitches are B and E, two of the three pitches introduced in 'A.' The 'C' section provides good continuity but uses new colors to develop the E tonality; by doing this, Jaco shows his skill at taking a simple sound and then using it in a new way, rather than simply repeating it. Overall, there is enough repetition in the piece to make it accessible to the average listener and enough compositional development to satisfy the artistic segment of the listening audience. 'Three Views of a Secret' is a very well crafted piece."

Night Passage also contains some other classic Jaco moments, including his furious walking lines on the uptempo "Fast City," his shuffle groove with Peter Erskine on the title cut, and his extended duet with percussionist Bobby Thomas on "Port of Entry," perhaps his most awesome display of chops on the album.

Ingrid continued to accompany Jaco during the tour to support *Night Passage*, but as Jaco's alcohol and cocaine consumption increased, the two began to fight a lot. "He was very possessive of me during those years," she says. "He would always make me stand stage left so he could keep an eye on me. I could never sit in the audience or go out by the sound man. Once when I went back to the dressing room while he was playing, he sent the road manager back to get me. After a while, this kind of thing got on my nerves."

Generally after an argument flared up between them, Jaco would storm out of the room and go get drunk, perhaps as a way of spite-fully getting back at Ingrid. On a tour of Japan, Jaco got so drunk after a fight with Ingrid that he was barely able to play the gig that evening. The next morning he apologized to Zawinul, who quickly forgave Jaco but warned him not to let it happen again. A few days later, in Osaka, Jaco was drunk by 11 o'clock in the morning. Zaw-inul contemplated firing him on the spot but once again relented.

Zawinul later told GQ: "By 1980, Jaco was always angry and drunk. He began to try to out-macho me, to out-drink me, as if it were a competition or something. Sure, I drank and occasionally did a little blow, but I liked myself too much to hurt myself. Jaco did everything to over-indulgence. Then his music began to slip. It was still perfect, but it wasn't fresh. It became a circus act. Jaco relied on tricks he had done before."

Meanwhile, the fights with Ingrid were getting more frequent and more violent. There were physical confrontations on the street, in restaurants, in hotel lobbies. Once, Ingrid punched Jaco squarely in the face and knocked him to the floor in front of a shocked Zawinul. Their fights were generally about Jaco's drinking, but another topic that inevitably fueled the arguments was Tracy. Jaco still carried an enormous burden of guilt for leaving his first wife and their two children, and in his more irrational moments he would blame Ingrid for breaking up his marriage.

"This became his pattern," said Pat Jordan in his GQ article, "to make each woman in his life suffer for his guilt at having left the previous one." Ingrid has a different take: "Deep down, I think Jaco

Courtesy Peter Erskine

had a general feeling of disdain for women, especially ambitious women. He wanted to keep them barefoot and pregnant but wasn't responsible once the babies came into the world. He was the one who wanted children. He wanted me to get pregnant. But once the kids arrived, he couldn't be bothered with the day-to-day drudgery."

Bobby Thomas, Jaco, and Ingrid Pastorius on Weather Report tour of Japan, circa 1980

Later in 1980, during their U.S. tour, Weather Report played a gig at the Sanger Theatre in New Orleans. On that swing through town, Jaco looked up two old friends from his C.C. Riders' days, Charlie Brent and Allyn Robinson. Brent vividly recalls his backstage encounter with Jaco and Zawinul that evening. "I went back after the show with Zigaboo Modeliste, the drummer from the Meters. Jaco saw us and got all excited. He said, 'I don't believe it! Wait right here!' He threw us in one of the dressing rooms and locked us in there. Then he came back with Zawinul and said to him, 'Do you know who this is? This is Charlie Brent and Zigaboo, the drummer from the fucking Meters!' And Joe plops down on his knees and starts kissing our hands. It was really weird, man."

Robinson also went backstage to visit Jaco. "We had been out of touch for the previous five years or so, and during those years I actually had no idea what he really thought of our days playing together with Wayne Cochran. Here he was an international star. He had reached such a high level. I was so proud of the guy—he was just this skinny little kid who had turned all his ambition and talent into something, and he was back in town as a big star."

Robinson was surprised to hear Jaco speak so highly of the Cochran band that evening. "He said he carried a gig tape from those days around with him all the time and played it for everybody. The roadies told me, 'Man, Jaco is driving us crazy with that tape. That's all he ever talks about—how great that band was.'" Jaco clung to that tape for years, because it reminded him of a time before he was "The World's Greatest Bass Player." Back then he was just a kid, learning and developing, still hungry. And more important, perhaps, it reminded him of a period in his life when he was probably the happiest he ever was.

"In the Cochran band, things were much simpler for him," affirms Robinson. "He didn't drink or do drugs. He was still married to Tracy and had two beautiful kids. After he got in Weather Report, he started drinking heavily and drugging a lot. He left his family, got divorced, remarried, started drinking more. His life just got so complicated. He was making big money and was this big celebrity and everything, but he didn't have the peace of mind that he had in the Cochran days. That's something he never found again."

Robinson says he saw a changed person that night in 1980. It was certainly not the Jaco he remembered from the C.C. Riders. After hanging out and exchanging small talk backstage, Robinson and Brent split to play a gig at a Bourbon Street nightclub. Always ready and willing to do the late-night hang, Jaco tagged along.

"Jaco dragged Peter Erskine and Zawinul and Wayne Shorter along

to our gig," Robinson recalls, "and the whole time he kept talking real loud during our set about how great we were. It was embarrassing. He seemed really different to me, so full of angry energy. At some point the rest of the guys in the band wanted to leave, but Jaco got mad and said he

Peter Erskine and Jaco during Weather Report tour of Japan, circa 1980

wanted to stay. He had a sort of temper tantrum right there in the club, and the other band members just got on the band bus and took off. They were going to leave him there. So Jaco runs out of the club and starts chasing the bus and hollering at the driver to stop. They finally stopped about two blocks away. And that was the last time I saw Jaco for a while, until he came back to town a couple of years later with his Word Of Mouth band. And each time he came back, he would look worse. I could see his gradual self-destruction happening right before my eyes. It was heartbreaking to watch."

Meanwhile, Jaco had been signed as a solo act to Warner Bros. Records. Hooking up with a rival label was a controversial move that infuriated Columbia, Weather Report's label and the parent company of Epic, the label that had put out Jaco's solo debut. Jaco soon became the focus of a bitter tug-of-war between the two corporate giants.

Record executive Ricky Schultz, who along with Michael Ostin was responsible for bringing Jaco to Warner Bros., says the company was expecting big things from their new star. "Partly in response to the success of the Mahavishnu Orchestra, Return To Forever, and Weather Report, jazz fusion suddenly had more currency within the industry. There was a period of time when the labels had a little bit of a bandwagon response, and a number of artists got pretty lucrative deals. Elektra signed John Klemmer, Columbia signed George Duke, and Warners signed Jaco. Obviously, when somebody gets a healthy deal, the expectations are somewhat in line with the investment.

"Michael and I had great enthusiasm for Jaco because he was clearly one of the happening guys on the scene. There was a big buzz about him. He was special, he was creative, he was innovative, he was making news. He definitely seemed to be the element that had pushed Weather Report to a new level of public awareness; their sales had doubled after Jaco joined the group. So the expectation was that Jaco was going to create some terrific contemporary jazz, based on his experience with Weather Report, which had made music that was pretty marketable and had a broad appeal and could cross over to a rock market while still having jazz credibility."

Jaco began work on his second solo album, *Word Of Mouth*, in August of 1980, assisted by engineer Peter Yianilos. "I had a 24-track mobile truck that I would pull up alongside his house in Deerfield Beach," recalls Yianilos. "He did a lot of the bass and percussion tracks right there in his music room at home. And sometimes for larger-scale things we would take the truck over to my warehouse and record there."

For several weeks, Jaco and Yianilos followed a daily routine: wake up at 5 AM, have a big breakfast, start recording at sunrise, and work straight through until noon. Then they would take a break, go down to the beach, and jump in the ocean. After a swim, they would resume recording until sunset, take a dinner break, and then come back and work until midnight.

"Jaco had a definite plan about how he wanted to do things in the studio, but to an outside observer it wouldn't appear that way at all," says Yianilos. "Sometimes it seemed as if he was totally improvising. He would jump up from the control board and do things instantly, as the mood struck him. He might say, 'Put up a new reel; we're going to do drums today.' I would ask him which song, and he would say, 'We'll see.' He was very impulsive, but usually his instincts were right on target."

Jaco went back and forth between Florida, Los Angeles, and New York to complete the recording of his first Warner Bros. album. As Erskine recalls, "When he came out to L.A. to work on the album, he stayed at my house. It was going to be two weeks, but he ended up staying for three months. In the beginning it was a very exciting, productive period. He was scoring a lot, copyists were coming over, messenger boys were coming and going, and music was flying all over the place. It was inspiring to watch him work."

The tune "Crisis" is a good example of just how involved this project got. Jaco's bass line was recorded in Florida. In New York, he had Jack DeJohnette, Michael Brecker, Herbie Hancock, Don Alias, and Bobby Thomas do overdubs. Each musician came in alone and played while listening to only the bass track. Back in Florida, Jaco had Erskine overdub a fast beat similar to "Teen Town." He then put the tape away. A few months later, he flew to L.A. and had Wayne Shorter and Hubert Laws overdub their parts, again while listening to just the bass line.

As Jaco told *Down Beat*: "I did it in a way similar to Jamaican dub music. For instance, while Wayne was playing I would sit at the control board and maybe slide a little of Herbie's piano into Wayne's headphones for a few bars, just so Wayne would react to it. It was a pretty strange way of recording, but it worked really well and I will definitely try something like it again."

It wasn't a very economical way to work. As the budget continued to balloon, Warners grew more and more impatient with their temperamental new star. And there was a major battle over the aptly titled "Crisis." In many ways, this volatile piece captures the anger and internal chaos that Jaco must have been experiencing at the time. To him, it was honest, expressive music that represented exactly how he felt. In essence, it was jazz with a capital J, albeit with some kind of dissonant post-Hendrix, post-Coltrane twist on the notion of playing in the moment.

Warners took one listen to "Crisis" and wanted it buried in the sequencing of the album. But the more they persisted, the more resolute Jaco became that he would lead off with that disturbing track. Pure suicide, the record execs reasoned—no one would get past this bunch of noise. After a while, they just threw up their arms and said, "Okay, we can't help you then."

Jaco had gotten his way, but he had alienated himself from his new record company in the process. "They drove Jaco nuts," says Peter Erskine. "And he was spending their money like crazy. They were pretty indulgent with him up to a certain point, but after a while they had had enough. They were used to dealing with people like Pat Metheny, who was on ECM, which at the time was a subsidiary of Warners. They would say stuff like, 'Pat's so nice. He comes in here, he remembers everybody's name, he shakes their hand.' And when it comes time to promote an album, they remember that kind of thing. Jaco was showing up drunk and creating havoc with the people in the Warners office. He did not have good public relations skills, to say the least."

For the album's orchestral version of "Three Views of a Secret," Jaco recorded the basic tracks in New York with himself on piano, Jack DeJohnette on drums, and Toots Thielemans on harmonica. In

L.A. he overdubbed strings, brass, woodwinds, voices, and his bass. For his rendition of Paul McCartney's "Blackbird," Jaco recorded his bass parts and the percussion tracks in Florida and then called on Thielemans to fill in the melody.

"Originally he wanted me to come to Miami to do my parts, but I told him I had engagements in Belgium," says Toots. "So he ended up taking the Concorde from Miami to Brussels for $5,000, just to bring the tapes to me. And I thought I was saving him bread by doing the session for free! But that was Jaco. He ended up staying at our house for a couple of days, and we had a ball. Of course, he was doing a lot of blow then. He kept saying to me, 'Hey Toots, you wanna toot?' And I kept telling him, 'Shit no, Jaco.' I never criticized him for what he put up his nose, but I've always been afraid of it myself. Maybe that's why I'm still alive."

Jaco concluded the "Blackbird" odyssey in Los Angeles, with Hubert Laws overdubbing four soprano and ten alto flutes in seven-part harmony.

Engineer Yianilos remembers one other particularly costly session. "We hired a 31-piece string section from the Los Angeles Philharmonic to play the charts for 'John and Mary' and 'Three Views of a Secret.' It cost about $9,000, and we ended up erasing all the tracks because Jaco was not satisfied with their performance. He felt they just didn't have the soul and commitment he was looking for. Later, we ended up getting seven of the best players from that session and having them overdub to create a 63-piece section. It was five hours of non-stop work, nine overdubs per person, and in the end Jaco finally got what he was looking for. That's the kind of perfectionist he was in the studio."

But his perfectionist tendencies ultimately got Jaco in deep trouble. "Jaco was really obsessing over the mixes," says Erskine. "This was before automation, and he would spend huge amounts of time in the studio trying to get things just right. Meanwhile, he was running around like a lunatic, freaking out the people from the L.A. Philharmonic he had brought in for the session. And even though he had flown in Michael Gibbs to conduct the strings and woodwinds, Jaco wouldn't let him in the room. He had us all wait in the control room and insisted on conducting himself. And he lost them all on the first downbeat. They didn't see anything they could follow, or anyone they could really respect. With orchestra guys, you have to get their attention and gain their respect. And Jaco could do neither at that point."

While he was working on his album, Jaco put together a quintet in New York with Michael Brecker and Bob Mintzer on saxophones, Don Alias on percussion, and Erskine on drums. Their first gig together was in the winter of 1980 at Seventh Avenue South, a popular jazz club in which the Brecker brothers had a financial interest. As Michael Brecker recalls, "For some reason, we couldn't advertise this gig. It had something to do with Jaco still honoring his commitment to Weather Report. As it turned out, the place was packed anyway. The news of that gig spread completely by word of mouth. And that was how Jaco got the title for the album and the name for his band."

Mintzer remembers that gig as a loose, jamming affair. "It was very much improvised. I had expected Jaco to provide us with all these incredibly thought-out charts, but it was exactly the opposite. There were no charts, and there was hardly any rehearsal at all. The whole thing was very characteristic of Jaco. His attitude for that gig was, 'We'll figure it out later.' He always let a lot of things happen on the bandstand."

The emergence of the Word Of Mouth band marked the beginning of the end for Jaco's deteriorating relationship with Weather Report. While on tour in 1981, he began exhibiting the kind of outrageous behavior that Zawinul found intolerable. Their strange father-son dynamic, which had been apparent from the outset, manifested itself most clearly on the flight over to Japan to begin that tour.

"Jaco had been working a long time on *Word Of Mouth*," says Erskine. "And he was particularly proud of this one tune, 'Liberty City,' which had Jack DeJohnette playing drums, Toots Thielemans on harmonica, Herbie Hancock playing an incredible piano solo, and a full horn section. So naturally he was anxious to play a rough mix of this cut for Joe, sort of looking for some kind of approval from *der meister*. Meanwhile, Joe had been harboring a certain amount of hostility toward Jaco. Just before we flew over, we had been rehearsing all this new material at Joe's house. And these were fairly involved tunes, so it took us a while to get it together. Wayne and I were there every day working hard, but Jaco kept disappearing at rehearsals, arguing with the management about money, and generally goofing off. Joe was getting a little frustrated by this.

"So at some point during this flight, Jaco hands a Walkman and headphones to Joe, asking him to check out this rough mix of 'Liberty City.' After the song is finished, Joe hands the headphones back to Jaco and says in his gruff manner, 'That sounds like some typical high school big band bullshit.' Jaco couldn't believe it. It stunned him, I think. Joe said it pretty coldly and didn't amplify his remarks with any other comments. It was devastating to Jaco."

Jaco handled this incident as he handled all rejection. "Jaco started getting drunk right away," continues Erskine. "He was hanging out with the road crew, sort of half-standing, half-sitting in the aisle. And I think they might've been doing some cocaine. A young Japanese girl had to walk by them to use the toilet, and all of a sudden this big scene went down—the mother was freaking out and accusing Jaco of improperly touching her daughter as she walked by. I don't know if he patted her or pinched her or what, but he did something he shouldn't have done.

"The captain of the plane was brought into this scene, and Joe had to get involved to cool things out. I might be playing armchair psychiatrist, but to me it was the son who has been rejected by the father going out and getting into trouble. And Jaco wouldn't stop. This woman was sitting in front of him, and he kept banging his knees into the back of her chair. His behavior was really getting out of control, and they wound up moving the mother and daughter up into first class. It was a weird scene—almost to the point where the police were going to meet the plane at the airport and arrest Jaco if things got any worse. But Joe did what he had to do to cool it out. And it was quickly forgotten."

Weather Report's first concert on that tour was at an outdoor park in Tokyo. Press interest in the band was at a peak, and all the Japanese critics showed up, eager to check out the new music (most of which ultimately ended up on the 1982 *Weather Report*

album). Ingrid, who was once again along for the tour, was trying to get Jaco to calm down and stop drinking, but to no avail. Instead, Jaco took the attitude of, "Oh yeah? You don't want me to drink? Well, watch this!"

Things turned ugly that first evening. As Erskine remembers, "The concert was a complete disaster. Jaco didn't play any of the tunes, any of the arrangements. It was the same kind of thing that he had pulled down in Havana with McLaughlin and Tony Williams, where he just started hitting the bass and feeding back, walking over to his amp, turning knobs—playing anything *but* the tunes. And the whole time Zawinul was just in total disbelief, completely freaking out and trying to carry on with the show. He would segue from tune to tune, just as he had planned, and Jaco would kind of be there for part of the tune, and then—*boom!*—he'd go off again with the feedback thing. It was apparent to everyone that the concert was a total fuck-up."

After the show, the road crew was concerned with keeping Jaco and Joe apart to avoid a backstage brawl. They left the area in separate cars. Zawinul stayed up all that night, still shaken from the nightmarish incident. "Joe was livid and heartbroken," says Erskine. "He felt Jaco had sabotaged all that we had worked so hard for in rehearsals."

Wayne Shorter, the band's resident Zen master, handled Jaco's outbursts in an entirely different manner. "Joe took a more active role in the day-to-day logistics of the band," says Erskine. "Wayne was generally more in the background, and he was informed of things by the road manager. Wayne is in his own orbit, sort of. I don't know if you could say he stayed above the fray, but he didn't get sucked into the psychodrama of it like Joe did. Wayne would sometimes comment on Jaco and say something that made it seem as if he had a greater understanding of his situation than anybody else."

After the Tokyo debacle, Zawinul decided he had to fire Jaco in order to salvage the tour and save face. First he put in a call to Tony Levin, the fine bassist he had seen with Peter Gabriel's band, but Levin wasn't available. He then considered hiring a Japanese bass player as a replacement. "We've got to get somebody. We can't cancel the tour," he told Erskine.

The next morning, Jaco came knocking on Zawinul's door, hat in hand, and apologized for his outrageous actions. Like the father taking the prodigal son back into the fold, Joe accepted the apology. The concert that night was a great success. The press was invited back a couple of days later to see the show again—and every journalist agreed not to review the first show. Weather Report finished

©Tom Copi, San Francisco

off the Japanese tour on a triumphant note and returned to the States to perform at the Playboy Jazz Festival in Los Angeles. Erskine remembers that gig as one of the band's most electrifying performances ever. "It was a late afternoon set, and we tore the place apart. The band just came out and killed."

Weather Report at the Playboy Jazz Festival, Hollywood Bowl, Los Angeles, 1981

Back in New York, they went into the Power Station to begin recording the music for the album *Weather Report*. On July 7, they held a luncheon at a fancy Italian restaurant in Manhattan to celebrate Zawinul's 49th birthday. Earlier in the day, Jaco had presented Joe with a rather extravagant gift. "He went up to Manny's on 48th Street and picked out the most expensive accordion they had," recalls Erskine. "It was ridiculously expensive—something like

$1,400. I remember Joe was touched, but he was also hurt by the way Jaco presented it to him. He knocked on the door, walked into Joe's room, kind of tossed this thing on the bed, thumped his chest, and said, 'Happy birthday, motherfucker. Check it out!' Then he walked out. Joe was amazed, but he told me later, 'Man, if he had just given me a birthday card, shook my hand, and said, "Happy birthday," I would have been more satisfied.'"

The strange father-son tension continued to play itself out later that day at the luncheon. Jaco brought along a couple of hangers-on, who didn't waste time grabbing seats at the table. "All of a sudden, we were two seats short," says Erskine. "Wayne and one of the road crew were left standing. Finally, someone walked up to these people and explained that there were only so many spots, so they would have to leave. Of course, Jaco took this as an opportunity to get offended and indicate that he had somehow been embarrassed, even though he had created this dumb situation by having these extra people come along.

"So Jaco got up and left the restaurant. The food arrived, and as we were eating occasionally one of us would go out to see if Jaco was hanging around outside. By the time we'd finished eating, it was late afternoon. As we were leaving the restaurant, we saw Jaco in his beautiful white silk suit, curled up in the fetal position in the gutter. We all felt bad, and we were kind of looking at Joe to do something. But Joe didn't know how to deal with it—and, of course, he wasn't Jaco's father."

Word Of Mouth was released in the summer of 1981 to critical acclaim, and it later earned Japan's Golden Disc Award as the top jazz recording of the year. In a strange bit of power politicking, CBS had come out of the woodwork at the last minute, just prior to the album's release, claiming that Jaco still owed them an album from the Epic deal. A huge corporate tug-of-war ensued. The matter was finally resolved with the provision that no CBS artists be listed in the album credits. This meant that the likes of Herbie Hancock,

©Tom Copi, San Francisco

Hubert Laws, Wayne Shorter, and Tom Scott could not be named anywhere on the album.

Jaco's response was typically defiant: "If they can't be listed, then nobody will be listed." So, on the first 50,000 copies of *Word Of Mouth* that were pressed, there were no credits. On subsequent copies, all the names were listed as Jaco had intended, with different colored lettering highlighting each guest artist.

When Ingrid became pregnant with twins in mid-September of 1981, she stopped following Jaco around on tour. To prepare herself for the double birth, she opted to return to Deerfield Beach to take care of her body. She had miscarried once before and was only taking a sensible precaution—but Jaco took her decision as a rejection. "After I stopped traveling with the band, that's really when things

Playboy Jazz Festival, Hollywood Bowl, 1981

got rough for Jaco," Ingrid says. "Having me around on tour sort of kept him more together. Being by himself, it was probably very hard not to get drunk or get high or maybe even deal with other women. This kind of thing would create another problem in his head, and he'd drown out his guilt with alcohol."

When Ingrid granted Jaco the freedom to make his own choices regarding groupies on the road, he took it as a sign that she didn't truly love him. This led to bouts of depression and, inevitably, to some serious bingeing. "Around this time was when I first heard the term 'manic depressive' regarding Jaco," Ingrid recalls. "Peter Erskine's father, Fred, who is a psychiatrist, suggested that Jaco might be suffering from this condition. Then I started noticing that when Jaco would come home, he would just lay low and sleep, not talk to anybody. He would take the phone off the hook and try to avoid people. Through it all there was a sense of depression. And then after a while the edge would come back, which triggered off a whole series of manic events. I remember watching this pattern of ups and downs with Jaco."

Jaco continued to tour and record with Weather Report, but by 1982 his role in the group had been significantly reduced. Not only was he not listed as co-producer for the album they released that year, but it's clear from even a cursory listen to the record that Zawinul was fighting to exert his dominance over the band. His layers of over-dubbed synth lines all but bury Jaco's bass on several cuts, reducing "The World's Greatest Bass Player" to a pedestrian sideman.

"There was a certain amount of tension between Jaco and Joe," observes Erskine. "I think Joe was getting tired of Jaco jumping around onstage and doing his Hendrix stuff, and Jaco was frustrated having to play all these written-out bass parts that Joe was composing for this new thing he was conceptualizing. And it drove Jaco nuts that Joe was doubling the bass with synth bass. He *really* hated that. So Jaco started committing himself to projects outside of Weather Report."

Feeling stifled by Zawinul's "technological overkill," as he called it, Jaco decided to leave the band in order to devote more time to his own Word Of Mouth project. From Zawinul's point of view, "It was time for him to go. He wanted to lead his own band, and he wanted to write for more horns."

Zawinul maintains that Jaco's departure from Weather Report was an amicable parting of the ways. "We had talked about it for a long time before he actually left. What happened was, we were all planning to take off the whole year of 1982. Wayne wanted to do something on his own, and I wanted to do a solo album myself. Jaco had been talking about taking a big band out on tour to play the charts he had been working on. So we said, 'Fine, no problem.' It was going to be our year away from Weather Report. Our plan was to regroup again in 1983 for another album and tour.

"But then our management told us we had to change our plans and go out on tour in the spring of 1982, because people had already put out a lot of money for publicity and for securing venues. Our managers had promised people, unbeknownst to us, that we would be back out on tour in April 1982, when we were all planning to take off that entire year. So we had to change our plans. Otherwise, Wayne and I would have had to pay penalties in excess of $70,000, just to pay people back. So we were stuck. We had to do the tour."

But Jaco was already committed to tour Europe and Japan with his Word Of Mouth band. "We had no choice," reasons Joe. "We had to find another bass player, which is how we got Victor Bailey into the band. Basically, Jaco went his way and we had to go ours."

FIVE

Word of Mouth

*"When you leave a group as big as Weather Report,
you really have to go out with a bang."*

FOR HIS 30TH BIRTHDAY, Jaco and a bunch of his pals threw a big party/jam at Mr. Pip's nightclub in Fort Lauderdale. The 23-piece big band included Michael Brecker and Bob Mintzer on tenor saxophones; Randy Brecker, Ken Faulk, Brian O'Flaherty, Brett Murphey and Melton Mustafa on trumpets; Dan Bonsanti, Gary Lindsay and Neal Bonsanti on woodwinds; Peter Eskine on drums; Don Alias, Bobby Thomas Jr. and Oscar Salas on percussion; Peter Gordon on French horn; Dave Bargeron on trombone and tuba; Peter Graves, Russ Freeland and Mike Katz on trombones; Randy Emerick on baritone sax; and Othello Molineaux and Paul Hornmüller on steel pans. Engineer Peter Yianilos pulled up his 24-track mobile recording facility alongside the club and documented the proceedings. By all accounts, Jaco was in peak form for this casual performance on December 1, 1981.

This event was essentially the debut of Jaco's Word Of Mouth big band. Floridian Larry Warrilow, who had worked closely with Jaco in scoring his music for the large ensemble, came up with a special arrangement of "Happy Birthday" just for the occasion. Dave Bargeron claims that Warrilow was an important behind-the-scenes contributor who rarely got the credit he deserved for his work. "Just like Quincy Jones has had a few ghost writers, Jaco had one in Larry Warrilow," says Bargeron. "This was a very unassuming guy from Fort Lauderdale who crafted these beautiful arrangements. You can't

take it all away from Jaco—I mean, he did come up with the tunes. But the actual magic of those arrangements came from Larry. It pissed me off that Jaco took credit for it, and the bubble kind of burst after that. In a way, it probably was good that he was knocked down a couple of pegs in my eyes. It made it easier to encompass him."

Warrilow, however, downplays his role. "I was basically the music copyist," he says. "He'd hand me a sketch or something, but all the notes would be there. We were usually under time constraints; we had to produce a lot of stuff on pretty short notice, whether it was for a session or a Word Of Mouth tour. Jaco would basically say, 'Hey, do this,' and I'd get it done. But it was all Jaco's stuff. He had a lot more things to worry about on those tours than getting the music on paper. And he and I had pretty much the same ideas about chord spacing and so forth, so it wasn't a case of me making up anything."

While on tour, Jaco would often write in fragments and then fax or mail Warrilow the handwritten material. "I'd get 16 bars on one sheet of paper, and then 16 bars of something else on some scrap of paper or napkin from a hotel lounge. When he'd get back home, he would crank out 30 or 40 bars on score pages. By the time I got the completed song, it would be a mishmash of paper and napkins and menus and everything else. But by and large, the ideas were all there. Basically, my job was getting those snippets of ideas onto paper and in front of the guys so they could play the music. But I can't take any substantial credit for the arrangements, with the exception of that chorale arrangement of 'Happy Birthday,' which I cooked up the afternoon before his 30th-birthday gig. I just tossed it in front of the brass players, and they sight-read it on the gig."

The party took place the day before one of the Word Of Mouth band members (who prefers to remain anonymous) checked into a rehabilitation hospital in West Palm Beach, Florida. "That was the beginning of my recovery period" he recalls. "I was grappling with a powerful addiction at that point, so my memories of the gig are very, very hazy. But I do remember Jaco visiting me in the hospital a few days later. He brought me a basketball and three juggling balls—but he showed up drunk, so it kind of defeated the purpose of his visit. They were reluctant to let him in, but eventually he got to see me for about two minutes. Believe it or not, he snuck back in after they kicked him out. He climbed over a fence and somehow got back in. I thanked him for the gifts and told him I was trying to get sober and asked him to leave. That was pretty much the end of it for me and Jaco. I couldn't associate with him after that."

The New York debut of the Word Of Mouth band took place on January 15, 1982, at the Savoy Theater. When the curtain went up, revealing a bespectacled Jaco fronting a 20-piece big band, the audience let out a collective gasp of surprise. Some had envisioned Jaco leading a power trio, while others expected some variation of the Weather Report formula—but Jaco threw everyone a curve by unveiling this swinging juggernaut.

The evening was full of surprises. For one thing, the building was not properly heated, forcing Randy Brecker to begin the show playing his trumpet with gloves on. But things soon heated up considerably. Dave Bargeron stepped forward to deliver an uncanny reading of "Donna Lee," navigating his way through the chops-busting head on *tuba*, no less. Othello Molineaux blew through the changes to Coltrane's "Giant Steps" on steel pans. Jaco delivered some raunchy vocals on Buster Brown's "Fannie Mae," an old R&B staple he had been jamming on since his early days with Woodchuck. Bob Mintzer and Randy Brecker were prominently featured as soloists that night, but Jaco took over the spotlight for his bass showcase, quoting liberally from Hendrix as he cranked up the distortion on his amp and filled the hall with a blistering barrage of feedback.

Perhaps the biggest surprise of the evening came when Jaco invited his father onstage to sing "Watch What Happens," a tune long associated with Frank Sinatra. Jack Pastorius was clearly in lounge singer's heaven, exuding the suave sophistication and Vegas-styled hipness of Ol' Blue Eyes himself while Jaco stood alongside, brimming with pride at the way Mr. Personality commanded the stage. For the finale, the band played Warrilow's arrangement of "Happy Birthday," which Jaco dedicated to Dr. Martin Luther King Jr. on the anniversary of his birth.

It was a triumphant debut and an impressive inauguration of Jaco's post-Weather Report career. Backstage after the show, he said, "When you leave a group as big as Weather Report, you really have to go out with a bang." And he did.

Following the Savoy gig, Word Of Mouth performed shows in Chicago, Los Angeles, and Miami before returning to New York for gigs at Birdland West and the Lone Star Cafe, which would soon

©Tom Copi, San Francisco

become a regular venue for Jaco. "That band was really happening in the beginning," remembers Dave Bargeron. "It was a very exciting time. Jaco was completely healthy and taking care of business. Of course, that didn't last too long."

Randy Brecker, Don Alias, Jaco, Peter Erskine, and Bob Mintzer at the Old Waldorf, San Francisco, January 1982

As Jaco resumed his marathon hanging, he began to unravel. At night, he would hold court at the 55 Grand, a hipster's hang in the SoHo section of Manhattan, where the cognac and cocaine flowed freely for all the musicians who stopped by to jam. The players who frequented those jams included saxophonist David Sanborn; guitarists Hiram Bullock, Mike Stern, and James Blood Ulmer; keyboardist Delmar Brown; and drummers Bob Moses, Rashied Ali, and Phillip Wilson. They would often get into 40-minute rave-ups on "All Blues," "So What," or "Impressions," sometimes taking a pause for the cause in the middle of a song.

During an extended drum solo, the rest of the band would often vacate the stage and head to the basement for another round of toot. On one such occasion, Jaco and Stern both returned with a crazed gleam in their eyes—for some bizarre reason, they had switched pants down in the basement, though few in the audience even noticed their quick-change act.

"I used to play at 55 with Mike Stern," recalls John Scofield. "It would be our two guitars with Peter Warren on bass and Victor Lewis on drums. Jaco would come into the place drunk, and we would all look at each other and go, 'Oh shit, here he comes.' He would get up onstage and want to sing 'Mustang Sally' and dance around. That whole scene was destructive for everyone involved, but Jaco was the biggest offender. By then, he was like a walking time bomb."

Early in 1982, Jaco had taken up residence in Mike and Leni Stern's loft, located directly above the 55 Grand. Jaco and Mike played duets together during the day and hung out together at the club at night, generally staying up until sunrise. Stern was playing in the Miles Davis group at the time and was fighting a serious addiction himself. "The prevailing attitude of that 55 Grand scene was, 'Who's got some blow? Go get some blow. When am I gonna have some blow?'" says Mike. "For me, it had been going on for years before that. My favorite drug was heroin, but that shit scared Jaco— he was afraid of needles. He mostly drank vodka and did a lot of coke, which kept him up for days at a time and allowed him to continue drinking. And all the while, he was trying to get me to leave Miles and join his band."

By the summer of 1982, during the Word Of Mouth big band's tour of Japan, Jaco's behavior had grown increasingly bizarre. It got to a point where his outrageous antics—ostensibly intended to amuse and entertain—began to elicit wholly different responses from both band mates and audiences. Some feared for his safety, while others began to question his sanity.

"That's when Jaco really started to get out of hand," says Peter Erskine. "It was a great band, with some of the best players in New York, but Jaco was completely sabotaging our efforts. A lot of us were pretty unnerved at the shows, because he got into painting his face, stripping off his clothes, and running around naked onstage. It was pretty awful—and it was scary. He seemed like a different person. He had a wild look in his eyes that had never been there before. Everything just seemed so ... *wrong*.

"I remember meeting him at the airport just before we took off for the tour that summer. At first, I was shocked because he had cut his hair really short; that long, shoulder-length hair was one of his trademarks, but he had had it cropped like a punk, really jagged and close to his head. I went over to talk to him, and he looked at me real nasty and said, 'Hi, fatso!' There was a hostile edge in his voice that was totally foreign to me."

Erskine grew more concerned during the flight to Japan. "On the plane, Jaco was sort of stalking up and down the aisles with colored plastic tape on his face. Finally, he sat down next to me. I was reading the sports section, and Jaco grabbed the paper from me and started circling words with a Magic Marker. Wherever there was a reference to the Minnesota Twins, he'd circle the word 'Twins,' because Ingrid was expecting twins. Where the paper mentioned something about second base, he circled the word 'base.' These words in the newspaper had suddenly taken on some kind of deeper significance to him."

Saxophonist Randy Emerick, who played baritone on that tour, concurs with Erskine's assessment of Jaco's behavior, adding, "He was doing a lot of bizarre things onstage. One day he confided that he felt he *had* to do crazy and unusual things because it was expected of him. He said it was his way of getting people's attention."

Alex Foster, who played alto sax in the band, witnessed one of these attention-getting episodes at a hotel bar in Tokyo. "Jaco had been drinking a lot, and suddenly he passed out at the bar. The hotel management brought in a wheelchair to get him back to his room. I was following behind as they wheeled him to the elevator. Jaco had his head down and was drooling. I bent over to see if he was all right, and he looked up at me and winked, like it was all some kind of gag."

Foster has his own theory about some of Jaco's strange behavior on that tour. "Right before we left, Jaco had spent a couple of weeks on a Miccosoukee Indian reservation, so he was really into that vibe. He had this Indian garb that he would wear onstage, and he got into painting his face like warpaint. He took a black Magic Marker to his arms one day. I don't know—I always had this impression that Jaco wanted to be black, so one day he just decided to paint himself black."

Dave Bargeron says, "All creative people have a certain level of eccentricity that we kind of accept. But by the end of that tour, when Jaco was painting his bass and coloring himself with Magic Markers, that's when the red flags started to go up. That's when I really started wondering, What the hell is going on here?"

Ironically, even as his behavior grew increasingly more bizarre and self-destructive, Jaco continued to earn accolades both in the United States and abroad. He was voted Best Jazz Bassist in the 1982 *Guitar Player* readers' poll. That same year, he was named Jazz Artist Of The Year by *Swing Journal*, and with that honor came a certain amount of respect from the promoters and other people around him in Japan.

"Jaco was acting crazy most of the time on that tour," says Alex Foster, "whether it was on the gig, at the hotel, or on the train. The only reason he wasn't arrested by security guards was that there were Japanese people escorting him who would explain to the cops that he wasn't just a total maniac. He may have been *acting* like a total maniac, but he was also Jazz Artist Of The Year in Japan, and they had great respect for him because of that."

During one show, Jaco walked offstage in the middle of a set. On another occasion, he threw his bass in Hiroshima Bay (which was front-page news in Tokyo). But none of his stunts could top the infamous "squid episode." As Foster recalls, "One day Jaco drove into the hotel lobby on a motorcycle, fell off the bike, and passed out.

When the hotel employees tried to revive him, they found a dead squid stuffed under his T-shirt."

In some twisted way, Jaco saw these antics as a means of release from the enormous pressures coming to bear on him at the time. There was the pressure of fronting his own band and taking charge as a leader. There was the pressure of living up to his reputation as "The World's Greatest Bass Player." And on that tour there was also the responsibility of watching over his daughter, Mary, who was 11 years old at the time. As Jaco later explained, "I promised her if she got straight A's in school I would take her along with me. She did, so I had to take her, because you should never lie to children."

Jaco's level of anxiety was also heightened by Ingrid's pregnancy. She finally gave birth to twin sons on June 9, 1982; the boys were named Julius Josef and Felix Xavier. Both not only inherited their

Charlie Haden, Wynton Marsalis, Jaco, and Carlos Santana in San Francisco, for the "Jazz at the Opera House" benefit, February 1982

father's double-jointed thumbs but grew up to bear a striking resemblance to him. In their honor, Jaco named the live double album documenting that 1982 tour *Twins*.

Jaco's mood swings grew more dramatic as the tour progressed. He would laugh hysterically one minute and cry uncontrollably the next. Alarmed, some of the people in his entourage began making plans to get him admitted to a hospital upon his return to the States.

After leaving Japan, the band spent a few days in Hawaii. Jaco disappeared for a day or so and was later picked up by the police. They found him in the mountains, naked, with axle grease smeared all over his body. The cops brought Jaco to the hotel room of trumpeter Jon Faddis, who was so concerned about Jaco's state of mind that he immediately put in a call to Ingrid back in Florida.

Upon returning to New York, Peter Erskine and others close to Jaco tried to convince him to check into a rehabilitation hospital. Jaco lashed out at his concerned friends, claiming that there was nothing wrong with him. "I'm perfectly healthy and I do not abuse drugs," he said. "That's just the way I am. I know who I am. I'm just being Jaco."

When Jaco returned to Florida, his constant drinking became a source of much frustration for Ingrid. As Geri Palladino remembers, "After those babies were born, it was like all hell broke loose. Ingrid didn't want Jaco around the house when he was drinking. She's not an easy woman to get along with, and he wasn't an easy man to get along with. Needless to say, they fought a lot."

In late 1982, Jaco left his home in Deerfield Beach and headed to New York City to recruit a smaller version of his Word Of Mouth band. From the ranks of the big band, he signed up saxophonist Alex Foster. The trumpeter was Elmer Brown; the percussionist was Carol Steele; and for keyboards Jaco picked one of his late-night buddies from the 55 Grand scene, Delmar Brown, who had gigged with Pat Martino and appeared on the guitarist's adventurous Warner Bros. fusion album, *Joyous Lake*.

©Tom Copi, San Francisco

"Jaco knew about me before I even hooked up with Pat Martino," says Brown, "because he was crashing at Pat's place in Philly when I sent a demo tape there for Pat to check out. Jaco listened to it and said to Pat, 'This guy can play!' So in a way, he recommended me for that gig. I met up with him later at the 55 Grand. I was sort of in a rut at the time. I was broke, had just broken up with a woman, didn't have a place to stay—and then Jaco came along. He had just come off the Weather Report gig. I was rolling this way; he was rolling that way. We were like two balls rolling down the street, and we ran into each other. He actually pulled me out of my rut and gave me new energy to play.

"Most of all, Jaco gave me a new feeling of confidence. At that time, I felt nobody wanted me to play. I'd ask to sit in and people wouldn't let me. They thought I was too 'out' or whatever. It was similar to what happened to Jaco later. People were very surprised that he took me."

On drums, Jaco recruited Kenwood Dennard, who had previously toured and recorded with Pat Martino and the British fusion band Brand X. "Of course, I knew who Jaco was," says Dennard, "but the first time I talked to him was when Delmar called and put him on the phone. Jaco's first words to me were, 'I'm taking you to Europe, motherfucker! So come down to 55 Grand tonight and we'll talk.' I told him, 'Oh, that sounds great. I really dig your music. But tonight I've got to do a session at the Daily Planet on 30th Street, and I'm just running out the door.' Jaco said, 'I'll be right there.' And he hung up."

Sure enough, Jaco showed up at the studio—much to the dismay of bassist Alex Blake, who had organized the session. "Jaco came down and disrupted the entire session by playing the drums and just being a pain in the ass," says Kenwood. "Nobody could believe it. I explained to them that it was Jaco, but as far as Alex was concerned he was just some guy who was fucking around. It was a pretty strange way to meet the cat. But afterwards we ended up jamming at 55 Grand, and it was instantaneous magic. It really worked extremely well right away."

It was around this time that I had my first official interview with Jaco, for a story in *Guitar Player* magazine. Jaco had designated the time and place: 3 PM at the 55 Grand. I arrived promptly, but Jaco was nowhere in sight. The bar wasn't even scheduled to open until 6 o'clock, but after I knocked on the locked door for several minutes, the clubowner let me in. He explained that Jaco had been up all night and was fast asleep upstairs in the Sterns' loft.

I had Mike Stern's phone number, so I walked to a corner telephone and called, waking Jaco on the seventh ring. Rather than being angry with me for disturbing his sleep, he apologized for missing our appointment and promised to do the interview right away. "Just give me 20 minutes to wash up and get myself together."

Two hours later, I was still waiting inside the bar for Jaco. Finally, out of sheer boredom, I decided to go for a stroll around SoHo, just to kill time. As I turned the corner a couple of blocks from the club, I spied a familiar figure in the distance. As he approached, I noticed he was barefoot and wearing shorts and a T-shirt—perfect attire for an afternoon at the beach in Fort Lauderdale. But this was a cold mid-November afternoon in New York City.

He greeted me with a hearty shout. "Hey, man. I just came from the record store. Guess what? They're sold out of Weather Report albums. That's good news, right? Hell, I bought ten of them myself yesterday and handed them out to people on the street. I may not be in the band anymore, but I'm still promoting our music."

He seemed to be in good spirits, but his eyes looked horribly blood-shot, his voice was hoarse, and his skin was pallid. My guess was that he had been drinking and snorting coke all night, probably hadn't slept more than an hour or two in the past few days, and hadn't eaten in a while. I was ready to blow off the interview, but Jaco insisted that we get to it … *"right now."*

He was cordial and cooperative for the first ten minutes or so, but his attention soon wandered. When I tried to get him to explain the specifics of his bass technique, he wanted to talk about the Ku Klux Klan and police brutality in Florida. When I brought up the triumphs of his Weather Report years, he changed the sub-ject to basketball, which became a kind of common ground in our conversation.

When I mentioned my interest in hoops, Jaco's competitive nature instantly kicked into high gear. "You play ball?" Before the interview could continue, I had to submit to a game of one-on-one at a nearby playground. Jaco hustled upstairs to the loft and returned with a basketball under his arm. As he stood in the door-way, he issued his challenge to me: "Let's go, motherfucker!"

After two hours of ugly, grueling B-ball, I felt a bond had been established. But there were still a few more obstacles to overcome.

First, we had to ride the A train up to Jerry Jemmott's house in Harlem. Then we had to take a cab back down to Greenwich Village and meet a certain mysterious friend of Jaco's in Washington Square Park (no doubt to cop some coke). When we returned to the 55 Grand, it was nearly time for Jaco's first set to begin. He told me to stick around, assuring me that we would squeeze in the interview between sets.

But during the breaks, Jaco was far too engaged in snorting cocaine down in the basement to bother with an interview. Determined to stick it out, I endured two more sets of meandering, drug-induced jamming before finally making my move. By 4 AM, the club had emptied out. Jaco turned to me and said, "Damn, you still here? You really must want to do this thing. Well, let's do it ... *right now*."

I ended up conducting the rest of the interview at Wo Hop's on Mott Street in Chinatown, over platters of spicy gung bo chicken and beef with Chinese vegetables. Jaco spoke of how successful his tour of Japan had been but added, "That tour was the highlight of my life as a leader, which is ironic because half of my friends wanted to have me put in a nuthouse when we got back. They thought I went crazy—but they had no fucking idea what kind of pressure I was under."

Jaco spoke excitedly about his new sextet and said they were going to "kick ass" on an upcoming European tour. He also mentioned that he wanted to steal Mike Stern from Miles Davis's band.

Jaco concluded our first interview with these thoughts: "You have to keep the humor up when you go out on tour, otherwise you'll go crazy. You just can't go from living in the ghetto one day to touring Europe and Japan the next day—it's too much of a shock to your system. You have to put on a disguise and go crazy once in a while, or the pressure will kill you. So I want to have fun on tour. I want to take risks. I want to stand on the edge, but in a safe place."

During a tour of Italy in December 1982, Jaco was indeed standing on the edge—but he was definitely not in a safe place. Alex Foster

remembers the tour as "just total madness, from the very beginning." It began with a press conference before the jazz festival in
Milano. Jaco, who had been up for three days drinking heavily, was
obnoxious and unreasonable. "He treated the whole press conference like a goof," says Foster. "He was just ranting and raving non-
sensically. One by one, the Italian journalists turned off their tape
recorders and crept out of the room, until there was nobody left."

That evening, the band was scheduled to perform in a huge
circus-type tent. A sellout crowd of 20,000 arrived early, fully
expecting to see "The World's Greatest Bass Player" perform his
magic. Jaco still hadn't gotten any sleep and was somewhat incoherent by showtime.

"We had no rehearsals," recalls Kenwood Dennard. "He kept
telling us there were going to be a couple of rehearsals, but it was like
the boy who cried, 'Wolf!' They never happened. The only rehearsal
we had before we flew over consisted of sitting around smoking pot
and talking about the blues. It was a nice party, but there were no
instruments to play. After we got there, I was pretty wasted from the
flight. All of a sudden, at about three in the morning, the phone
rings. It's Jaco. 'Kenwood! You're late! Get your ass over here to my
room … *right now*! We're rehearsing.' I thought, Shit, this cat has
some kind of energy to call a rehearsal at 3 AM.

"So I went up to Jaco's room, and there he was in the fucking bath-
tub playing with a rubber duck. In the other room, a tape player was
blaring out some of the music we were going to do. Jaco was a little
incoherent. So I sat and listened to this music for a while and then
fell asleep. That was all the rehearsal we had.

"The next day at soundcheck, I was waiting for Jaco to whip out
these incredible charts for us to sight-read on the gig, but he never
did. What did happen was very weird. All of a sudden, Jaco got
incredibly angry about something. He and Delmar exchanged
words, and Jaco threw his bass at Delmar. Delmar had to duck to get
out of the way, or he might've been pretty badly injured. They

ended up on the floor fighting. This was my first gig with Jaco, and I was sitting there thinking, Damn, what kind of shit is this? I had never seen anything like it."

That night the show began on time. Jaco, barefoot, counted off "Invitation" at a brisk tempo, and the band kicked in. Suddenly, in the middle of the song, Jaco launched into a long, crazed feedback solo. People in the crowd began booing, which visibly upset Jaco. He threw down his bass, gave the audience the finger, and stormed off the stage. Backstage, the nervous promoter approached Jaco, who had assumed the fetal position. Meanwhile, the crowd was beginning to get unruly, chanting *"Shaimo! Shaimo! Shaimo!"*

The promoter begged Jaco to go back onstage and finish the show, but his reply was, "I'm not playing unless I get $10,000 in cash … *American!"* The crowd grew louder and angrier by the minute. Jaco's road manager, Michael Knuckles, alerted the band members that they should be ready to make a quick exit. The tour bus pulled up behind the stage just as the Italian riot police launched a salvo of tear gas into the mob. Backstage, paparazzi hovered around Jaco, snapping pictures of "The World's Greatest Bass Player" pathetically curled up on the floor.

"I started pushing these cameramen away, yelling, 'Get the fuck outta here!'" says Delmar Brown. "A riot had broken out, 20,000 people were screaming, and the tear gas was burning our eyes. Suddenly Jaco got up on his feet, winked at me, and said, 'We got 'em now.'"

In the midst of the chaos, Jaco had an altercation with percussionist Carol Steele. As one member of the entourage remembers, "Basically, he told her, 'Gimme some pussy or you're fired.' And this was in the middle of a riot. When she refused, he locked her in the dressing room."

The promoter was running around frantically and wondering how in the world he could get out of this mess. He approached Alex Foster and pleaded, "Can't you do something?" Alex surveyed the scene and replied, "I'm not going out there." Finally, the promoter and Knuckles cornered Delmar Brown and demanded, "You've got to go on. Play something!" A hailstorm of cans and bottles was raining down on the stage.

"The whole stage was moving," recalls Brown. "They were shaking the foundation pillars and rocking the stage. I looked over my shoulder, and there was Jaco, back on the floor in the fetal position—and this time he wasn't winking. Meanwhile, Carol's locked in the dressing room, the riot police are running around with nightsticks, bottles and bricks are flying—it was like some kind of wild theater piece."

Delmar gathered his wits, took a huge swig from a bottle of cognac, and bravely walked onstage to face the frenzy alone, like Daniel going into the lion's den. "I cranked up my amplifier to the max and hit the highest note I could sing. It was the only way I was gonna get the crowd's attention. I held this note for a long time and then dropped down into a tune I wrote called 'Promise Land,' which was one of Jaco's favorite songs. So I started singing this kind of gospel-flavored tune, and everybody got into it and began to cool out."

Jaco regained his composure, walked back onstage, strapped on his bass, and began playing along. "Everybody was cheering by then, and Jaco looked like he was cool," says Brown. "We played through the whole tune, and suddenly we were back in favor with the crowd. We did a couple more tunes, and then all of a sudden Jaco made another checkout. He turned up his bass and started playing loud and totally out of context. Then he threw down his bass and went back to making all kinds of demands on the promoter. 'Where's my money? And I want my wife and kids flown in on the Concorde … *right now!*'"

Once again, the Italians went wild, shaking the stage and throwing bottles with even more vehemence. Giving up all hope of salvaging the gig, the band jumped on the tour bus to make a quick getaway. "People were jumping on top of the bus and trying to overturn it," says Brown. "The cops were fighting off the crowd with their bare hands. We barely got out of there alive."

The Word Of Mouth traveling circus moved on to Rome. Along the way, Jaco indulged in yet another series of "total wipes." As Alex Foster explains, "Jaco would sit in the back of the bus and fake that he had fallen out the back door. We'd be cruising down the highway at 100 kilometers per hour, and all of a sudden you'd hear this decompression kind of sound coming from the back door being opened. Then you'd hear a scream and a big thud. The door would be wide open, and there'd be no Jaco in sight. We'd look at each other and say, 'Oh shit! He jumped off the bus!' And we'd all run back to see if he was lying in the road. Jaco would be crouched down behind one of the seats with this big grin on his face, saying, 'What a wipe!' That was his thing, pulling these pranks. It happened several times on the tour."

In Rome, the band played four concerts that went relatively smoothly. But a few days later, in Rimini, the tour came to an abrupt halt when Jaco slipped off a balcony at the hotel and fell 16 feet to the ground, causing serious injuries.

"The concert was put on by an Italian jazz society," says Foster. "They had spent their entire annual budget on this one show, and they were treating us like kings. They took us to this castle to eat pasta and drink homemade wine, and they treated Jaco like a big star, which he was in Italy.

"That night, Jaco was the coolest of all," says Delmar Brown. "He was clean, wearing a sport jacket, saying nothing. But that was the time to worry with Jaco—it was like the calm before the storm. I'd look at him and say, 'You all right?' and he'd just nod. But he was being too fucking quiet. Whenever he got that super-serious look on his face, with his lower lip sticking out, I'd think, 'Uh-oh. He's gonna blow any minute!'"

Everybody in the band got pretty drunk that night. Back at the hotel, Michael Knuckles held a party in his room on the second floor. Brown was just down the hall. "My door was open, and I was sprawled out on the bed, completely out of it," he says. "They were partying and I was sleeping. At some point, I opened my eyes and there was Jaco standing over me with nothing on but a towel. He said, 'We got 'em now!' Then he took off running down the hall."

Jaco entered Knuckles's room, where the party was still going strong. "For some reason, he decided he would do some tightrope walking on the banister out on the balcony," recalls Alex Foster. "The next thing I knew, he was kind of hanging from the banister, and we all thought he was kidding. We thought it was just another of his wipes, so we didn't pay much attention to him. Suddenly, I heard a thud and this cry for help. I went out on the balcony and looked down—there was Jaco, sprawled out on the pavement with only a fucking towel on. It was raining like hell. At first, I thought he had somehow gotten back in the window, run downstairs, and laid down on the ground, pretending that he had fallen. Knuckles said, 'Oh shit! I think he's really hurt this time.' But I told him, 'No, man. He's just faking again.'

"We took the elevator down, and there was Jaco lying on the ground. He was moaning, 'Uh-oh. The World's Greatest Bass Player just broke his arm.' Then he looked around and said, 'Well, maybe not the greatest . . . .' I shook him and said, 'Get up, man. Stop kidding. Enough already!' But then I realized he was really in pain. He really had fallen off that balcony!"

An ambulance arrived to take the fallen hero to the local hospital. As they placed Jaco on the stretcher, he yelled to Dennard, "Woody! Get me a cognac!"

The first hospital set Jaco's arm improperly. He was promptly taken to a second hospital in a nearby town, where they corrected the problem. The next week, Jaco flew back to the States with a six-inch stainless-steel pin in his arm and a large cast on his right wrist. His pelvis was also cracked in four places—but that didn't stop him from playing. A week later, he was back at the 55 Grand, jamming with the cats.

Later that year, Jaco regrouped and toured Japan again with Brown, Dennard, Foster, percussionist Don Alias, trumpeter Ron Tooley, and steel-pans virtuoso Othello Molineaux. Dennard says that one of the band's peak performances happened in Nagoya. "This particular gig was so extreme it was physically dangerous—but that was the story of Jaco's life. His genius and musicality, his creativity and spontaneity, were so extreme that it was dangerous. We had been out on the road for two weeks, and everybody was loose. Alex Foster sounded like John Coltrane that night. I remember how fluent and spiritual he sounded—like fire. When he finished one long solo, half the audience was in a trance from the energy we were putting out. But it kept going higher.

"It came time for Delmar's keyboard solo, and he took the energy up a notch further. He was shaking his dreadlocks and playing with super speed. By this time, I was getting physically tired from all this playing. Then came Jaco's solo, and he launched into some stuff that was sensitive yet still blazing. He was playing a lot of fast harmonics, but he was so subtle about it. Then he walked over to his amp and with one sweep of his arm turned everything up full blast and launched into the solo of doom. He played his heart out, bringing so much of his pain and his joy to bear on that solo. By the time he finished, I was in a trance, too.

"Then Jaco pointed to me and said, 'Take it!' So I had to come up with *something*, building to yet another climax. By the time I finished my solo, I was physically ill. I felt dizzy. I couldn't continue. I had to lie down and get some oxygen. I was physically exhausted from the level of intensity we had hit on that song. Jaco had a way of pushing things to the extreme like that. I felt like the bionic drummer that night—and after that concert, Jaco started calling me 'The Boya From Nagoya.'"

In the summer of 1983, Jaco finally enlisted Mike Stern, who had been bounced from Miles Davis's band. "Miles asked me to leave because I was really fucking up," says Stern. "I was showing up late

and drunk for every gig. I couldn't get it together, and Miles wasn't going to wait for me. He used to say, 'Mike didn't get high, he *stayed* high.' And he was right."

Stern took Molineaux's spot on a European tour that was marked by an outrageous partying spirit, onstage and off. As Delmar Brown puts it, "We started the Hang Dynasty Club with me, Alex [Foster], Jaco, and Stern. There were some wild times, but that was also a killer band."

The group returned from Europe and put on a dynamic outdoor show at Pier 84 in New York City. Then, from October through the end of November, they made a grueling bus tour of the States.

"There was all this craziness happening, night after night," says Foster. "It began as kind of a competitive thing, trying to see who could be the 'out'-est. During his time, believe it or not, Jaco was acting as a kind of stabilizing influence on Stern, watching over him like a big brother. I remember we did a Halloween concert in Ann Arbor, Michigan, and Stern was really out of it. He probably doesn't remember anything about it, but he started acting wild and trashing the dressing room, and Jaco had to calm him down."

By this time, trumpeter Melton Mustafa, an old friend of Jaco's from Florida, had replaced Ron Tooley. "In the early '70s, Jaco used to come by my place in Liberty City to practice," recalls Mustafa. "He would just work out things, mostly jazz standards and R&B tunes. He did a lot of stuff down in that area, working with black artists there. He did some recording with Little Beaver and was tapped into the same little circuit I was in. I guess it was because of that association that he later named one of his tunes 'Liberty City.'"

During those years, Jaco and Mustafa had done some gigging together at a club called the Windjammer in Fort Lauderdale. "I distinctly remember him being a profound player, even back then. And he was so energetic. He would take the tempos at twice the speed, just to be different. And he never lagged on his time."

Mustafa says he lost touch with Jaco after he joined Weather Report. "I wasn't aware of the things he had been doing from the time in Liberty City until we got back together in New York. And when I found out, I couldn't believe it. But the music we played in the Word Of Mouth sextet was the most inspiring music I had been involved with up to that point. It was always aggressive and very dynamic in presentation."

The sextet had some triumphant gigs, including one memorable performance in New Orleans. Allyn Robinson says he was shocked by Jaco's appearance at that show, though. "Jaco looked pretty good during the show, but afterwards he just looked horrible. It was heartbreaking to see him going through that transformation. I was trying to figure it out in my own mind. I wanted to say, 'Jaco, what are you doing to yourself?' But I didn't pursue it with him at that point."

Earlier in the year, Warner Bros. had issued *Invitation*, an edited single-LP version of the *Twins* double album. Soon after the release, word began to leak out that the label was planning to drop Jaco. As Ricky Schultz explains, "Jaco had gone way over budget on his *Word Of Mouth* album, and for his second release he delivered *Holiday for Pans*, which the label rejected. They were expecting something more in the commercial fusion vein, like *Return To Forever* or something along the lines of Weather Report's *Mr. Gone*. But *Holiday for Pans* was extremely esoteric—it was basically a vehicle for Othello Molineaux that Jaco had produced. It wasn't very well received by the powers at the label."

Warner Bros. eventually confirmed the rumors by officially releasing Jaco from his contract. The decision was based not only on poor record sales but on Jaco's increasingly erratic behavior, which had been widely reported throughout the industry. By late 1983, the word on Jaco in industry circles was simple: Hands off!

"A number of incidents had happened, and there were constant reports of his bizarre behavior on the road," says Schultz. "He was getting some black marks against him. At one point he actually got banned from the East Coast Warners' offices for harassing a receptionist, intimidating employees, and throwing chairs in the lobby. That kind of behavior was something that [label head] Mo Ostin simply wouldn't tolerate, no matter who it was."

As Warner Bros. publicist Donna Russo so succinctly puts it, "These executives today are strictly bottom-line guys. They don't take shit from Prince or Madonna. And they certainly weren't going to take it from Jaco Pastorius."

Getting dumped from Warners left Jaco in a state of confusion and deep depression. He was also angry—something that he made clear with his disturbing performance at the 1984 Playboy Jazz Festival. "It was kind of hard to believe," recalls Melton Mustafa. "We had a format, we had a program, we had a plan. We had discussed what we were going to do in the hotel before the gig. But when we went out there and started to play, after about five or ten minutes it just went in a totally different direction."

The Hollywood Bowl was packed with music-industry dignitaries for this concert. Word Of Mouth started off with its usual opener, "Dania," a swinging Jaco original with tight, tricky horn lines. Things were going along fine, and then all of a sudden Jaco turned up his amplifier and began playing notes that were outside of what was happening harmonically, getting louder and more dissonant with each chorus.

"Everybody in the band was wondering what was happening," says Mustafa. "His playing was so out of context that it was actually embarrassing." The crowd started booing. Then, one by one, the other members of the band started walking off the stage. "Don Alias was so embarrassed," says Alex Foster. "He told me, 'God, in all the years I've played music I have never been booed off the stage.' And I told him, 'Hey man, they weren't booing you. We just happened to be up there.'"

Eventually, only Jaco and Kenwood Dennard remained onstage. The crowd continued to boo. Jaco screamed through his instrument as the drummer struggled to make sense of it. Then Dennard stopped playing and walked off, leaving Jaco alone.

Incredibly, Jaco kept playing, oblivious to the crowd's reaction as he thrashed wildly around the stage, knocking over equipment. Finally Bill Cosby, who was acting as master of ceremonies for the event, signaled the stage crew to give Jaco the hook. The revolving stage spun around, moving Jaco out of sight. Cosby stepped to the microphone, apologized to the crowd, and introduced the next band.

"As Jaco was coming off the stage," Mustafa recalls, "he said, 'I can't understand it. I played every note *perfect!*' It was sort of a humorous comment, but it was clear he was losing touch with reality at that point. That gig was a real turning point in Jaco's life. That's when everything started getting out of control.

"But it also seemed to be sort of a political act on Jaco's part. It seemed as if he was rebelling against the system and trying to make the point that what the music industry was doing to musicians was wrong. I believe Jaco really felt there was a conspiracy against him at that point, and this was his way of making a statement, of speaking out against it."

Following this debacle, Jaco broke up his band and returned to New York to recruit a new cast of players.

SIX

The Dark Years

"We were both out of our minds at that point.
But I was trying to save my life and he wasn't."

BY JANUARY OF 1985, Jaco was back in New York and gigging under the Word Of Mouth name. The band's lineup would change from night to night, depending on who was available and not feuding with him at the time.

Delmar Brown had left to tour Europe with his own band, Bushrock, but he would move back into Jaco's inner circle later in the year. Melton Mustafa had returned to Florida. Kenwood Dennard went on the road with Harry Belafonte. And Don Alias, still embarrassed by the Playboy Jazz Festival fiasco, got more involved in the lucrative New York studio scene. Only saxophonist Alex Foster remained from the old Word Of Mouth band.

Through January and February, Jaco and Mike Stern could still be seen ripping it up with pickup bands at 55 Grand and playing the occasional duet gig at Bradley's, where their 40-minute set consisted of everything from "Teen Town" to "All the Things You Are." During the breaks they would disappear, only to return for the next set red-eyed and sweaty. Some who had been following their druggy behavior for the past year began to wonder aloud about how long they could keep it up.

Stern was the first to crack, and he checked himself into a rehabilitation hospital in an attempt to overcome his serious drug and alcohol problem. "At that point, we were both out of our minds," says Mike. "I finally realized I had to get some help."

Jaco rented a car and drove Stern to the Pennsylvania treatment center, but he refused to consider checking in himself. "He continued doing what he was doing, mostly cocaine and drinking," says Mike. "He had this uncanny ability to cool out for maybe a week, and then everybody would start saying, 'Oh, Jaco's looking so good. He's doing great.' But it was just an act. It wasn't long before the whole cycle would start up again."

While Jaco sometimes spoke with pride about Stern's attempt to cool out, he also seemed threatened by it, as if Mike had deserted the cause and gone over to the other camp. "I had been evicted from my loft on Grand Street and was living at the Gramercy Park Hotel," recalls Stern. "Jaco had helped me to move in. He had also helped me with some money, but he wasn't particularly helpful in getting me to straighten out. I was wrestling with my addiction. I was trying to learn how to survive without drugs or alcohol, but I had been doing them for so long I didn't know if I could live without them. I didn't even know how to hold a normal conversation without a drink. And in the midst of all this, Jaco would come to visit me in the hospital and say shit like, 'Hey, man, when are you getting out? I'll be there with a fifth of vodka for you.' He was kidding, but I didn't think it was very funny."

Before Stern checked into the hospital, Jaco had been making plans for a tour of Japan with a trio featuring Mike on guitar and Kenwood Dennard on drums. After returning from rehab, Stern was more than a little leery about hanging out with Jaco at all, let alone going on the road with him. "Jaco wasn't taking into account the whole picture of my addiction," says Mike. "He wasn't seeing *his* part in it. His behavior was enormously self-destructive, and I just couldn't be around him during my period of recovery. You couldn't deal with Jaco without going his way, which was unmanageable for

©1985 John Driscoll

me at that point. He was totally 'out,' and I was trying to *Jaco and Mike* stay straight. And he didn't like the fact that I was cooled *Stern at the 55* out, because he couldn't do it himself." *Bar, New York*

This clash of attitudes ultimately led to a dramatic part- *1985* ing of the ways. The scene was the 55 Bar, an intimate, inconspicuous jazz club on Christopher Street off Sheridan Square in the West Village. (Not to be confused with 55 Grand, although the coincidence is striking.) It served as the perfect little hideaway for Stern, a place where he could gradually get his confidence and chops back together while maintaining a low profile. He was playing there on Monday and Wednesday nights with a trio, working on standards like "Stella by Starlight," "Autumn Leaves," and "If You Could See Me Now."

"One night Jaco came by the 55 Bar to sit in," recalls Stern. "Afterwards, he started talking about our tour of Japan. I told him I couldn't do it—boy, did that piss him off. He grabbed me and started crying and yelling, 'You said we had a deal!' It was a terrible scene. But it was obvious we were on separate paths at that point. Basically, I was trying to survive and he wasn't."

Around this time, Jaco began playing with drummer Ricky Sebastian, who had come to town from New Orleans the previous summer. They had met one night at the 55 Bar. "I was playing a trio gig there with Stern and [bassist] Jeff Andrews when Jaco walked in looking a little 'out.' He walked right up to Jeff and stared him down, with his arms folded across his chest in a sort of intimidating way, until Jeff gave him the bass and sat down. We were playing a straightahead jazz-blues in F, and in the first three or four notes he played, Jaco changed the whole vibe of the tune. He took the energy level up a few notches."

They played three songs together that night, ending with "Donna Lee." Impressed by Sebastian's ability to swing and also lay down some funky New Orleans rhythms, Jaco immediately offered the drummer a gig. "Man, you're playing your ass off," he told him. "What are you doing Monday night? I got a gig here and I want you to play."

Ricky took a cool stance, trying not to appear like a flustered rookie to "The World's Greatest Bass Player." "So I asked him, 'Well, how much does it pay?' And he looked at me like I was crazy, like I should've done the gig for free or something just because of who he was. But I think he actually took more of a liking to me because I copped that kind of cool attitude."

Jaco offered Sebastian $80 for the gig and he agreed. After a firm handshake to cement the deal, Ricky strolled out of the club, turned the corner, and waited until he was well of earshot before letting out a yell. "This was more than just another $80 gig," he says. "Being able to play with Jaco was a dream come true. When I was living down in New Orleans, there were two cats I always dreamed of playing with some day: Miles Davis and Jaco. And now I had one of them."

©1984 Ebet Roberts

Jaco and Sebastian had much in common. Both had been raised in the Deep South and had hung out with black musicians when they were growing up. Both had strict Catholic upbringings, and both had played professionally with Charlie Brent. As Ricky recalls, "I used to tell Jaco, 'Man, it's unbelievable how much you and Charlie look alike. Y'all could be brothers.' The resemblance was uncanny."

Jaco and Mike Stern at the Blue Note, New York City, February 1984

Jaco was staying in a sublet on Mercer Street in SoHo when he met Sebastian. "I was living right across the street at the time," says Ricky, "and he used to call me up and say, 'Man, I don't have any hot water. Can I come over and take a shower?' So I would see him almost every day."

Ricky remembers one especially dynamic gig with Jaco during that period. The venue was Razzmatazz, in the Village. "The band was me, Jaco, Jerry González, and Jerry's brother Andy on upright bass.

Andy covered the bass lines, and Jaco played like the lead instrument all night. It was phenomenal."

With a constantly changing lineup, Word Of Mouth continued to play at Seventh Avenue South, Razzmatazz, the Bottom Line, the Blue Note, and more regularly at the Lone Star Cafe on 13th Street and Fifth Avenue. In their ads in the *Village Voice*, the Lone Star billed Jaco as "The Bad Boy Of Jazz," a title he held with a certain punk pride.

On April 16, Jaco played a concert down in Fort Lauderdale at the Musicians Exchange. Ingrid Pastorius showed up for the gig with the twins. Before the show, she went backstage to talk to Jaco and caught him in his dressing room doing lines of coke with "some slimy drug dealer." Without speaking a word, she slapped him in the face, grabbed the kids, and went home. Later that night, Ingrid got a call from Tracy, warning her that Jaco was on the rampage and headed her way. After Jaco careened into the house and passed out in the bedroom, Ingrid gathered up the kids and split for good.

Over the next few days, Jaco made frequent overtures to Ingrid and tried to patch up their marriage. But Ingrid was determined to keep her distance. Whenever he'd call with drunken declarations of love, she would invariably put him off. "You're lost," she'd tell him. "Go find yourself."

In May, Jaco took a break from his marital troubles and the New York scene by touring Japan as a special guest with the Gil Evans Orchestra. Trumpeter Miles Evans (Gil's son) remembers that tour as a very unsettling experience. "The first place we played was Open Theatre East, outside of Tokyo," says Miles, who was on his first major tour with the band. "About 20,000 people showed up for the concert, and Jaco went on half an hour early as a solo act. He was playing loud rock & roll bass and just acting crazy. At one point, he threw his bass about 20 feet in the air and let it crash. The wood split, and we didn't have another bass on hand. So the orchestra went on without Jaco. We played for about 20 minutes, and then

Jaco came running out onstage with warpaint and mud all over him. It was really weird."

On the bus trip back to the hotel, Jaco threw a tantrum because the promoters had provided light beer instead of regular beer. "We were 45 minutes outside of Tokyo, and Jaco had them stop the bus," says Miles. "He yelled, 'What's this light beer shit?' Then he got off the bus and started walking."

Jaco's behavior remained erratic throughout the tour. "He would go from being totally crazy one day to playing very, very well and handling himself beautifully the next day. It was hard to predict his mood swings. There were some excellent nights. I remember one concert where Jaco and [guitarist] Hiram Bullock started the show by walking down the aisles, wearing wireless rigs and playing Herbie Hancock's 'Dolphin Dance.' Now *that* was a really great entrance."

When Jaco returned to the States, he resumed his musical relationship with Delmar Brown, who had just come back from a tour of Italy and Israel with Bushrock. Alex Foster and Jerry González were still members of the band, and on some occasions the lineup would be augmented by trumpeters Miles Evans, Lew Soloff, and Jon Faddis; saxophonist Lou Marini; and tuba player Dave Bargeron.

Near the end of June, Jaco began laying down tracks at the Kampo Cultural Center, a Japanese-owned recording studio on Bond Street that was just a couple of blocks from New York's notorious rock venue, CBGB's. On the strength of his name alone, Jaco was able to block several days of time. For this open-ended session, he called in drummer Rashied Ali and tenor saxophonist Pharoah Sanders, both of whom had played with John Coltrane in his latter exploratory years. He had also hired a top-notch New York string section and recruited pianist Joanne Brackeen, saxophonist Alex Foster, and trumpeter Randy Brecker. Ultimately, none of them would be paid and the tapes documenting the sessions would be left floating in limbo.

Jaco had promised Sanders $5,000 for the session. Alex Foster says, "Pharoah had some woman—I think it might've been his old lady—

acting as his manager at the time. She got a union contract and insisted that Pharoah would not play a note until it was signed. Jaco was hedging. He didn't want to sign the contract. Finally he said, 'Okay, fine,' but it was obvious at that point that it meant nothing for him to sign a contract, since he didn't have any money anyway. Whatever money he had coming in, he was blowing immediately. He was buying a lot of cocaine, tipping cab drivers a couple of hundred bucks for a $5 fare, and giving away money to people on the basketball court."

Jaco managed to get several tunes on tape. The material ranged from loose blues jams with street performer Royal Blue on vocals to highly orchestrated compositions with strings and a children's choir. One track featured Jaco overdubbing fuzzed-out solos on top of his own drums. And in a nostalgic look back to his C.C. Riders' days, he did a party-in-the-studio cover of the funky Wayne Cochran-Charlie Brent tune "Somebody Been Cutting In on My Groove."

When the management of the Kampo studios pressed Jaco for payment, he simply walked off, leaving the tapes behind. It was not an uncommon scenario for Jaco at that time: he would throw together a jam at some studio, roll tape, and then split when it came time to pay. Ricky Sebastian recalls one such session at the Power Station: "There were as many as 15 people in the studio at one point, including cats like Lew Soloff [trumpet], Michael Shrieve [drums], Ronnie Cuber [baritone sax], Michael Lewy [violin], Alex Foster [alto sax], and Royal Blue [vocals]. There were some really terrible moments where we would just be goofing off, but there were also some really high moments. They had two sets of drums in the studio, and at one point Jaco and I did a 20-minute duet on drums. I would really like to hear that."

One strange session that happened around this time featured the unlikely pairing of Jaco with Muhammed Ali. Kenwood Dennard was the connection for this rap session in Los Angeles. A drum student of his, Scott Weinberger, who was Ali's agent, brought Kenwood in on the project. The proceeds of the recording were supposed to go to an organization dedicated to fighting hunger. Los Angeles Mayor Tom Bradley had recruited 15 underprivileged kids from around the city to participate in this session, and they cheered on Ali as he rapped:

> *I'm gonna tell you about my biggest fight*
> *Let's get together and whup hunger tonight*
> *Wars on nations were fought to change maps*
> *But wars on hunger were fought to map change*

Jaco was excited about meeting his boyhood hero. But instead of playing it humble, he showed up at the session slightly intoxicated and chose to break the ice with a lewd and wholly inappropriate joke. "Jaco walked into the control room where Ali was sitting," recalls Dennard, "and his first words to him were, 'Muhammed, how do you know if your roommate is gay? 'Cause his dick tastes like shit.' And Ali looks over with this really disdainful expression and says, 'Is this guy gonna be on *my* record?'"

Jaco ended up playing some funky bass alongside Dennard's slamming backbeats on that session, but the record never came out due to business hassles that arose between Ali's management and the label. Looking back on that day, Dennard comments that Jaco and Ali had at least one thing on common. "I think a lot of historically significant people seem to have this thing, where they're always *on*, 24 hours a day. They've got some kind of magic going all the time. And in the case of Jaco and Ali, they were both natural-born entertainers."

In August 1984, Jaco appeared on the cover of *Guitar Player* magazine. Based on my interviews with him on several occasions, this article not only gave Jaco a morale boost at a time when musicians and clubowners around town were turning their backs on him, it also sent a message to his fans all over the world: namely, that everything was cool and Jaco was indeed on top of his game. Only those in New York who had seen his erratic behavior in nightclubs and on the streets of Greenwich Village knew the truth about Jaco's mental and physical decline.

When this issue of *Guitar Player* hit the newsstands, Jaco used it as ammunition against his detractors. He bought copies and proudly passed them out, as if to say, "See, I'm not crazy. I'm on the cover of a major music magazine. That *proves* I'm not crazy." Months later, he was still gloating about all the attention *Guitar Player* had given to him. At one point, he confided in me, "You know, that story saved my life. Everybody was counting me out, but you believed in me. You brought me back from the dead with that article."

Jaco began touting me as "The #1 Jazz Writer" to all of his street pals from Washington Square Park and the West Fourth Street bas-

©1984 Mark Brady

ketball court. In retrospect, I believe the timing of that story may have done more harm than good to Jaco. Its publication only perpetuated the Jaco myth at a time when he should have been confronting the reality of his self-destructive lifestyle. In essence, by glorifying him, it gave Jaco license to continue his nasty habits, which he did with impunity.

Ricky Sebastian says, "Around that time I got a road gig with Blood, Sweat & Tears, so I would only see Jaco when I came back to town. And each time I came back, I could tell he was getting more and more 'out.'" By the winter of 1984, both the Bottom Line and the Blue Note had stopped booking Jaco because of the crazy, destructive stunts he had pulled at those venues. His only regular outlets were Seventh Avenue South and the Lone Star Cafe, where they continued to bill him as "The Bad Boy Of Jazz."

In November, Jaco began playing piano/bass gigs with Delmar Brown, Kirk Lightsey, or Michael Gerber, a blind pianist from Florida. One regular venue for these duets was a small SoHo restaurant called 5 & 10 No Exaggeration, which was the site of a sad encounter with Joni Mitchell. As Joni related in *Musician* magazine: "I went to an art opening with a group of people. We came out and were looking for a place to eat. We saw this little restaurant across the street with a hand-painted sign: 'Jaco Pastorius Tonight.' So I went across to see him. We all walked in, and he was sitting at the bar. I went up and tapped him on the shoulder. When he turned his face to me he was just ... gone. It was a 'gone' face. He said my name and we hugged. He hugged me like he was drowning. Then he started yelling my name around the club. 'Joni Mitchell is the baddest! She's the only woman this, she's the only woman that,' until it was embarrassing. Everyone concerned was embarrassed. He kept hollering my name. It was a very small club, and there were maybe ten people present.

"Anyway, we ended up jamming for a minute. I just got up and started improvising on this electric piano. Then I started singing and let Jaco take the lead. He used to play 'out' a lot, but there's out and then there's *out*. This was not good. It was frustrating. It was heartbreaking. And so I just let him play and followed him and sang along. That way, no matter where he went I could try and be supportive. But he was not in the mood to be supportive. That particular evening, he was a saboteur."

In mid-December of 1984, Jaco and Rashied Ali traveled to Guadeloupe to conduct clinics and play a series of concerts. Their performance on December 19 was broadcast over French radio. A bootleg CD, stolen off the radio feed, emerged several years later in Japan as *Blackbird*. (The disc was manufactured by Alfa Jazz and distributed by Timeless Records.) And though the recording is far from audiophile quality, the duet performances of Ornette Coleman's "Broadway Blues," Jimi Hendrix's "Purple Haze," Tadd Dameron's "If You

Could See Me Now," Paul McCartney's "Blackbird," and John Coltrane's "Naima" include some exhilarating moments. On two tracks—"Donna Lee" and "Continuum"—Jaco and Rashied are joined by some accomplished bass students who had attended the clinic earlier in the day.

Jaco sounds focused and on top of his game during the course of this one-hour performance. He nonchalantly tosses off his famous licks from "Liberty City," "Portrait of Tracy," "Barbary Coast," "Teen Town" and "(Used to Be a) Cha-Cha" while dropping in quotes from "The Sound of Music," "The High and the Mighty," "Alfie," and "If I Only Had a Brain." And the drummer reacts to every statement Jaco throws his way. ("We had a really good hookup," says Rashied. "You take two guys who are really good at what they do and love what they do—they can't help but sound good together.")

On his way back from that gig, Jaco stopped off at his home in Deerfield Beach, where he remained for a week or so. Coincidentally, his old comrade, drummer Bob Moses, happened to be in Florida on vacation. "I was chilling out on Sanibel Island," recalls Moses. "I had driven down from Boston—just a slow, leisurely excursion with my girlfriend. I didn't expect to see Jaco. I didn't know if he was back in New York or down in Florida at the time, but I was clear across the state from Fort Lauderdale."

On the drive back, Moses stopped off in Melbourne, in central Florida, to pay a visit to Jaco's brother Gregory. While he was there, Jaco just happened to call. "He was really surprised to hear me. It was right before New Year's Eve, and Jaco said, 'Hey, man, you wanna play a New Year's Eve gig in Fort Lauderdale?' It was always a trip to play with Jaco, and I figured it was going to be an adventure I couldn't pass up, musically or otherwise. So I told him, 'Sure, man, let's do it.'

"We drove down and got to Jaco's house at about 5 PM. There was nobody home. I walked out to the backyard and noticed this big German acoustic bass lying there on his lawn—no case, nothing.

This cat really had some trust in the fates to leave an instrument like that. The other unusual thing I noticed was that there were monkeys in the grapefruit trees around his house. So I came upon this kind of bizarre scene—African monkeys, a bass lying on the lawn, and no Jaco." Moses hung out for about half an hour and then split to get something to eat. He returned around 7:30.

"Jaco was home by then, so I asked him about the gig. He said, 'Gig? Man, that's a great idea!'

"I said, 'Come on, man! You pulled us all the way here, and there's no gig?'

"'Man, if I told you I have a gig, I'm gonna have a gig. You wait right here.'"

Jaco left Moses and his girlfriend in the backyard with the monkeys and the bass and took off on his motorcycle. "At this point I'm laughing to myself," recalls Moses. "Here it is, 8 PM on New Year's Eve, and he's out looking for a gig on the busiest night of the year. New Year's Eve gigs are booked months in advance, but Jaco seemed so determined I just let him go."

An hour passed before Jaco returned. Somehow, he had booked a gig at an Irish bar called Tipperary's that was located in a Fort Lauderdale shopping mall. The band consisted of Moses on drums, Jaco on bass, and Othello Molineaux on steel pans. Moses recalls that Molineaux came over to Jaco's house so Jaco could show him how to play "It's a Long Way to Tipperary" on the pans, just so they would have at least one song the crowd could relate to.

"Jaco had me playing a samba beat underneath this tune, and it was cooking. It was incredible how fast it all came together. So we went to play the gig, and the club turned out to be a redneck bar. The vibe was ugly. Some of these cats were saying shit like, 'Fuckin' hippie music. What the fuck is this?' Ingrid's brother Peter wanted to get in a fight with these cats because they were calling us faggots, and we had to restrain him. But Jaco kind of fought them with the music. He turned up his amp real loud and started playing 'America the Beautiful.' The walls were shaking, and those redneck cats just stood there with their mouths open. They couldn't say anything after that. I mean, these were the kind of cats who had American flags stitched on their jackets and baseball caps. And Jaco's attitude was, 'All right, I'll give you America, motherfuckers!' It was beautiful."

When he returned to New York, Jaco found it hard to get work. "People were starting to say Jaco couldn't play anymore, that his bass playing sucked," says Miles Evans. "They were saying you shouldn't go to see him, that he was just doing the same old clichés he had been doing for the past five years. And they were right, to some degree. He was very erratic at this point—some nights he would be great, other nights he would be horrible. It depended on what was happening in his personal life at the time."

By this time, Theresa Nagell had entered Jaco's life. A tall, exotic beauty of Japanese-German ancestry, she quickly became Jaco's latest obsession. Terry and Jaco were an extremely volatile combination: Both were strong-willed, streetwise individuals with jealous natures, and neither would back down from a fight. Both drank to excess, and Terry was also using hard drugs. They went from extreme highs to horrific lows, often culminating in violent confrontations that involved slapping, biting, kicking, and hair-pulling incidents. Every fight would be followed by a truce, a make-up period, and another romantic interlude. It was an emotional roller-coaster ride.

Ingrid Pastorius says, "I can understand why Jaco was attracted to Theresa, but those feelings stemmed from some very warped and unresolved things that happened when he was young. She represented a lot of the stuff he had some sort of attraction to, which had something to do with claiming to be white trash and feeling good about being dirty. He was proud of telling stories about living on the railroad tracks and eating rats with the bums. So she represented this kind of dangerous element that he was attracted to. And whether they were good for each other—it was beyond that. Jaco wasn't good for himself. I mean, I never would have left him if he hadn't been so abusive and self-destructive. I wasn't surprised when Theresa came into his life. I think they were just two needy people, and neither one of them would have been with the other if they were both sane."

On January 15, 1985, Jaco made an appearance at the Lone Star with a 12-piece version of his Word Of Mouth big band, featuring special guest Toots Thielemans on harmonica. As my wife sat and watched Jaco's performance, she turned to me and said, "He just tears me up," referring to the fragile balance of anguish and joy that he wore like a badge of honor. By this time, it was clear that Jaco was bordering on psychosis. His performances had become pathetic rituals of alcoholic rage and catharsis, often devoid of any musical coherence. And yet, the small contingent of Jaco groupies who flocked to every one of these sad displays continued to stroke his ego by telling him, "You're the baddest, Jaco!"

In the terminology of Alcoholic Anonymous, these people were enablers. By ignoring the fact that Jaco had a serious problem, they enabled him to continue indulging in cocaine and alcohol. Some even hastened his descent by providing drinks and drugs after his sub-par outings. Occasionally, Jaco would summon up the fortitude to pull himself together and deliver an excellent performance. But that, says Mike Stern, only obscured a deeper problem.

"Jaco's enormous talent allows him to get away with murder," Stern told me around that time. "All he has to do is have one good night, and everybody is patting him on the back and telling him how good he's doing. But I don't buy that. You can't fool another alcoholic. When he looks good for one day, I don't buy into it. Because the only way Jaco is going to look good to me is if he has had at least 90 days of complete sobriety. And the only way that is going to happen is if he goes into a rehabilitation program."

The key, Stern stressed, was that Jaco would have to make that move on his own. "You can't force him into a hospital. He has to recognize that he has a problem and go in voluntarily. Right now, he's still in denial. He thinks he's okay, and sometimes he's pretty convincing. But it's all bullshit. Take it from someone who's been there. Ultimately, it's up to him. He has got to see that things are fucked up and that rehab is what he needs. But Jaco doesn't see it yet."

Jaco lost his prized '62 Fender Jazz Bass around this time. He often carried his axe around town with him, without a case, and he had a tendency to leave it unattended while he played basketball or when he fell asleep in Washington Square Park. On one such occasion, it was stolen.

Dave Bargeron came to Jaco's rescue for one Lone Star gig. "I had this gorgeous pre-CBS Jazz Bass that had been appraised at a couple thousand dollars," he recalls. "I knew better, but I ended up loaning it to Jaco, knowing full well that it was basically the same as giving it to him. I had never done anything like that before in my life, but he was a dear friend of mine. It was such a joy being around him in the early years, so this was kind of my personal tribute to Jaco. At the time, our understanding was that I was lending the bass to him and that he could pay me for it whenever he got the money. Of course, I never saw that bass again, and he never paid me a cent."

In February 1985, Alex Foster finally decided to part company with Jaco. "It was getting too weird," he says. "He would show up for gigs without a bass and play piano for 15 minutes while the audience sat there in dead silence. Or he would have a temper tantrum onstage and turn up his bass all the way and let it feed back for ten minutes. What amazed me was that the people sitting right in the front row would not get up and leave. I could not believe that. It was so loud I would leave the bandstand—unbearable noise, just painful to hear. I couldn't put up with that any longer. As far as I was concerned, it was over."

It was also over between Jaco and Ingrid, who filed for a divorce on the grounds of mental and physical cruelty. "When I divorced him," she says in retrospect, "I did it not because I was in love with someone else or because I didn't love him. To this day, I still love Jaco. It was just that I needed to protect the children. The marriage wasn't conducive to a healthy environment for the children. I was subjected, many times, to watching him take one of the babies under his arm and run off into the night when he wasn't in such great shape. I just couldn't bear the thought that at any time something terrible might happen. So I did what I had to do."

That spring, Jaco went on a brief tour of Europe with a young drummer from San Francisco named Brian Melvin. They had met the previous year, when Jaco went to the Bay Area to play on Melvin's debut album, *Night Food*. Melvin recounts the circumstances: "Todd Barkin, who was the ex-owner of the Keystone Korner jazz club in San Francisco, had put out the word around New York that I wanted to get Jaco on my album. It was purely a wish kind of thing for me. Todd had asked me, kind of hypothetically, if I could choose one guy to have on my album, who would it be. And without hesitating I had said, 'Jaco.'"

A few days later, Melvin was awakened at 4 AM by a ringing telephone. The caller was gruff and to the point: "Hey, Brian Melvin, I hear you need a bass player for your album. Well, this is Jaco Pastorius, The World's Greatest Bass Player. I'd love to play on your album. Put me on a plane ... *now!*"

The next day, after borrowing his mother's credit card, Melvin purchased a round-trip ticket to San Francisco. Unfortunately, Jaco missed the flight. He called again: "Listen, I didn't make it. I got hung up. Get me another one."

A second ticket was arranged, and Melvin drove out to meet Jaco at the airport. "He looked tired. His hair was cut really short. He had no shoes on, and he was wearing a pair of loose karate pants and a colorful shirt. He was carrying a book with him, Mary Shelley's *Frankenstein*. And the first thing he said was, 'You gotta get me a bass.' I told him, 'No problem,' and took him back to my mom's house for a nice Italian dinner and a little rest."

They recorded at a little 8-track studio in San Francisco. Most of the tunes were originals composed by Melvin or saxophonist Rick Smith, and they also cut a version of "Continuum." Melvin says, "That was my first record date as a leader. I didn't know anything about it, really. I was green to the world of recording. I was more of a street musician, a garage musician who had never had any formal training. But Jaco just dug me as a person. There was something we had in common that was extra-musical. We had both gone to Catholic schools, and we had both played sports, so we were coming from the jock-music thing. And I think somewhere along the line his mom and dad had had a tough time, and he suffered from that. I had gone through that in my family, too. So there were a lot of similarities. I think it was because of those things that we developed a very tight relationship."

Through connections in Amsterdam, Melvin had gotten a deal with Timeless Records, and Timeless sponsored Melvin's band on a swing through Europe to promote the new album. The band included Azar Lawrence on sax, Jon Davis on piano, and Paul Mousavi on guitar. Jaco agreed to tour as a sideman on the condition that his name not be used in any of the promotion for the concerts. But once the band got to Europe, an unscrupulous promoter put Jaco's name in large type on the posters, with Melvin's name set far below in minuscule letters. To make matters worse, Jaco was in a particularly unstable frame of mind.

"This was a drastic period in Jaco's life," says Melvin. "Things were starting to get a little hazy with him. I sensed that Jaco's deepest emotional problems stemmed from a family thing that probably went all the way back to the time when he was a little kid. I could see that he missed his own children a lot, and I also saw how much he loved his mother. He would call her all the time when we were in Europe, just to say, 'I love you, Mom.' Sometimes he would be very sincere, other times he would be really high and childlike, crying over the phone to her."

Melvin was only 25 years old at the time. He felt a lot of pressure on him as the bandleader, and Jaco made matters worse with his erratic, unpredictable behavior. "Jaco had a way of pulling these little power plays," says Melvin. "He would get you to a point where you needed him, and then he would throw you a curve. Right before a show, he might demand more money or threaten to leave if his demands weren't met."

The tour started in Stockholm, Sweden. The gig was a complete disaster, and it was written up in the local papers as one of the worst jazz concerts in memory. Jaco played very little bass during the show, preferring to take over the drums while Melvin played bass. The concert a few days later in a small town outside Paris was even worse. "Jaco had gotten a message that Ingrid's divorce had gone through," recalls Melvin, "so he went out and started drinking heavily. He got really animalistic. He threw a plate in my dressing room, just barely missing me, and he cut his right index finger in the process. He was so frustrated about the divorce and about cutting himself that he started crying. But he didn't cancel the gig. He taped his finger, went out onstage, and started playing some solo bass, just to see how his finger would respond. But it was very painful for him. He couldn't play.

"The audience didn't know he had cut his finger, so they got impatient and started booing him. This freaked out Jaco to the point where he threw his bass into the crowd. Then he grabbed the microphone and yelled, 'You French live in hell!' You can imagine how that went over."

Thousands of feet were stomping as the crowd began chanting in unison, *"Reimbursement! Reimbursement!"* Backstage, the band made a quick getaway.

The next gig was at a club in Paris called New Morning. "Jaco started spitting at people in the audience, and at that point I went over and almost decked him. I said, 'Jaco, you can't do this. My name is on this shit, too.' Jaco turned to the promoter, pointed at me, and said, 'Either he goes or I go.' The promoter couldn't afford to have Jaco leave, so they found some other drummer to finish the rest of the tour. It was like a mutiny. In essence, I got aced out of my own gig."

After returning to New York, Jaco resumed his regular gigs at the Lone Star. On April 30, he invited Led Zeppelin guitarist Jimmy Page onstage to jam. Geri Palladino recalls that entire day as a special event. "Jaco called me at 6 AM and said, 'Geraldine, I need my hair done. Be at Anita Evans's house at 7.' So I went over there. Jaco said he wanted eight braids around his head, and on the bottom I lined it with beads so it would be colorful and make noise when he shook his head. The whole process took about three hours, and then Jaco asked me to hang out with him for the rest of the day. He offered to pay my regular day rate, which was $100. So we hung out all morning and afternoon, drinking champagne at Anita's.

"In early evening, we headed over to the Lone Star. When Jaco came onstage with his band, he had a hat on, and I thought to myself, I did all that work and he covers it up with a hat? But Jaco always liked surprises, and he liked to be noticed. So after they played a few songs, he whipped off the hat to reveal this beautiful hairstyle. He looked hot."

Jaco spotted Page in the audience and invited him up to jam. "At first you could see that Jimmy was intimidated," Geri recalls. "He started to play kind of slow, but Jaco kept prodding and pushing him until finally Jimmy got into the groove, and the two of them took off into this cosmic jam."

At this point, Jaco was living in an apartment on Jones Street in the heart of the Village, just a few blocks away from the basketball court on West Fourth Street, where he spent most of his waking hours. He had taken on as his manager a man named Jose Fuentes, a shady street character he had met at the basketball court.

Through Fuentes, I arranged to conduct a Blindfold Test with Jaco for *Down Beat* magazine. (A regular feature of the magazine since the

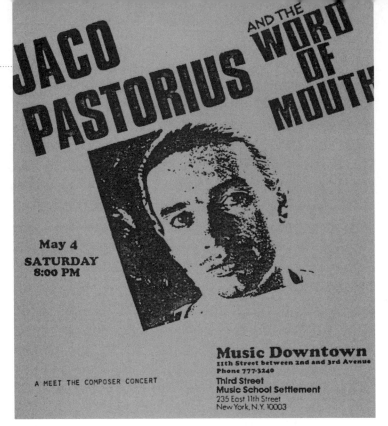

Program for performance at the Third Street Music School Settlement

'40s, the Blindfold Test is a listening session. Without seeing the records being played, the subject is asked to identify the performers and offer comments.) Our appointment was scheduled for 7 PM on May 1 at Jaco's apartment. I knocked on the door. No answer. I waited in the pouring rain for 20 minutes before calling Fuentes to find out what had happened. He assured me, "Don't worry, Jaco is on his way. Just hang on a few more minutes. He'll be there." By 9 o'clock there was still no sign of Jaco, and the rain was coming down harder than ever. I left.

Three days later, Jaco appeared at the Third Street Music School Settlement as part of its Meet The Composer series. This state-funded program was designed to give students a chance to talk to working professionals and learn more about music. Jaco was the lone representative of jazz in the series. The parents who accompanied their kids to this lecture-demonstration were probably expecting some kindly elder statesman like Dave Brubeck. Instead they got Jaco, whose nickname in musician circles had become "Whacko." True to form, Jaco showed up in a drunken, disheveled state. He had been up for a couple of days and had drunk a whole carafe of wine at a restaurant just before arriving.

A piano was set up alongside the drum kit. There was no bass or bass amp in sight. Jaco entered the space barefoot and sweaty, with a faraway look in his eyes. He began the program on piano, noodling a gospel vamp while singing in a hoarse voice that had some of the audience shifting nervously in their seats. The other musicians— Jerry González on congas, Scott Brown on piano, René McLean on tenor sax, and Manny Montura on drums—stood by, waiting for a cue, looking as confused as the audience.

Jaco jumped up from the piano and broke into a crazed shuffle step, laughing and giggling to himself. He sat down again and rambled on at the keyboard for a few more minutes, until someone yelled, "Play the bass!" Jaco responded by giving the heckler the finger, saying, "When I do this, it means I love you."

The crowd was clearly shocked. Some concerned parents in the audience grabbed their children by the hand and escorted them out of the hall. Just as the exodus began, Royal Blue wandered out to center stage. A sharp dresser with a hip street demeanor, Blue greeted Jaco with a high five and distracted the crowd by getting them to clap along to the beat. That succeeded momentarily, but in the middle of the next song, Jaco turned mean. He stood up from the piano and started yelling at Manny Montura, telling him precisely what beat to play. The drummer, who obviously wanted to please Jaco, tried hard to make sense out of Jaco's wild arm-waving. Finally, Jaco rushed across the stage, grabbed a drumstick, and started banging and crashing rudely on cymbals while screaming obscenities at Montura.

By this time, most of the crowd had left. The voyeurs stayed behind to see how far Jaco would take it, like race fans hoping for a car crash. René McLean shook his head and walked off the stage. Finally, Jaco threw down the drumsticks and stormed out of the hall. The principal of the music school, a matronly woman who was clearly outraged by this chaotic display, announced that the concert was over and that refunds would be given at the box office. She had already placed a phone call to the police, fearing that Jaco might turn his violent outbursts on the audience.

As the crowd filed out, I spotted a young man with long hair and a headband—obviously a Jaco fan from the Weather Report days. This aspiring bass player had traveled all the way from Connecticut, and he was visibly upset by what had taken place. When I spoke to him, all he could say was, "Jaco was my hero!" as tears rolled down his face. Jerry González tried to console him, saying, "Jaco's been having some mental problems lately."

Two policemen were stationed outside the principal's office, where Jaco was cooling out. He was sitting behind a desk, and he had painted both his hands white with some correction fluid he had found inside a desk drawer. He barked at a young woman he had introduced to me as his daughter, ordering her to go get him a beer. When Jaco saw me, he said, "Hey, man, we're gonna go out there and do that Blindfold Test right now, onstage, in front of everybody."

His "daughter" looked down at him and said, in a tone of contempt, "Jaco, everybody's *gone*."

A week later, I witnessed more bizarre behavior by Jaco, this time on the streets of Greenwich Village. I was attending an afternoon press conference at the Blue Note, where representatives of the Japan Victor Corporation were announcing their sponsorship of what had previously been the Kool Jazz Festival. I was standing at the bar when I heard a commotion behind me at the door. Someone was trying to crash the press conference. In the midst of the scuffle, I heard a familiar voice yell out, "I'm Jaco Pastorius!"

Jaco looked sick, and he screamed out an unintelligible threat as he slammed the door. I left the Blue Note and followed him. Jaco wandered up Third Street like a wounded animal, lurching forward as he prowled the sidewalk, ranting and spitting at pedestrians along the way. When I caught up to him, I grabbed him by the shoulder and spun him around. He seemed momentarily startled, and then a slow grin broke across his face. "You found me!" he screamed, as if we were playing a game of hide and seek. He yelled, "Come on, let's go!" and took off down the block.

I followed a couple of steps behind him, watching as he poked his head into every boutique and restaurant along Third Street and yelled out some garbled obscenity. We came to a pizza stand on the corner of McDougal and Third. Jaco asked me to buy him a slice. He took three bites, flung the remains against a wall, and then continued trudging along Third Street, his eyes bloodshot, his hair greasy and stringy. It was unseasonably warm that day, about 80 degrees, but Jaco was wearing a shirt, a sweater, and a denim jacket. He had masking tape wrapped around his knees on the outside of his pants, and all of his fingers were wrapped in tape.

I continued to follow Jaco, observing the shocked faces of pedestrians who caught a glimpse of this menacing figure. He veered over to Bleecker Street, a popular strip of folk, rock, and blues nightclubs.

Ironically, that very afternoon had been set for the press preview of *Mayor*, a new musical at the Village Gate based on the charismatic then-mayor of New York City, Edward I. Koch, who was in attendance. Jaco's Bowery-bum attire was at odds with the formal dress code for this gala affair. Nevertheless, he was determined to crash the party. Without breaking stride, he somehow got past the doormen and wandered onto the packed terrace of the Village Gate.

Jaco cast a bloodshot eye around the room, sizing up the elite crowd, and then yelled, "Tell Mayor Koch that Jaco owns this town!" The high-society types let out a collective gasp as Jaco stalked through the crowd and headed back to the street. I continued to trail him as he headed for the Apple Spa, just around the corner from the Village Gate. The attendant seemed to know Jaco, and he let him pass through to the men's locker room. I watched him soap up his face and walk into the sauna with all his clothes on, sitting down right next to two businessmen with towels over their laps and astonished looks on their faces. Jaco sat there stone-faced, like a deranged mime, not even acknowledging their presence. Finally, he got up and headed to the showers. He poked his head under a shower to rinse off the soap and then ambled over to Washington Square Park, his safe haven.

As more and more colleagues began to turn their backs on Jaco, he sought out the company of the homeless people who hung out in Washington Square Park. Jaco had a strange affinity for these street characters. Once, while sitting in the park, he looked around at the assembly of derelicts, drug dealers, and street hustlers, threw out his arms, and declared with a wide grin on his face, "*This* is my family!"

The Jaco horror stories began to pile up. He had removed the door of his apartment and used it to sleep on. He had tried to flood his apartment to create a swimming pool. He was seen passing out $20 bills to members of his street "family."

I was hanging with him one night when he tried to score some cocaine from dealers in Washington Square Park. He introduced himself, as he always did around this time, as "Jaco, the bass player from Weather Report," even though it had been more than three years since he had left the band. The two dealers seemed vaguely aware of Weather Report and agreed to go back to Jaco's apartment. With the skillful, streetwise delivery of a flim-flam man, Jaco persuaded these young hustlers to lay out several lines for him to sample.

Soon after Jaco snorted the lines, the phone rang. It was Ingrid calling from Florida, asking about his alimony payments. Jaco yelled, "I told you yesterday you'll get the money!" He tugged violently on the cord, ripping the phone out of the wall, and then he threw it across the room. The drug dealers looked impressed. Proclaiming the coke to meet his standards, Jaco continued his bluff. "I'll take an ounce. But first I have go get the cash. My friend is storing it for me in his safe over on Carmine Street. I'll be right back."

©1985 Ebet Roberts

Leaving me behind as collateral, Jaco dashed out the *Kenwood Dennard,*
door. We waited in his apartment for 20 uncomfortable *Jerry Jemmott, and*
minutes. The dealers nervously paced the floor, smacking *Jaco filming*
their fists into their palms as they wondered aloud if they *instructional video*
had been scammed. Eventually, they turned their wrath on me. One
of them grabbed me, put me up against the wall, and yelled, "You
tell your friend he's in serious trouble." They smashed a couple of
windows on their way out.

By the summer of 1985, Jaco had hit a new low. He was financially
strapped and had been evicted from his apartment. At that point, he
was literally living on the West Fourth Street basketball court. He
roamed the streets in a daze, using his former ties to Weather Report
as a means of panhandling money from passersby. "It hurts me to
see him this way," said one colleague. "It's pathetic."

Miraculously, Jaco filmed an instructional video called *Modern*

Electric Bass that summer. Rob Wallis and Paul Siegel, who had founded the Drummers Collective in 1977 and created the DCI Video business several years later, arranged for Jaco to stay at the Chelsea Hotel on 23rd Street for three days prior to the shooting. They watched over Jaco, making sure that he never came in contact with alcohol or drugs.

For the video shoot, they had arranged for Jerry Jemmott to interview Jaco on camera. In his opening appraisal of Jaco's talents and contributions to the bass, Jemmott says: "Jaco, a lot's been said about you. But the main thing is that people recognize that you're able to play, with real sincerity, every style of music. Not only every style, but you can play all parts of a given piece at the same time on just one instrument, the bass. Now because of this, a lot of people have gone crazy trying to duplicate what you do. You've given the bass quite a bit of attention. How do you feel about that?"

After a pregnant pause and a sly smirk, Jaco replied, "Gimme a gig."

Following the interview/clinic segment of the video, Jaco jammed in the studio with John Scofield and Kenwood Dennard. This trio was in essence a working model of the group that Jaco had once envisioned for himself, with Dennard and Mike Stern. It also anticipated the trio he would later form with Dennard and Hiram Bullock.

"Jaco was cool that day," says Scofield. "He was drinking a couple of beers toward the end of the filming, but he wasn't out of it. We did the video and everything went pretty smoothly. And for me, that really offered some hope that Jaco was on his way back."

But it didn't last long. A couple of weeks later, Jaco, eyebrows shaved off, stormed into the DCI offices ranting about payment for the video shoot and yelling something about visiting with the spirit of Jimi Hendrix.

It was around this time that Jaco moved into an apartment on 31st Street with James Cannings, an itinerant guitarist/singer from Trinidad who also worked as an engineer. Cannings was unaware of Jaco's fame, and this actually served as the basis of a strong and last-

ing friendship between them. "Jaco appreciated the fact that I wasn't sucking up to him because of his fame," says James. "I was always straight up with him. At one point he said, 'That's all I need. I need someone to relate to me as just another person and not as Jaco Pastorius.'"

John Scofield, Kenwood Dennard, and Jaco filming instructional video

Cannings arranged for Jaco to meet with the vice president of New England Digital, the corporation that manufactured the Synclavier. Cannings hoped that Jaco could get an endorsement deal with the company, and he used some connections to set up the meeting. It turned out to be yet another fiasco.

Cannings says, "He came in late wearing the baggy white beach pants that he always wore. His eyebrows and his underarms were shaved. We're sitting there in this office with the vice president and a corporate lawyer, and Jaco looks at me and says, 'Hey, James. Do you know who dances for Michael Jackson in the 'Thriller' video?

Me. They paint me black and I do all the steps. I'm the stunt dancer. That's why I had to shave down here.' Then he pulls down his pants to show that he had also shaved his pubic hair. And that blew the whole deal right there—the vice president and the lawyer got up and left the room."

Cannings tried to get Jaco to take stock of himself and turn his life around, but to no avail. At the end of August, Jaco was seen wandering around the Village with two black eyes, looking like a total wreck. A fellow musician relates this story: "I was walking through Washington Square Park when I heard Weather Report's 'Birdland' blaring on a boom box in the distance. I walked closer to the source, trying to find out who was playing it. And there, sitting under the archway, was Jaco, looking terrible. His hair was all greasy and stringy, like he hadn't slept or taken a bath in days. It was hot, but he was wearing a sweater and a heavy coat over that. His face was full of cuts and one eye was blackened. He had obviously been beaten up.

"He was sitting with his head hung down, kind of hovering over this little boom box playing *Heavy Weather*. And he had laid a hat in front of him to collect change from people passing by. I approached him and called out his name. He looked up but didn't seem to recognize me. I said, 'Hey, Jaco, you all right?' And he said, 'Yeah, man, I'm fine. You got a quarter?' I gave him a dollar and left. I just couldn't bear to see him that way."

To anyone who would listen to him at that point, Jaco would complain about having "two wives, two houses, and no place to sleep." He would also go on at length about how so many bass players were stealing his style but he couldn't get a gig anywhere except the Lone Star and Seventh Avenue South.

Jaco's situation paralleled the frustration that Charlie Parker felt toward the end of his life, when he heard many imitators capitalizing on the style of playing he had invented. In his book *Jazz Is* [Avon], Nat Hentoff recounts this exchange between Parker and

singer Babs Gonzalez: "When Babs tried to persuade Parker to get off drugs, Bird's answer was, 'Wait until everybody gets rich off your style and you don't have any bread. Then lecture me about drugs.'"

The pressure of being broke, homeless, and estranged from his children built up to a point where Jaco finally cracked. In September 1985, he went to Philadelphia to visit his father and was arrested while trying to break into the house while Jack was away. After he was released, Jaco agreed to go into a hospital in Pennsylvania to get some help.

After a brief stay, Jaco emerged from the hospital relatively stable but somewhat sedated by the lithium the doctors had prescribed for him. The lithium prevented his enormous mood swings, but it had a number of bad side effects. The drug caused numbness in Jaco's fingers, made his hands shake, and left him in a chronic state of exhaustion. It also rendered him impotent. ("And you know that ain't right," he complained.)

Jaco returned to New York and took up residence with Geri Palladino and her teenager daughter, Michelle, in the apartment they were subletting from James Cannings, who had gone to Jamaica on business. "Jaco was really glassy-eyed when he came to live with us," says Palladino. "And he slept a lot. It was strange to see him in that condition—most people knew Jaco for this incredible roaring spirit he had. He was always going, from morning until late at night. Seeing him sedated like that was kind of sad."

On December 1, 1985, Jaco celebrated his 34th birthday at Seventh Avenue South. At one point during the festivities, he turned to James Cannings and commented, "I can't believe I'm still alive," almost sounding sad at the thought. When James asked him why, Jaco replied, "Because I wanted to be like Jesus. I expected that at 33 I would be off the planet."

Around this time, Jaco became friends with the young gypsy guitarist Bireli Lagrene. He attended a Lagrene performance at Fat Tuesday's on December 7, and after the last set the two showed up at a private party held at S.I.R. studios following a blues show at Carnegie Hall featuring guitarists Roy Buchanan, Lonnie Mack, and Albert Collins. Jaco got drunk at the party and ended up sitting in with Albert Collins, guitarist Eddie Martinez, and keyboardist Paul Shaffer for a rendition of "Further on Up the Road" sung by Lonnie Mack. Some critics in the audience were outraged by what they perceived as Jaco's grandstanding in the presence of the blues greats, and they dismissed him as an egotistical showoff.

On Christmas night, Jaco fell into a deep depression. While walking home from a visit to Anita Evans's place, he stopped in his tracks and started crying. James Cannings asked him what was wrong, and

he said, "You don't understand! It's Christmas, and I've got two kids that I can't see. If I go to Florida, Ingrid will call the cops and have me arrested for nonpayment of alimony. It's very hard, as a father, to go through Christmas without seeing your kids."

Albert Collins, Jaco, and Eddie Martinez at S.I.R. studios

By this time, Jaco had begun gigging in a trio with Kenwood Dennard and Hiram Bullock. Dennard and Jaco had, of course, developed a close working relationship during the tumultuous Word Of Mouth tours. But Jaco's relationship with Bullock went back even farther, as the guitarist explains: "When I was going to the University of Miami back around '73–'74, I took bass lessons from Jaco. His son John had just been born and he was poor, man—he was just trying to get by, which is why he began teaching. Will Lee's father, who was dean of the music school, got Jaco onto the part-time faculty. He had 15 or 20 students, and out of those maybe two or three were anywhere near close to being professional bass players. This was very frustrating to Jaco. I'd walk in for my lesson, and he'd say, 'Hiram, man, they're driving me crazy. They can't even play a G scale.' Jaco was not a great teacher, because he didn't have any patience. He was a genius, and he didn't understand why everybody else wasn't like him. To him, it wasn't any big deal. He'd always say things like, 'It's simple, man. Just look at it!' But what he was doing at the time was way over the heads of his students."

Bullock was the only student of Jaco's who got an A, although he remembers the lessons as being kind of vague. "We'd both have basses in our hands, and we'd start playing a standard, maybe 'Autumn Leaves' or 'Stella by Starlight.' Jaco would solo for 45 minutes while I walked behind him. Or he would start one of his patented grooves, and I would cop it; once I had it under my fingers, he would take off and solo on top of it. That was basically the gist of my lessons with him."

Bullock says that Jaco used to come by and sit in on his gig with singer Phyllis Hyman. "And I just hated it. His concept of sitting in with local guys was to blow them out of the water, to play some shit so complex and hip that they didn't know what the fuck was going on. That was his way of weeding out the lame-o's. He'd be playing seven against eight or whatever. For me, at that time, it was intimidating."

A little more than ten years later, Bullock and Jaco were back on the bandstand together. "When he came back from treatment, he gave me a buzz and said, 'Can you help me out?' He didn't even have a bass. And he had been banned from just about every club in the Village—he had either thrown shit through the windows or run up big tabs. He was dead in the water, so to speak. So I booked a gig for us at Seventh Avenue South."

Victor Lewis was on drums that night, and the music—a mixture of R&B covers and Bullock originals with some Weather Report and Jaco tunes thrown in—went over pretty well. But the next morning, Hiram got a call from the club. "The guy said, 'Hey, man, can you come and get Jaco. He's still here.' So I walked over there and found him passed out on the bar. I woke him up and walked him over to my place, which was just about a block away. On the way, he pulled his bass out of the case in the middle of Seventh Avenue. I eventually dragged him in and laid him on my couch."

At the next gig Dennard took over the drum chair, and the trio became known as PDB, which represented both an acronym for their last names (Pastorius, Dennard, Bullock) and their slogan (Pretty Damn Bad). Working with Jaco proved to be a trial for Bullock. "I lived in this nervous state, where I was trying to make sure he was okay for the gig and in a safe situation with his personal life. I guess I was sort of mothering him at the time. The playing was the easiest part of dealing with Jaco. Playing the bass was the part he was really locked in on. It was all the rest of the shit, the living part, that he was having trouble with. And I worried that at some point he was gonna fuck up—that he would hit somebody on the street and something ugly would happen."

PDB closed out the year with a week-long engagement at Seventh Avenue South. During that gig, Jaco was uncharacteristically understated and somewhat restrained. He was still taking his medication, and it was clearly having adverse effects, leaving him dazed. For the final night of the engagement, on New Year's Eve, the trio was augmented by Mitch Forman on keyboards and Michael Brecker playing tenor sax and a new synthesizer called an EWI (Electronic Wind Instrument).

"That was right before the club closed down," recalls Brecker. "The lithium seemed to stop Jaco's mood swings, but what remained was an extremely depressed person, like a shell of his former self. He just seemed like he was fighting to stay glued together, that he could fall apart at any moment. But he was still able to function through the lithium haze. In fact, there were some moments on that gig when he really reminded me of the old Jaco. He was playing like he used to back in 1979."

Miles Evans confirms that Jaco sounded good that week. "I started getting optimistic about Jaco's career. I thought he was on the verge of turning his life around. People had been saying that he was all washed up, that he couldn't play anymore. But he showed everyone that week. It was some of the best playing Jaco did in the latter part of his life. He had perfect time, perfect tone, perfect feeling. Seeing him play that well made me very hopeful."

At the rehearsal for that eventful New Year's Eve performance, Jaco showed up roaring drunk. "He was totally wasted and started crying when he heard Brecker playing," recalls Bullock. "He kept crying and saying, 'Oh, man, this band is so good!' And my deal with Jaco was, I didn't really care if he was drunk or not, as long as he was playing well. And he wasn't playing well at this rehearsal. He wasn't reading the music. He was basically stepping on his dick as far as I was concerned, and I told him so. I laid into him, and he said, 'I'm Jaco, dammit!' I told him, 'I know who you are, motherfucker. But you sound like shit right now, and you'd better get it together.'"

Brecker took a more Zen approach. Bullock says, "Michael's attitude was, 'Well, if he's drunk, he's drunk. If he's not, he's not. If he shows up, he shows up. If he doesn't, he doesn't.' But that whole attitude was foreign to me at the time. I really wanted it to be a good gig, and I was doing everything I could to make sure it was."

Brecker says the bouncer at Seventh Avenue South gave Jaco further motivation for getting his act together. "This was a tough guy and a sober guy," says Michael. "After that drunken rehearsal, he came up to Jaco and said, 'If you fuck up again, I'll eat your fucking eyeballs.' Needless to say, Jaco showed up for the gig sober."

The following week, during a Bushrock gig at S.O.B.'s, Jaco and I spoke about what it would take for him to make a comeback. He seemed sincere. He listened intently to what I had to say and pledged that he would make an effort to return to his former glory. He talked enthusiastically about a project he had in mind. "I want to do an album of ballads with strings," he said. "Beautiful standards

Stanley Turrentine and Jaco at the Blue Note

like 'Angel Eyes,' 'The Days of Wine and Roses,' 'The Shadow of Your Smile,' 'All the Things You Are,' and 'Stella by Starlight.' And I have the perfect title. I want to call it *For Lovers Only*."

I liked his idea and encouraged him to pursue it. In spite of his erratic behavior, I still believed in Jaco and hoped he could turn his life around. I had never formalized any kind of client-manager relationship with him, but I did promise to help him in any way that I could. After that, Jaco would call me every day, just to check in and hear what progress I was making with his career. And his expectations were unrealistically high.

Meanwhile, Jaco continued to hang out on the basketball court and get bombed on beer. At this point, it took very little alcohol to get him drunk. He would routinely get completely inebriated after chugging just one can of beer. This abnormal reaction suggested that something was seriously wrong with him, but no one knew what it was—and Jaco himself didn't have a clue.

Geri Palladino says, "I was working in an office in SoHo at the time, and during my lunch break I would run over to the courts to check on Jaco. One time when I got there, he was passed out on the ground. I kneeled down and said a prayer for him, and then my friend Scotty Brown came by. I said, 'I've got to go back to work, but whatever you do, don't leave him until he wakes up.' Scotty and I ended up being his biggest baby-sitters, but it was never a burden. It always made me feel good if I could help Jaco."

But nobody was able to look out for Jaco when he went on a brief European tour with Bireli Lagrene in March 1986. Jaco took Terry with him on that four-week swing through Germany and France, and they fought off and on the entire time. As he had done in the past after arguments with Ingrid, Jaco would storm off and get drunk after fighting with Terry. On one occasion, Lagrene and the rest of the band sided with Terry during a confrontation. In frustration, Jaco jumped off the tour bus and ran for hours, until he finally collapsed from exhaustion. The local police in a small German town found Jaco sleeping in the snow and brought him in for questioning. He had no passport or other identification on him. At the police station, Jaco placed a call to Ingrid in Florida, and she eventually contacted the right people to straighten out the matter. Jaco missed the rest of the tour.

Back in New York, Jaco got a chance to renew his friendship with Joe Zawinul, who was in town for an April 26 performance at Carnegie Hall. This was a one-man show in which Zawinul utilized his sophisticated MIDI setup to create the sound of a full band. Jaco was on his best behavior for this event: he was clean, dressed in a new suit, and sober. He hung out with Zawinul during the soundcheck, and they exchanged some hugs and laughs, although Jaco seemed disappointed that Joe did not ask him to sit in. (During the show, he must have gained some satisfaction when a heckler shouted, "Where's Jaco?")

Two days later, Jaco and I met with Bruce Lundvall, the head of Blue Note Records. I had been speaking to Bruce on Jaco's behalf, trying to get him to consider recording Jaco. Lundvall and Jaco were old friends from Bruce's days at Columbia Records during the height of Jaco's glory years with Weather Report. Because of that, Lundvall felt a certain loyalty to Jaco—but he had heard many tales of Jaco's antics and was wary of dealing with him.

I was able to convince Bruce to meet with us. In part, this was because I had helped him to sign guitarist Stanley Jordan, whose albums had been quite successful for Blue Note. I spoke enthusiastically about the "new Jaco" (who had been sober for several days and was practicing again), and Lundvall seemed intrigued. He was well aware of Jaco's genius, but he didn't want to be saddled with the chore of having to baby-sit him should he lose control again.

I met Jaco at 10 AM at James Cannings's apartment on 31st Street. He looked clean and had a positive outlook. We walked up Sixth Avenue toward the Blue Note offices on 55th Street. Along the way, we stopped in at Sam Ash, a popular music store on 48th Street. Jim Godwynn, an old friend of Jaco's from Florida, was working there as a salesman. Jaco and Godwynn had played together in Las Olas Brass back in the late '60s. They hugged and exchanged small talk, and then Godwynn showed Jaco a new instrument: a bass-to-MIDI controller. Jaco seemed mildly amused by the possibility of triggering flute, violin, and trumpet samples from the bass—but after playing it for a few minutes, he dismissed it as a gimmick.

Godwynn then took Jaco to an area where several sampling keyboards were on display. On one of the instruments, he called up a programmed sound that was called "Jaco Bass." Again, Jaco seemed amused. Godwynn turned up the amplifier, and Jaco played the riff to "Teen Town" on this keyboard as a crowd gathered around him in the store. One kid tapped me on the shoulder and said, "Hey, man, do you know who that is?"

Meanwhile, the clock was ticking away. I told Jaco we had to leave, but he was caught up in Showtime. He kept playing. Finally, I grabbed him, pulled him aside, and persuaded him to leave.

As we walked up Sixth Avenue, Jaco suddenly grew nervous. By the time we reached 55th Street, he said, "Let's have just one drink before we go into that meeting."

I told him he was crazy and that drinking could blow the whole deal. But Jaco was persistent. He promised, "Just one drink."

We ducked into a nearby tavern called the Chicago Bar. Jaco ordered a scotch on the rocks, drank it down, and quickly ordered another. I looked up at the clock. It was just a few minutes before 11. I paid for the drinks, grabbed Jaco, and ushered him out of the bar.

While we waited in the Blue Note lobby, Jaco began flirting with the receptionist, whom he remembered from her days at Columbia Records. She told me, "Yeah, Jaco and I go way back. We're old friends." And as Lundvall's personal secretary led us back to the meeting, she shouted out, "Good luck, Jaco. I hope you'll be coming to this company. We'd love to have you as part of the family."

The meeting went well. Lundvall seemed genuinely pleased to see Jaco looking so clean. They renewed their acquaintance, shared some small talk, and then got down to business. Although Jaco had downed those two shots of scotch, he was still on his best behavior. He was relaxed, cogent, and a capable negotiator.

Lundvall talked enthusiastically about forming a trio around Jaco. He mentioned the possibility of using Bireli Lagrene on guitar and Kenwood Dennard on drums, envisioning this unit as the "Mahavishnu Orchestra for the '80s." Before we left, Lundvall agreed to finance the recording of a professional-quality demo tape.

After the meeting, Jaco and I slipped into a nearby conference room, where he made a call to Terry. She was very upset. Apparently,

Ingrid had called, and any mention of Ingrid's name would enrage Terry. Jaco hung up the phone and immediately placed a long-distance call to Florida to confront his ex-wife. He began yelling at her over the phone. A few Blue Note employees strolled into the conference room to see what all the commotion was about. Jaco was so angry he wanted to pull the phone out of the wall and throw it across the room, but I convinced him that wasn't a good idea. He finally put down the phone, and we left.

Later that night, Jaco and Terry made up, and I joined them at the Lone Star Cafe to see Jerry Lee Lewis. Jaco was convinced that Jerry Lee knew him. "Yeah, when I was with Wayne Cochran, we used to open up for Jerry Lee a lot. He'll definitely remember me."

We went downstairs to the dressing room, where Jerry Lee was entertaining a busty middle-aged Southern woman with a towering beehive hairdo. He was decked out in a white ruffled shirt, black jeans, and pointy cowboy boots. When Jaco mentioned Wayne Cochran & the C.C. Riders, Jerry Lee's ears perked up. "Oh yeah, I remember you, boy," he said, while lighting up a massive cigar. 'Why don't you sit in on the next set?'"

Unfortunately, Jerry Lee had mistaken Jaco for Charlie Brent. (As Ricky Sebastian had mentioned, the two did look very much alike.) During the next set, Jerry Lee invited Jaco up onstage. As he strapped on a guitar, he directed Jaco to the piano, remembering that Brent was an accomplished rock & roll pianist. They launched into a boogie woogie, with Jerry Lee singing and playing guitar. Meanwhile, Jaco was noodling around on the piano and coming up with altered chords and dissonant voicings that would've been more appropriate on a gig with Sun Ra than with The Killer.

As the band continued to grind out the rhythm, Jerry Lee shot Jaco an astonished look and yelled, "What the hell are you doing there, boy? That ain't no way to play a piano!" He put down his guitar and literally booted Jaco off the piano bench. Jaco rolled off the stage like a rag doll as Jerry Lee began pumping away at the keyboard. Fortunately, Jaco took the whole episode in stride, and we all had a good laugh about it later.

Jaco and Terry had been staying at James Cannings's apartment while James was away. They fought often, shouting and cursing at each other and disturbing the neighbors. When Cannings returned from his trip, he was threatened with eviction by his landlord. "I remember seeing clumps of Terry's hair around the apartment," he says, "so I knew that something pretty violent had gone down while I was away. I had a talk with Jaco and told him that that was not the way to treat a woman. He said he only did it because he loved her.

"Terry had her own apartment, but Jaco insisted that she stay with him at my place. Finally, I explained the situation with the landlord to Terry and asked her to leave. Jaco got very upset with me for sending her away. One night he came over to my apartment with a couple of guys from the basketball court, packed all of his things, and walked out. About an hour later, Terry called me and said, 'James, Jaco is selling his clothes on the corner. What happened?' It was his way of raising money to buy beers for himself and his pals."

After this incident, Jaco moved in with a blues harmonica player by the name of Styve. But it wasn't long before he overstayed his welcome there, too. By the summer of '86, Jaco was living in a van owned by Lenny Charles, a guitarist from Denver who had jammed with Jaco on the street a couple of times. Lenny parked his van in the vicinity of the West Fourth Street basketball court, and Jaco usually slept either in the van or on the court. By day, he would use the corner pay phone to receive calls from anyone still interested in "The World's Greatest Bass Player." If a promoter from Europe or Japan called, one of Jaco's street pals would answer as if he were Jaco's secretary and then call Jaco to the phone. Invariably, he would be involved in a basketball game, and the gang would have to halt the action while Jaco went over to try to do some business.

I received a phone call on May 20 from Bruce Theriott, an accountant with Blue Note Records. He had been authorized to cut a check for $5,000 for the recording of a demo tape, and he wanted Jaco to come by and pick it up. I tried to tell Jaco the good news, but he was nowhere to be found. He had vanished from the scene, and nobody seemed to know how to reach him.

Two days later, I found Jaco at the basketball court and gave him the news. He looked horrible. It was early in the morning, and he was already drunk. He looked at me, folded his arms across his chest, stuck out his lower lip, and declared, "You tell Lundvall that I want $150,000! And tell him to send a limo to pick me up. Those are my terms ... *period!*"

I knew the deal was gone. There wasn't going to be any record contract, and there wasn't going to be any comeback. Jaco had returned to the streets once again.

I continued to see Jaco almost every day, mostly at the basketball court. One night, after playing basketball all afternoon, we walked over to S.O.B.'s to see Loremil Machado's samba band. Delmar Brown was in the group, and Jaco was in a particularly good mood. He introduced me to a Brazilian drink called a *caipirinha*, a specialty of the house at S.O.B.'s. As he pounded down this powerful concoction of rum and sugar, I noticed his mood shifting from high to low. Soon he was weeping openly. When I asked him what was wrong, he hugged me and said, "Jorge Dalto's got cancer, man," referring to the great Argentinean pianist who had come to prominence in the States as a sideman to guitarist George Benson. Jaco and Jorge, apparently, had jammed together on a few occasions.

But it wasn't long before the tears subsided and Jaco's mischievous streak kicked into high gear. With a basketball tucked under one arm, he headed to the dance floor. The music was hot and grooving, and Jaco got into the feeling, stutter-stepping in front of the bandstand while bouncing his basketball to the samba beat. The band and some of the patrons seemed genuinely amused by Jaco's basketball dance; unfortunately, the club's manager, Larry Gold, wasn't. After signaling for a couple of bouncers, he put an abrupt halt to

Jaco's antics. As Jaco was being escorted out, Gold said, "Jaco has bounced his last ball in this place!"

Things continued to go downhill from there. On June 29, Jaco tried to jump onstage during an outdoor concert by the Chick Corea Elektric Band at Pier 84. The stagehands dragged him off. A few days later, Jaco appeared at the offices of Blue Note Records, demanding to see Bruce Lundvall. When he was rebuffed at the door, he took his clothes off and began running around the lobby naked. Lundvall says, sadly, "I had no choice. I had to call the cops."

The following week, on the Fourth of July, Jaco performed "The Star-Spangled Banner" on the West Fourth Street basketball court.

Jaco's brother Gregory and Ingrid came to town a week later, after getting reports that Jaco was endangering himself on the streets. Gregory followed Jaco around for a day, just to confirm the reports. After witnessing several incidents where Jaco harassed pedestrians, pulled down his pants, and screamed obscenities, Gregory realized he had to do something. With Ingrid's help, he persuaded Jaco to check himself into the psychiatric ward of Bellevue Hospital on July 16, 1986.

SEVEN

The Finale

"I'm just in here for a rest, man. I'm not nuts."

T HEY TOOK JACO TO BELLEVUE in a straitjacket. After a series of examinations, he was diagnosed as manic-depressive, a mental illness characterized by wild mood swings in which periods of manic excitation and supreme confidence alternate with melancholic depression. (It was no small coincidence, then, that Mike Stern had picked "Mood Swings" for the title of the track he and Jaco had recorded together just two months earlier for Stern's 1986 Atlantic Records debut, *Upside Downside*).

At Bellevue, Dr. Kenneth Alper explained that Jaco's illness was probably genetic and was bound to surface when the stresses of his life became intense. He also detailed the seven symptoms of a manic-depressive:

1. Relentless activity
2. Excessive talkativeness
3. Fanciful visions
4. Inflated self-esteem
5. Decreased need for sleep
6. Diminished attention span
7. Involvement in self-destructive activities such as drugs, alcohol, or dangerous physical feats

It sounded like a description of Jaco.

And yet, denial was perhaps his biggest problem of all. Even while undergoing examination in the hospital, Jaco continued to delude himself into believing everything was cool. "They did all these tests on me," he confided. "They had me hooked up to something that looked like the mixing board at the Power Station. They had electrodes all over my face, but they didn't find a thing wrong with me."

Jaco dismissed the significance of his stay at Bellevue, calling it "just a vacation." He even referred to the hospital as the "Bellevue Spa & Casino Hotel."

Dr. Alper believed that some brain atrophy had taken place. He also theorized that Jaco was haunted by demons and used alcohol as a means of self-medication to drive those demons away. As Ingrid explained it to Pat Jordan in *GQ*: "Jaco was born with music in his head. He heard music in everything. He said music went through him, as if he were a conductor. He couldn't stop it."

Lithium drove the demons away, but it also sapped Jaco's creativity and left him depressed. Noting this, Dr. Alper prescribed the drug Tegretol. It stabilized Jaco, as long as he continued to take it on a regular basis. But Jaco was hardly an ideal patient. By all reports, he was uncooperative, argumentative, and hostile toward the nurses. He threatened to punch one of the attending nurses, and then vehemently denied it. When confronted in therapy with questions about his behavior, he would storm out of the room, complaining that the sessions were boring and useless.

One of the last things Jaco had told Peter Erskine before he went into Bellevue was, "I burned every bridge I possibly could." Erskine, still loyal, lamented, "In a lot of ways, I feel like I haven't done enough to help a dear old friend. But it's tough when a guy sets out to join the ranks of the jazz legends who completely fucked up their lives."

There was a steady stream of visitors up to the 19th floor at Bellevue to see Jaco. Jeff Andrews brought a fretless bass. Miles Evans came with some Charlie Parker transcription books. Hiram Bullock and Kenwood Dennard dropped in to lift Jaco's spirits. A variety of street characters stopped by to pay their respects, signing the guest book with names like "Humpty Dumpty" and "Mother Goose." The regular visitors included James Cannings, Geri Palladino, Theresa Nagell, and Styve.

Since I lived only a few blocks away, a visit to the "Bellevue Spa & Casino Hotel" became a daily ritual for me. Jaco would call me early in the morning, usually requesting Italian hero sandwiches from the outside world. I would also bring a roll of quarters so he could feed the pay phone down the hall. Jaco would spend a large portion of his day on the telephone, desperately reaching out to anyone who might be in a position to either get him out of Bellevue or get him a record deal. Sometimes he'd call collect, but most often he'd pump quarters into the phone to make calls to the West Coast, trying in vain to reach industry heavyweights like Ted Templeman and Mo Ostin at Warner Bros. or Quincy Jones, whom he was convinced would rescue him.

Jaco also made several attempts to reach Kareem Abdul-Jabbar, the Los Angeles Lakers basketball star who was reportedly negotiating to start up his own jazz label, Cranberry Records. "Yeah, Kareem knows me. We're pals from way back," Jaco insisted. He also explained that the basketball he had carried around with him that summer was a gift from Abdul-Jabbar. But at that point, you tended to doubt him.

During my first visit to Bellevue on July 22, Jaco greeted me with a smile. He was wearing a standard-issue hospital robe, slippers, and a wide-brimmed straw hat. Under one arm he carried a Yamaha portable keyboard, a gift from Michael Brecker. Brecker says, "I checked with his doctor first, to see if it was all right to give him that keyboard. In that kind of situation, a doctor might say that an instrument would be counter-productive, because they wanted him to focus on his emotional side and not on music. But the doctor gave his approval, and Jaco seemed to appreciate the gesture. But it was still very upsetting to see him there."

Jaco roamed the halls of the psychiatric ward cheering up his fellow patients with corny jokes and encouraging words, like Babe Ruth making the rounds in a children's hospital. He addressed them by first name and always said, "Who loves ya, babe."

Sitting at the piano in the recreation room, Jaco would present concerts for the small crowds that invariably gathered to hear him play. When the mood struck, he'd get up from the piano and instruct a few of them on the finer points of a new dance he'd developed, which he called "The Thorazine Shuffle."

Watching Jaco strut around Bellevue with his sly grin and knowing wink reminded me of Jack Nicholson's portrayal of R. P. McMurphy in *One Flew Over the Cuckoo's Nest*. Like McMurphy, Jaco considered himself "the head nut in the psycho ward," an appellation he wore with mock pride.

Jaco's disarming charisma and down-home demeanor had an immediate effect on at least one other patient, a nervous young man who had been plotting to blow up the New York subway system before checking himself into Bellevue. As he put it, "Jaco is really popular around here. He's mellowed everybody out."

There were a number of people on the outside rooting for Jaco to get well, get his act together, and make a triumphant return to the scene. As Peter Erskine said at the time, "Joe Zawinul and I have faith that Jaco's going to make a comeback. And when he does, no matter how many bridges it seems like he burned, he will be welcomed back with open arms by everyone." Jaco firmly held onto that belief, too, although he may have been deluding himself just a touch when he said, "Everybody wants me. They're standing in line to sign me."

Jaco would cruise up and down the halls of the 19th floor in his outrageous hat, robe, and slippers, chanting his mantra for the Second Coming of Jaco: "I'm ready to burn, man. I'm good to go. Straight as an arrow, strong as a bull, and ready to get back to work. I'm ready to make records again. I'm playing better than ever. This new stuff I got is killin'. I mean, it's frightening. I want Ted Templeman to give it a listen. Maybe he'll produce something for me."

But the record industry had basically declared Jaco *persona non grata*. As one insider at Warner Bros. noted, "It's a small industry, even though it's big in terms of dollars. Everybody knows everybody else's business. Word gets around quickly, and the word is out about Jaco. Nobody will touch him. It's not a question of talent. If it was just that, they'd be falling all over themselves to sign him. The problem has never been the music he makes; the problem is his brain."

Another record-company spokesman confided, "Everybody knows the Jaco horror stories—blowing his advance money, showing up wrecked for gigs, walking around the streets barefoot, panhandling and all that shit. Jaco chose to live in a certain way, and that's cool. But in this business you have to work with people. There's a lot of ass-kissing and diplomacy involved, and Jaco doesn't know how to do that. He just doesn't know how to deal with people."

During one visit to Bellevue, I met Peter Erskine's father, a psychiatrist based in Atlantic City, New Jersey. Jaco greatly respected Dr. Fred Erskine, and their friendship went back to the Weather Report years. During his visit, Dr. Erskine reprimanded Jaco for not being more cooperative with the nurses, and Jaco flew into a defensive rage, yelling, "Oh, so now you're on *their* side."

That afternoon over lunch, Dr. Erskine offered his thoughts on the case. "I think Jaco is where he should be now," he said. "He needs to cool off and be made to realize that some of his behavior over the past months has been potentially self-destructive. The way he's been acting-out on the streets could get him seriously hurt, or worse, if he confronts the wrong character. In Bellevue, at least he's safe."

But Jaco's defense mechanism was strong, as Dr. Erskine noted. "There is a lot of denial there. He simply does not have the insight at this point to recognize his situation. Right now, Jaco is dealing from a very superior point of view. He believes that he's right and everybody else is wrong. But he's got to come around."

As we parted company that afternoon, Dr. Erskine added, "I told the senior resident physician who is handling him that it's probably the most challenging case he will ever see. I just hope he can get through to Jaco."

But Jaco continued to cling defiantly to his basic rap: "Man, I'm cool. I'm not worried about nothin' because I'm on top. I'm just in here for a rest, man. I'm not nuts. Everybody in this place is fuckin' nuts except me. They're calling me nuts, but I'm saner than anybody. I'm just being Jaco, that's all. I'm not gonna change."

And yet, a storm was brewing on the inside. What Jaco had expected to be a weekend stay turned into a week, and then two weeks. By the third week, his patience was wearing thin and the medication had begun to chip away at his swaggering attitude. He began to turn inward, becoming embittered and despondent. "[Promoter] George Wein owes me a million dollars," he would snarl. "ASCAP owes me at least $30 million. Every promoter in Europe owes me at least $40,000 each."

Jaco continued to pound the telephone lines. He would sit at the end of the hall, dominating one of the two pay phones. If anyone else tried to use the phone when Jaco was in calling mode, he'd growl at them like a Rottweiler guarding the mansion. Besides phoning all the record companies in the free world, he also placed calls to close friends like Anita Evans and Allyn Robinson.

"During his years with Weather Report, Jaco would call me from the road in the middle of the night," says Robinson. "I'd pick up the phone and hear, 'Robinson, you're the baddest!' Then he'd play one of our old C.C. Riders' gig tapes over the phone. On one hand, I was flattered he felt that attachment to me, but it also seemed like he really clung to that period, almost out of desperation. Whenever he was getting to a point where he felt totally alienated, he would give me a call and talk about the old days—how we did this and that, how he couldn't find anybody to play like that, how nothing could compare to the old days.

"Then one day he called to tell me he had checked himself into

Bellevue. He said he was trying to prove to people that he wasn't nuts. He told me, 'Hey, this is just the way I am, whether I'm under the influence or straight. I'm just a nutty kind of guy.' And I thought that was so sad. He seemed trapped by this need to play the role of Jaco, as if it were a game or something. Meanwhile, he was losing touch with his real self, with that person I had known back in Florida. It seemed like such a waste."

Peter Graves, Jaco's employer from his Bachelors III days in Fort Lauderdale, also received some late-night calls. "I remember one time when he called—collect, of course—and sounded very lucid one minute and made no sense at all the next. He would drop the phone, walk away, come back with his bass, and play it through the phone to me for ten minutes. It was tough to communicate with him then."

But Graves stuck by his old friend, even after things started looking bleak. "People kept telling me, 'You have to get away from him, just cut your losses and get away.' But I hung in there with Jaco. Part of me wanted to help him, and part of me was saying, 'Don't get too close, because all you are going to do is open yourself up to more pain.' Sometimes I questioned whether I should've tried to do more. But I watched his own family try to help, and they got rebuffed too."

Ricky Sebastian would call Jaco from the road while he was out touring with blues-harp master Paul Butterfield. "There was a period just before Jaco checked into the hospital when he and Paul would walk up and down Bleecker Street drinking in all the bars," says Ricky. "They definitely had those two things in common— drinking and a love of the blues. Whenever I'd call him from the road, Jaco would talk about wanting to play in Paul's band when he got out of Bellevue."

Jaco also began harboring great expectations for his *Holiday for Pans* master tapes, which had been sitting on the shelf since Warner Bros. rejected them back in 1983. The album was a showcase for Jaco's longtime friend and associate Othello Molineaux, whose virtuosity on the steel pans was highlighted on stirring renditions of Wayne Shorter's "Elegant People," John Coltrane's "Giant Steps," a sparse, fragile version of the Beatles' "She's Leaving Home," and three Jaco originals: "Good Morning Annya," "City of Angels," and "Birth of Island." Also included was an excerpt from Allan Hovaness's contemporary classical masterpiece "Mysterious Mountain," with an orchestration by Michael Gibbs played by members of the L.A. Philharmonic strings. The title track was Jaco's clever steel-pans arrangement of the giddy David Rose theme, "Holiday for Strings."

An adventurous project, to be sure—and far more esoteric than anything a major record company was likely to invest in. Yet Jaco considered it his ticket out of Bellevue and back into the limelight. His idea was to mix a quick demo tape onto cassette, dupe it, and send out copies to all the industry heavyweights he could think of.

Jaco had been storing the nine *Holiday for Pans* master tapes in a closet at the Drummers Collective on Sixth Avenue and 23rd Street in Manhattan since the previous summer. In the summer of '86, before he checked into Bellevue, Jaco took all the master tapes back to his apartment on Jones Street in the Village, but when he was evicted he needed another place to store them. And this is where the saga of the *Holiday for Pans* tapes turns into a convoluted mess.

During the period when Jaco was sleeping in the van owned by Lenny Charles, he decided to store the tapes there. Unfortunately, the van was later impounded by the New Jersey police for a number of unpaid traffic tickets. So as Jaco sat up on the 19th floor of Bellevue plotting his next move, his prized master tapes were stashed in the back of a beat-up van somewhere in New Jersey.

One day, Jaco called and asked me to rescue the tapes. Not having a car at the time, I called on my friend Ed Maguire, a bass player who had gigged on the street with Lenny Charles. He was a devout Jaco fan—and he owned a car. Ed agreed to drive out to Jersey and rescue the master tapes from the back of Lenny's van, drive them back to Manhattan, and drop them off at a small jingle studio on the Upper

$1,000 REWARD

FOR THE RETURN OF JACO'S BASSES :

- '62 Fender fretless with sunburst body and inscription on back of neck: "Custom refinished for Jaco Pastorius by Kevin Kaufman, Palm Beach, FLA, '86."
- '62 Fender fretted with baby blue body and pickguard.

NO QUESTIONS ASKED
CALL THE DRUMMERS COLLEC.
(212) 741-1203

East Side where I had arranged for a quick mixdown session with Jaco. The place was run at night by Kenny Jackel, an apprentice engineer and guitarist whom I had met at a few informal jam sessions.

Two of Jaco's basses were stolen shortly before he entered Bellevue; they were never recovered

The plan was to get Jaco out of Bellevue on a two-hour pass, rendezvous with Maguire at the studio, and have Jackel mix the masters down to a cassette copy under Jaco's direction. On the night of September 11, 1986, we did precisely that. And I distinctly remember Jackel expressing excitement over the prospect of meeting Jaco for the first time. Yet a few years later, after he went into hiding with the master tapes and then emerged with legal council, Jackel would insist he was the original engineer for those sessions recorded between 1980 and 1982, and he would demand compensation from the Pastorius estate. In effect, he held the tapes hostage until he could collect a ransom from the highest bidder.

Jaco arrived at Jackel's studio with his girlfriend Theresa. There were breezy introductions and a bit of small talk, but once Kenny put up the tape Jaco got down to business. He picked four tunes to mix—"Elegant People," "Good Morning Annya," "Holiday for Pans," and the excerpt from "Mysterious Mountain." We all watched with amazement as Jaco manned the mixing board, manipulating the faders expertly and bringing up particular sounds at just the right moment. He made decisions with catlike quickness. Another engineer trying to deal with those tapes would have been totally confused, but Jaco had the big picture in his head.

When the two hours were up, Jaco returned to Bellevue, leaving the master tapes behind at the studio. He would later call Jackel from Bellevue on a daily basis, telling him, "Hold onto those tapes! Just hold onto those tapes! Don't give them up to anybody except me! Not even my ex-wives or my brothers or my mother. Don't listen to anybody but me."

Back in Bellevue, Jaco grew impatient with what he came to perceive as a cruel and unnecessary incarceration. By the end of the fourth week he was bored and angry. By the end of the fifth week he was depressed. And by the end of the sixth week his spirit was broken.

In some regards, Jaco's situation at Bellevue paralleled Charlie Parker's stay at Camarillo State Hospital some 40 years earlier. Following a breakdown, Bird remained in the psychiatric ward at Camarillo for six months. He was eventually released into the custody of entrepreneur Ross Russell, who immediately recorded Bird on his Dial label. Those February 1947 sessions yielded Parker's sinuous blues "Relaxin' at Camarillo," a soulful paean to his period of recovery. To his credit, Russell took a chance on Bird when other industry types had written him off as being hopelessly out of control and all washed up.

Unfortunately, there was no Ross Russell waiting for Jaco when he finally checked out of Bellevue on September 15, 1986, after a seven-week stay. He was released to Brian Melvin, the young San Francisco drummer who had recruited Jaco back in 1984 for his first album. "I went to visit Jaco at Bellevue," recalls Melvin, "and he seemed dejected. I said, 'What's the deal?' And he said, 'I don't belong in here, man. I'm not nuts.' I think in his heart he felt a lot of people had let him down by allowing him to be locked up like that. That really hurt him. It hurt me, too. I mean, you don't let one of the greats go down like that."

Melvin and his mother had to undergo a barrage of questioning from the psychiatrists before Jaco was released to them. Apparently, they made a favorable impression. Jaco arrived at their San Francisco house in good spirits, ready to begin his new life. "We took it very slow," says Melvin. "During the day we would go to the beach and swim, or we would go to the gym and exercise or play basketball. At night we would jam. And I was supposed to make sure he was taking his medication."

Melvin, who had been friendly for years with members of the Grateful Dead, introduced Jaco to Dead singer-guitarist Bob Weir. They participated in casual jams together and later laid down some tracks at Different Fur Studios. Among other things, those sessions yielded soulful versions of "Fever" and Joe Zawinul's "Mercy, Mercy, Mercy," with Weir on lead vocals and Jaco on bass. Both tracks later appeared on Melvin's *Nightfood* album, released in 1988 on the Global Pacific label.

Brian also introduced Jaco to members of the West Coast pop band Pablo Cruise. "Corey Lerios of Pablo Cruise had a huge studio with an incredible MIDI keyboard setup," he says. "And one night Corey took Jaco over there. Jaco kind of barricaded himself into the studio and wouldn't let anybody in while he was working. About 20 minutes later he opened the door and said, 'You can all come in now.' He was smiling like a little kid, and he said, 'Look what I just did.' Then he pressed a button, and out came the heaviest shit you'd ever heard in your life, like Stravinsky or something. He had programmed drums, keyboard parts, bass—everything—in just 20 minutes. I'm telling you, he could've done an album in a week. He was just one of those amazing guys."

Melvin looks back at this post-Bellevue period as almost completely positive for Jaco. "He was having a good time, eating good food, getting exercise, and playing music. And he enjoyed the San Francisco ambiance. It's a different kind of groove than New York—it's a little slower, and there's a higher consciousness. I really do think there is something about San Francisco that's very spiritual. New York is strictly about hustling, ripping off people, and doing drugs. That kind of lifestyle was destructive for Jaco. At one point, Jaco even said, 'Maybe I'll live out my life here. Maybe San Francisco is my kind of place.' He seemed really inspired for the first couple of weeks he was here."

The only negative Melvin saw in Jaco's life during that period was his girlfriend Terry, who had come to live with him. "She was trouble," he says. "She had a jealous streak a mile long. If Jaco looked at another lady or said hello to some girl, she immediately flew into this wild rap: 'What do you want with her? Is she better than me?' Her jealousy was crazy."

James Cannings confirms Terry's jealous nature—and its effect on Jaco. "One time, Jaco called his mother to reassure her that he was not drinking so much, that he was taking care of himself. All through the conversation he was holding my hand, and Terry got so jealous at this. She hated the fact that Jaco was leaning on me instead of her. So she started a big scene—they began arguing, and it got to the point where Jaco couldn't take it anymore. He picked up his bass and threw it out the window, and then he went out to get drunk."

Cannings witnessed many such scenes of domestic violence between Jaco and Terry. "One time, Terry ripped his brand-new sweater," he recalls. "Jaco started crying and said, 'I'm trying to be good. I'm trying to get better. But this woman keeps dragging me back down.' It was always like that between those two."

Geri Palladino somehow managed to remain on friendly terms with all of the women in Jaco's life, even Terry. "Terry had a problem with drugs and alcohol herself," she says. "She was doing a lot of heroin and cocaine. She was a beautiful woman and a kind woman when she wasn't under the influence, but those times were few and far between. Jaco and Terry fought, and a lot of it was pretty nasty."

Jaco often referred to Terry as a "groove-killer." Anyone who upset his flow of fun-in-the-moment was considered a groove-killer—and Terry had a talent for pushing Jaco's buttons. "She was very violent," says Brian Melvin. "I can remember them having fist fights in the back of my car while I was driving. I would have to pull off the highway to break them up. They would antagonize each other to the point where they'd both go crazy. But Jaco always treated her like a queen. He told me he loved her. But if that was love … well, maybe I haven't experienced love."

The couple's constant bickering took a toll on Melvin's mother. "The things that Terry put Jaco through were mind-blowing, and they were really upsetting to my mother," says Brian. "She loved Jaco and hated to see the pain that Terry caused him. She couldn't stand to see another woman, under her roof, treat this guy so horribly. So one night she took Terry aside and told her to straighten out her act or leave the house."

Soon after that ultimatum, another incident occurred. Jaco and Brian had gone to a nearby bar to watch a basketball game on TV. Terry followed them there and started an argument with Jaco. His reaction to this confrontation was, of course, to start drinking. "The next thing you knew, they were outside fighting on the sidewalk," says Melvin. "Jaco had her in a headlock, and she was biting him. People on the street were totally shocked. Finally, he ran back to my house. She followed him, and they started fighting again. He ended up calling the cops on *her*. By the time I got back to my house, the police were escorting Terry away."

After that episode, Terry returned to New York. Jaco remained in

San Francisco to honor his commitment to Melvin. They finished recording material for the *Nightfood* album and also cut a bunch of straightahead trio tunes with pianist Jon Davis. (That material later appeared on Melvin's *Standards Zone* album on Global Pacific.) But Jaco missed Terry and soon grew depressed without her by his side.

"There were times after she left when he got so low he actually scared me," says Melvin. "He would get that faraway look in his eyes and say stuff like, 'Brian, man, I don't even feel like living. I don't know what to do anymore.' He would become very withdrawn. It was hard to reach him at that point."

Ironically, in the midst of all this turmoil and personal anguish, Jaco won Best Jazz Bass for the fifth time in the annual *Guitar Player* readers' poll, automatically qualifying him for entry into the magazine's Gallery Of The Greats.

In mid-November, I received a desperate call from Jaco. He was still in San Francisco and sounding drunker than I had ever heard him, crying and begging me to call Terry for him. "You gotta call her. You gotta do this for me. Just call her and tell her I love her."

Terry seemed exhausted and frustrated when I spoke to her on the phone that evening. "I just can't stand it anymore," she said. "I've got to get away from him." But she couldn't.

A week later, Jaco was back in New York. He and Terry had reconciled and were staying with James Cannings at his new apartment on Second Avenue and 23rd Street, just a few blocks from Bellevue. The three had Thanksgiving dinner together at the apartment, and Cannings remembers it as a genuinely warm, peaceful evening. "Jaco seemed very relaxed and contented. I put on a gospel record by the Edwin Hawkins Singers, 'Oh Happy Day,' and he seemed to like it a lot. Later that evening, he went out and passed out money to the bums on the street. He had $300 when he left, and he came back with nothing."

Around that time, Cannings was playing a house gig at Magoo's, a workingman's bar below Canal Street. Jaco came by and sat in on a few occasions, including the night of December 1, 1986—his 35th birthday. Ricky Sebastian dropped by to help Jaco celebrate, and the two later headed over to a Greenwich Village bar called the Front for more jamming. "That was the last time I saw Jaco," says Sebastian.

Bob Mintzer also ran into Jaco around this time. "I was working a gig at the Blue Note, and he was hanging out around the corner with these street characters. He was still oblivious to the fact that he was not in great shape, and he was talking like everything was fine. I said to him, 'Man, you're really making me sad. I see you killing yourself. I know you're not going to hear what I'm saying, but I have to say it anyway, because I care about you.' And he said, 'What are you talking about, man? I'm in great shape.' He tried to avoid the whole issue. But something told me that was the last time I was going to see him."

Late in December, Jaco embarked on his second tour of Europe with Bireli Lagrene. Earlier in the year, a record documenting Jaco and Bireli's work together had come out on the German Jazzpoint label. Entitled *Stuttgart Aria*, it contained a blazing version of "Donna Lee," a funky rendition of Jimi Hendrix's "Third Stone from the Sun," and a tender, swinging treatment of the romantic Johnny Mercer-Henry Mancini ballad, "The Days of Wine and Roses." It also had a waltz Jaco had written while in Bellevue, titled "Theresa." Jaco's playing was not up to par on *Stuttgart Aria*, but the album was well received in Europe and later made its way to the U.S. as an import.

After his tour with Lagrene, Jaco returned to the States and headed down to Florida, intent on seeing his children and patching up his relationship with Ingrid. Strangely, he brought Terry with him.

Jaco and Terry took up residence in the home of Jaco's mother, and Terry supported them by working as a waitress. Both seemed to enjoy the warmer climate, and Jaco appeared to be making an effort to clean up his act. Randy Bernsen says, "We got into a regular routine where we would wake up, go for a swim, and then play music for hours. He looked great, and he was playing great. He sat in with my band a couple of times at the Musicians Exchange, and we even did some duet gigs. It was an inspiring time. His spirit seemed so strong."

Bernsen told Ricky Schultz about Jaco's improved condition. Schultz, who had been instrumental in signing Jaco to Warner Bros. in 1981, was by this time heading Zebra Records, the jazz-fusion subsidiary of MCA Records. He had signed Bernsen to a deal and put out *Music for Planets, People & Washing Machines* in 1984 and *Mo' Wasabi* in 1986. Both albums featured solid guest appearances by Jaco.

"Ricky had always been a Jaco believer," says Bernsen, "but he was being cautious. No one would touch Jaco with a ten-foot pole at this time, but Ricky was at least willing to listen. I called him and said, 'Look, man, he's playing phenomenally. His chops are back, and he's really getting it together.' I was excited about a Jaco comeback. And I would have been honored to help him get back into the scene."

Bernsen's encouraging reports inspired Schultz to fly down to Fort Lauderdale and get a first-hand impression. "I met with Jaco," he says, "and I told him, 'Look, man, I think you can have it all again. You've still got your shit happening, but you have to realize that you've got bridges to rebuild on the business side. Nobody wants to deal with you. I'd like to work with you, but there's just got to be something happening here.'"

Schultz's recommendation to Jaco was that he and Bernsen start a band together. "I told him, 'Jaco, you should consider being the co-leader of a group. Just go out with this band, make the dates, blow people away with your playing, and don't cause any trouble. Let the promoters and clubowners see you've got your act together again. Show them that you're not a menace, that you're not flipped out, and everything will be cool.' And he seemed to understand what I was telling him."

Jaco talked it over with Bernsen, and he even came up with a name for the band. "Jaco wanted to call it the Holy Ghost," says Randy, "which only goes to show that he was still very much in touch with spirituality. Right up until the end, Jaco was a devout Catholic."

Unfortunately, this hopeful period in Jaco's life didn't last long. At his mother's birthday party in February 1987, he and Terry got into another violent argument. Jaco stormed out and went on a drinking binge that lasted for several days. By March, all of his positive momentum was gone, and he began crashing with different people. At first, he moved in with Kevin Kaufman, the bassist and luthier who had done all of Jaco's repair work for several years. He stayed there for about a month, until Kaufman reluctantly asked him to leave. "He broke into my house one night and took every record I had with him on it. He claimed they were his. He pulled the same stunt at some of the local record stores. But what really upset me was when he ran up an $1,100 bill in long-distance phone calls to people all over the world."

Several of those calls were to me back in New York. Jaco would call frequently just to talk about music and hear what was happening back in the Big Apple. He mentioned that he was planning to record a blues album called *Dixie Highway*. "Yeah, it's time to go back to the roots," he declared. Jaco also inquired about the *Holiday for Pans* tapes, which remained tucked away in a closet of Kenny Jackel's studio. At his urging, I had sent out the cassette demos that he had mixed the night we got him out of Bellevue. The general response was the typical industry brush-off: "Thank you for your submission, but we have decided to pass at this time."

On April 8, 1987, I got a collect call from Jaco. He was in jail—arrested, he explained, on a mere technicality. "There I was playing basketball and having a barbecue at Holiday Park when these two rookie cops came over because they had gotten a noise complaint from some neighbors. They asked me my name, so I told them. They fed my name into their computer and found out that I had all these outstanding parking tickets from four years ago. So they busted me."

Jaco remained in the Pompano Beach jail for ten days. On the day after he was released, he created a disturbance at a gig he had booked at the Sunset Lounge in Palm Beach. Billed as a Word Of Mouth show, it was a trio with Jaco on bass, Randy Bernsen on guitar, and Bill Bollard on drums. According to reports, Jaco looked wired and seemed particularly hostile. The set was chaotic, and whenever Jaco became frustrated—which was often—he would turn up his amp and play a distorted rendition of "America the Beautiful" or "Purple Haze." At one point, Jaco grabbed the microphone and chided the crowd. "You came to hear jazz, didn't ya? Well, that's what I'm playing." Halfway through the set, he boasted: "Me, Stanley Clarke, and Ron Carter—the greatest bass players in the world. Flip a coin. There ain't nobody else. We're holding it down."

The audience looked on in utter amazement as Jaco closed the show by drop-kicking his bass (which had been loaned to him by Kevin Kaufman) off the stage. At that point, the irate clubowner grabbed Jaco and physically ejected him from the place. On his way out, Jaco screamed incoherently and even spat at a few shocked patrons.

By this time, Jaco had alienated himself from nearly all of the relatives and friends who had been trying to help him. He began hanging out at Holiday Park, playing basketball and chugging beers by day and sleeping on the ground at night, just as he had done the summer before on the West Fourth Street court back in Greenwich Village. Because of his dirty appearance and erratic behavior, he was banned from many nightclubs around the Fort Lauderdale area.

Reports of Jaco's recidivism reached Ricky Schultz, who became increasingly dubious about the prospect of a comeback. As he put it at the time, "I want to help him save his life. He's a genius, but he has an uncanny ability to be difficult with people. I don't know if I want to subject my staff to Jaco yet, but I'm ready to do battle with him." Jaco's response was: "All Ricky Schultz is interested in is new shoes and season tickets to Lakers' games."

In spite of the bad reports coming out of Florida, Schultz began formulating a plan for dealing with Jaco. "My motivation," he explained at the time, "is that a possible record deal with Zebra might be a chance to save a great artist's life. But I want to do it right. I want to set up a trust account and administer it for him. We would put him in a house and cover his rent for six months. We would pay his food expenses and give him minimal pocket money. Basically, I want to avoid the danger of giving him too much cash all at once, because you'd be reading about him in the obituaries a week later. Give him $3 and he'll go out and chug three beers, so you can imagine what might happen if you gave him $25,000.

On the morning of May 1, I got a collect call from Jaco. He was in jail again. The charge this time was trespassing; he had apparently been sleeping on a stretch of private beach when he was picked up. Not long after that, he was arrested once more for falling asleep naked on top of a garbage truck. When he called (collect, of course) to tell me about it, he said, "Man, the guy in the cell next to me has AIDS and tuberculosis. They got him on a strict diet of pancakes and flounder—it's the only thing they can slide under the door."

Up to that point, Jaco had somehow managed to keep his sense of humor despite his miserable plight. Then, on June 13, he received a devastating blow. Bob Herzog, Jaco's high school pal and early R&B mentor, died suddenly of a heart attack at the age of 35. Herzog had been the singer and drummer in Woodchuck, and he had co-written "Come On, Come Over" with Jaco.

The news of Herzog's death sent Jaco into a deep depression. Drummer Scott Kirkpatrick, Jaco's former rhythm-section partner in Tommy Strand & the Upper Hand, saw him around that time. "I was playing at Bootleggers one night, and Jaco walked in. I hadn't seen him in quite a while and, my God, he was a gruesome sight. I had never seen a human being transform himself from someone with brilliance and humanity into something completely the opposite. I mean, it was like looking at a bag person."

Jaco was barefoot and dirty. His teeth had become crooked, his feet were swollen, his eyes were bloodshot, and his skin was burned from overexposure to the sun. And he was drunk. "He just walked up to me," says Kirkpatrick, "and started sobbing and saying shit like, 'Man, Herzog's gone! Fuck the world, fuck everybody!' He was really losing control, so I told him, 'Jaco, get a hold of yourself. Hang out and I'll see you during my break.' But he started making a racket and upsetting people. He got thrown out of the club before our set was over. And that was the last time I saw him."

The day of Herzog's funeral, Jaco arrived hours before everyone else. He grabbed a broom and proceeded to sweep every inch of the church, as if to cleanse it. Then he vanished. When he returned, he disrupted the service by coming in late and drumming with his hands on the casket before announcing, "Bob Herzog taught me everything I know about music ... *period*!"

Herzog's widow was neither shocked nor offended by Jaco's strange behavior. "Some people didn't know what to make of it," recalls Janis Herzog. "They kept coming up to me and saying, 'I'll get rid of him if you want me to.' But I said, 'No, don't usher him out. He needs to be here just as much as I do.' Jaco really needed to let all that out. Afterwards, I thought about how much it took for him to get up there and say that in front of all these sad people. I saw a strength in Jaco that day. It made me think, Well, this is it. This is the thing that's going to scare the shit out of him and get him to pull himself together. I saw a glimmer of hope there."

But that glimmer was quickly snuffed out. The bizarre episodes continued, and reports circulated of a hopelessly deranged Jaco on the rampage, sabotaging gigs and picking fights in biker bars. Bob Bobbing says that the Jaco he saw during this period was nothing like the Jaco he grew up with in Fort Lauderdale. "It was sad to see his talents decline like that. When Jaco was allowed to sit in with local bands, his playing was very sloppy. He couldn't make the changes. He seemed lost onstage, and he'd look dazed and confused in the middle of a song. It was like seeing the champ, Muhammed Ali, getting beat up and slurring his words."

Concerned about Jaco's condition, brothers Rory and Gregory went around to the local pubs and pleaded with the bartenders to cut him off. Many of the bartenders complied, but Jaco usually found a way around that obstacle. He would con some unsuspecting patron (often an aspiring young bassist) into sneaking a drink outside to him; the payoff was a chance to hang with "The World's Greatest Bass Player"—or what was left of him.

Bobbing became involved in the effort to keep Jaco from drinking, and he would comb the Fort Lauderdale bars in search of him. "When I showed up, he'd get this 'Oh shit!' expression on his face," says Bob. "Sometimes he'd try to run away. But I'd always grab him by the hair, put him in a headlock, and drag him away."

One night, while driving along, Bobbing spotted a familiar figure dashing out of a Peaches record store near the beach in Fort Lauderdale. Jaco had grabbed a stack of Weather Report and Word Of Mouth records and made a run for it out the front door, with an employee in hot pursuit. Outside the store was the Walk of Stars, a strip of hand prints and signatures set in concrete. Jaco, a local boy who had made good, had his own place there, alongside the likes of Peter Frampton, Charlie Daniels, and Luciano Pavarotti. Jaco's hand prints, with the double-jointed thumbs bent backwards, were next to an inscription that read: "Hometown Record Store Makes Good. Love, Jaco." As he raced along the Walk of Stars, Jaco dumped the armful of stolen records onto his own little slab of concrete. Then he took off into the darkness.

A few days after that, following another ugly incident, Bobbing decided to take matters into his own hands. "Jaco called me late one night. He was crying. Apparently, someone had punched him out in a bar. I drove out there and found him. One front tooth was broken in half, and his face was black and blue. I took one look at him and just grabbed him, tied him up with a microphone cord I had in the trunk, and threw him in my car. Basically, I kidnapped him. My plan was to drive him down to the Florida Keys to cool him out for a few days. I put him in a room, had room service bring some food, and sat there with him, waiting for him to sober up."

Bob had brought his bass along, hoping that Jaco would get back into playing while he was recuperating. Jaco began practicing and made remarkable progress; by the third day, he had his confidence back and was sitting in at local nightclubs. "He was really ripping it up," says Bobbing. "He was like the Jaco of old."

On the return trip to Fort Lauderdale, they stopped at a gas station. While Bobbing was pumping gas, Jaco managed to sneak into a nearby convenience store and buy a beer, which he quickly chugged before Bob found out. Bobbing says, "By the time he came back to the car, he was laughing like a court jester. It was like Dr. Jekyll turning into Mr. Hyde—two minutes out of my sight and he was totally smashed! I couldn't believe it."

In July, Jaco received another crushing blow. Another close friend from his teenage years, Alex Sadkin, was killed in a car crash in Mexico City. Jaco and Sadkin had gone to high school together, and they had played in Las Olas Brass back in 1967. After he became an engineer at Criteria Studios in Miami, Sadkin had worked the board for the demo tape that led to Jaco's solo debut, and he eventually went on to international renown as a producer of such big-name pop acts as Foreigner, Simply Red, and Duran Duran.

Sadkin's death seemed to sap more of Jaco's spirit. It also worried Jaco's mother, Stephanie, and she said to family members at the time, "Things come in threes. I just hope Jaco's not next."

On August 3, 1987, I received a phone call from a Florida entrepreneur named Gary Byrd. He claimed to be a childhood friend of Jaco's and said he was concerned about his welfare. He went on to explain that he and a partner were building a digital recording facility in Orlando and that he had just put up $5,000 to bail Jaco out of yet another legal predicament. He added that Jaco had signed a contract granting him rights to the *Holiday for Pans* tapes. Byrd wanted to secure the tapes and make a deal with some record company to raise capital to pay off Jaco's debts and get him into a Palm Beach detox center. Furthermore, he wanted to set up a trust fund for Jaco, "since he is obviously incapable of making decisions or handling money at this point."

Jaco called me a couple of days later and scoffed at Gary Byrd's story. "I just signed his contract to get out of jail," he said.

In late August, Jaco continued to call me collect from various spots around Florida, but he rarely made much sense. On one occasion, he said he was calling from a hotel in Fort Lauderdale; he claimed that he and Terry had just gotten married and were on their honeymoon, even though I knew she had left Jaco and started dating other men. Another time he insisted he wanted to get an official announcement printed in *Down Beat*. "Guess what!" he barked. "Me and Zawinul and Shorter are getting back together for a reunion tour ... *write it down!*"

When a report reached New York that Jaco had fallen asleep on the railroad tracks that ran along Dixie Highway, we all sensed the end was near. Kevin Kaufman had confronted Jaco after this stunt. "I asked him if he had a death wish," says Kaufman. "He said, 'No, don't be stupid.' But the truth seemed obvious to me."

Scott Brown, a keyboardist who had played in one of Jaco's last New York bands in 1986, saw Jaco in Fort Lauderdale late in August. He brought back a sad report. "Jaco seemed like he had lost the will to live by then. When he was in New York, he always had this drive; he was always psyched up to be hanging in New York. He might have been self-destructive, but he didn't want to die. But when I saw him in Florida, it was like he had given up."

Around that time, Jaco paid an unexpected visit to engineer Peter Yianilos. "I came home one night and found Jaco asleep in my back-yard, lying in a hammock," he says. "I brought him in. He looked like he had been out on the streets for a while, so I told him to take a shower. I gave him some clean clothes and my bicycle, so he could get around. We sat down and had a nice, calm talk. It reminded me of the old days."

On September 6, James Cannings flew to Fort Lauderdale to pay a visit to Jaco. Gregory Pastorius picked him up at the airport and informed him that Jaco was in jail on a breaking-and-entering charge. Jaco, of course, had his own version of the story. He claimed he had been riding along the coast on Yianilos's bike when it had started to rain. He took shelter in what he thought was an abandoned shack and fell asleep, only to be awakened by the police. They ran a computer check on him and found out he was wanted in Miami for car theft. Jaco insisted he was innocent of that charge as well, explaining that he had once helped some strangers push a car along the road, not realizing it was a stolen vehicle. "When the cops pulled up, they ran," he explained. "I didn't know what was going on, so I got caught."

The next day, Cannings went to court to see Jaco. "His teeth were all broken, and they had him in handcuffs. He said to me, 'This is where I'm at, but when I get out of here, which should be today, I'm gonna show you a great time.'"

During their brief conversation, Jaco asked Cannings for a glass of water. By the time he returned with it, the police were leading Jaco back to his cell. "I yelled out, 'Hey, Jaco, do you want this water?' And he said to me, 'Don't worry, man. Where I'm going there's gonna be plenty of water.' That was his last statement to me, which I took to be a clairvoyant thought."

On September 8, Jaco was visited by a mystery woman named Ute. She had flown all the way from Germany to see him. She told James Cannings and Gregory Pastorius that she had dreamed of Jaco. In her dream Jaco was a shepherd, and he was trying to round up all the sheep into one flock. (Pastorius, of course, means "shepherd" in Latin.) While Ute didn't know exactly what to make of this dream, she felt compelled to come to Florida, even though she had no friends there and didn't know the Pastorius family.

Ute arrived at the Fort Lauderdale airport and simply looked up the name Pastorius in the phone book. She called Gregory. After listening to her story, Gregory picked Ute up at the airport and took her to the court, where she made an appeal to the judge on Jaco's behalf. She explained that Jaco was a great artist and a famous musician who had given a great deal of happiness to many people, and she pointed out how cruel it was to ignore an artist in his hour of need. The judge, who happened to be a cousin of the jazz-funk pianist Richard Tee, listened to Ute's plea and agreed to release Jaco on his own recognizance.

Jaco and Ute hung out together for a few hours after that courtroom scene. At a nearby nightclub that happened to have a piano, he played her a song he had written in jail and asked her to buy him a few beers. When she tried to cut him off, Jaco got angry and left. Ute searched the area, but Jaco was nowhere to be found.

On September 10, Jaco paid a surprise visit to Randy Bernsen. "He came by the studio where I was working on my next album. He said, 'Yeah, man, what's happening. Play me something.' I was struggling with an edit on one song, trying to get it perfect. Jaco's advice was, 'Don't be so nit-picky. Just let it go. We used to do it that way with Weather Report all the time. Let it go, man.' Then he started telling me about his plans to record the *Dixie Highway* album. He seemed so excited about it. He said, 'I got a session scheduled for Monday. I want you to be there.' And then he just walked off."

That night Jaco arrived at Ingrid's doorstep. "He was barefoot, so I gave him a pair of my father's shoes," she recalls. "He had just gotten out of jail and said he didn't have any money to pay for the cab, so I paid." Jaco pointed his finger at Ingrid and declared, "You and me are gonna get married again ... *right now!*"

Ingrid was not about to honor that demand, but she ended up accompanying Jaco to a place down the street called Pickle's 4 O'Clock Pub. "We played pool there. Jaco was being very abusive to these biker guys sitting at the bar, just looking to get his ass kicked," she says. "It was a pretty weird scene. And that was the last time I saw him."

On the morning of September 11, Jaco called Terry. They had been estranged for some time, but she agreed to meet him for lunch at the Bangkok Inn, a Thai restaurant. At some point in their conversation, Terry asked Jaco if he could arrange to get tickets for her and her new boyfriend to that night's Santana concert at the Sunrise Music Theater. Jaco agreed.

When Terry and her boyfriend arrived at the theater, they found tickets waiting for them at the box office. During the concert, Jaco jumped onstage after a solo by bassist Alphonso Johnson (ironically, the person he had replaced 11 years earlier in Weather Report). Carlos Santana says, "Jaco walked over to Alphonso and held his hand up in the air, the way a referee does in the boxing ring to signify the winner. But the bouncers didn't know who Jaco was, so they wrestled him off the stage and took him outside."

On his way out, according to Pat Jordan in *GQ*, Jaco spotted Terry and said, "I hope you and your blond-haired boyfriend are very happy together." Then he paused and added, "I'm dead."

About an hour after the concert, Jaco was still waiting around outside when Carlos Santana came out. "I walked over to him, and he gave me a hug," recalls Carlos. "He said, 'Man, you played your ass off.' Then we talked a little bit about Jesus. And that was the last thing I heard from him."

Jaco wandered over to the Midnight Bottle Club, an after-hours bar located in a shopping complex in Wilton Manors, a suburb of Fort Lauderdale. According to the club's bouncer, a 25-year-old martial-arts expert by the name of Luc Havan, Jaco was denied entry because he was drunk and abusive. A scuffle ensued. When Wilton Manors police arrived on the scene at 4 AM on September 12, 1987, they found Jaco lying face down in a pool of blood. His skull had been fractured. Several facial bones were fractured. His right eye was ruptured and dislodged from its socket, and there was massive internal bleeding.

Havan claimed he had shoved Jaco, causing him to fall backward and hit his head on the concrete. The police report listed the cause of injury as "blunt trauma to the head." But *Miami Herald* reporter Tom Moon was skeptical of the police report. He told me, "It had to be false. It looked like somebody had bashed his head on the concrete repeatedly, far more than necessary to cause unconsciousness."

Jaco was admitted to the Broward County General Medical Center at about 4:20 AM. He had lost a lot of blood and was in a coma. It was also discovered that he had pneumonia. Doctors told the family that Jaco would probably not regain the use of his left arm or right eye.

Havan was charged with aggravated battery. He posted a $5,000 bond and was released. The general reaction among those who knew Jaco was one of shock but not surprise. As Ricky Schultz put it, "He finally gave some shit to the wrong dude."

Jaco lay in the hospital for six days. During that time, he remained in a coma but was able to respond to simple commands like "squeeze my finger" and "wiggle your toe." The doctors told his family that Jaco would probably be sitting up and eating out of a spoon within a few days.

Back in New York, Geri Palladino consulted a psychic in an attempt to communicate with Jaco's spirit. "I had a reading, and Jaco accepted the reading in his coma," she says. "The one thing he kept saying through the channel was, 'Geri, please remember the good times. Don't deal with negativity.' During the reading, I asked the psychic, 'How much time? How long is he going to be this way?' And she saw everything; she saw his injuries and pinpointed things that were wrong with him. She was there in the room with him. If I had been in the room with Jaco, I would have grabbed hold of him and said, 'Don't go, pal! It's going to be all right! Come on, man, I'll take care of you!'"

On the night of September 17, Jaco stopped reacting to stimuli, but his mother remained hopeful. "He could still feel my presence," she says. "I knew he was trying to say something. He could hear but he couldn't respond."

Ingrid remembers seeing Ute at Jaco's bedside. "From the two times I had met her, I could tell she was very much in love with Jaco. She thought he was Jesus—that's what she told me. And I heard her pray at his bedside, something like, 'We'll be together soon.'"

On the evening of September 19, a blood vessel burst in Jaco's brain. By the next day, there was no brain activity.

In the early evening of September 21, Jaco's family made the decision to remove him from life support. Ingrid, however, was still holding onto the hope that he would make a miraculous comeback. "I would tickle him on the arm and he'd get goose bumps," she said, "but the nurse told me it was purely involuntary. Even so, I was against taking him off life support."

When they finally removed the life support, Jaco's breathing ceased but his heart continued to beat for three more hours. Jack Pastorius, never at a loss for levity, said, "Man, I knew Jaco had good rhythm, but this is ridiculous." He cradled his son in his arms and crooned "Watch What Happens" as Jaco's final heartbeats ticked by:

> Let someone start believing in you
> Let him hold out his hand
> Let him touch you
> And watch what happens.

Jaco was officially pronounced dead at 9:25 PM. The sad news was delivered to me at 2 AM by Jeff Andrews. All around the planet, Jaco's fans mourned the passing of "The World's Greatest Bass Player."

The following evening, I had a vivid dream about Jaco. Here's how I described it in my journal entry for September 22:

> I was at a concert in a big concert hall somewhere. Suddenly, a stranger came up behind me and tapped me on the shoulder. I turned around, and he said, "Jaco is waiting for you." He pointed to a door. I walked through it, and there in this kind of clinical waiting room was Jaco lying on an operating table, totally still, eyes closed. He heard me enter and called out,

"Who's there?" I approached him. He kept repeating, "Touch my hand, touch my hand." Jaco reached out his hand, and when mine touched his there was a spark, as if my life force had jump-started him into an awakened state. He opened his eyes, sat up, looked at me, and grinned. "Milkowski! Yeah! Let's do that Blindfold Test … *right now!*" He slid off the table and began strutting around and boasting, "I told you they couldn't get rid of me so easy. You know what I'm talkin' about. I'm still Jaco. I'm still the baddest bass player in the world. Don't worry, man. They can't stop me. I'll always be around."

We stood there and talked for a while in that empty white room, and then I noticed a startled expression flash across his face, as if he had heard someone calling him. "I gotta go," he said in a serious tone. He smiled, slapped me five, hugged me, and climbed back onto the stainless-steel operating table. Then he laid down and closed his eyes, and the lights in the room suddenly dimmed. At that point I woke up. I was tingling all over.

On September 24, I flew down to Fort Lauderdale to attend Jaco's funeral. On the night of the wake at the Kalis Funeral Home, located along Dixie Highway, friends and relatives gathered to say prayers for Jaco. Flowers filled the room. In one corner there was a huge, exotic bouquet sent by Joni Mitchell. Propped up next to the closed casket was an arrangement of red carnations in the shape of a bass guitar, bearing the familiar Jaco slogan: Who Loves Ya, Babe!

One by one, the mourners filed slowly past the casket. As the priest offered a prayer, a train rolled by outside, the sound of its lonely whistle filtering into the funeral home and growing fainter as it sped along the tracks. I immediately thought of "Barbary Coast." Then it struck me—he really was gone. It was almost too much to fathom. As Bobby Economou later put it, "I still can't picture him lying in his coffin. All that energy—I cannot picture him gone."

The last one to walk by Jaco's casket was his father. He paused for a moment, knelt down, and said a prayer. Then, reverting to his Mr.

In Loving Memory of

JACO

December 1, 1951
September 21, 1987

MOST merciful Father, we com-
mend our departed into your
hands. We are filled with the sure
hope that our departed will rise
again on the Last Day with all who
have died in Christ. We thank you
for all the good things you have
given during our departed's earthly
life.

O Father, in your great mercy,
accept our prayer that the Gates of
Paradise may be opened for your
servant. In our turn, may we too be
comforted by the words of faith
until we greet Christ in glory and
are united with you and our departed.

Through Christ our Lord, Amen.

KALIS FUNERAL HOME
Wilton Manors
Fort Lauderdale, Florida

PRIMA series

Personality ways, he banged out a brief drum solo on the coffin lid before saying, "Hey Jaco, we gotta go. Turn out the lights after we leave, okay?"

After the wake, I drove with bassist Jeff Berlin to a local nightclub called La T's, where a few of Jaco's musician friends paid tribute to him. Berlin, Scott Brown, and Othello Molineaux played "All the Things You Are," and then Jeff made a moving speech about his fallen colleague before dedicating a stunning solo-bass rendition of "Dixie" to Jaco. At the bar, Joe Zawinul and Wayne Shorter sat drinking with Jack Pastorius, toasting Jaco's memory.

Later, Jack got up to sing with the band. During a swinging rendition of "Watch What Happens," he broke from his normally cool character and yelled emotionally into the microphone, "That guy murdered my son!" Everyone in the place felt his anger.

Between sets, the club deejay played tapes of Jaco's music through the house sound system. At one point, he cued up the hauntingly beautiful Zawinul ballad "A Remark You Made," and the sound of Jaco's fretless bass filled the room like a spiritual presence. Randy Bernsen looked at me and said, "Listen! We've still got him! His spirit is still here. It's in his music. He'll always be here."

In the wee hours of the morning, Rory Pastorius drove me to his mother's house to look at old photos and newspaper clippings of Jaco that she had been meticulously pasting into scrapbooks over the years. Along the way, he pointed out places where he and Gregory and Jaco used to play. He showed me Jaco's old paper route, the football field where they spent endless hours as kids, and the places where they used to hide. Then we drove by the Midnight Bottle Club.

The funeral mass on the morning of September 25 at St. Clement's Church, where Jaco had served as an altar boy, was a profoundly moving affair. Guitarist Bernsen, bassist Dave Wilkerson, and drummer Rich Franks performed a gentle acoustic rendition of Jaco's "Las Olas" during the consecration. During the Holy Communion, a nine-piece horn ensemble directed by Peter Graves played a Larry Warrilow arrangement of "Continuum." Then those nine horns blended together on a version of "Three Views of a Secret" as the pallbearers—Randy Bernsen, Dave Wilkerson, Charles Norkus, Peter Yianilos, Wayne Shorter, and Joe Zawinul—led the procession of mourners out of the church.

At the cemetery, we all stood in silence, reflecting on Jaco's talent and torment. "Brilliant goods in a damaged package," is how one mourner put it. As the priest gave his final blessing, Jaco's five-year-old twin sons, Felix and Julius, romped in the grass, oblivious to the somber proceedings. Their striking resemblance to Jaco made the scene all the more poignant.

"After everyone else had left," recalls Ingrid, "the only ones still standing at the grave were Othello, Ute, Bobby Thomas, and Pat Metheny. The twins were still running around, playing and laughing.

Finally the crew came, four or five guys, and they prepared to put the coffin in the ground. Julius and Felix decided to stay for that—they knew their father was in that coffin, and I think they needed to see where he went."

Ute and Othello Molineaux hugged each other as Jaco was lowered into the ground. Metheny remained alone by the grave for several minutes, wiping away tears and shaking his head as he stared into that dark, lonesome hole.

Several close friends of the family retired to Tracy's house following the ceremony to sit and reminisce about Jaco while listening to records that Stephanie Pastorius had brought over from her personal archives. For many, it was their first opportunity to hear rarities like the 1974 Paul Bley session or the 1976 live album with German trombonist Albert Mangelsdorff and drummer Alphonse Mouzon.

Outside on the patio, Zawinul, Erskine, and Shorter toasted their fallen comrade with shots of Jack Daniel's as they flipped through Erskine's personal snapshot book from the Weather Report days. As "Opus Pocus" played in the background, Zawinul threw back another shot and proclaimed, "He was a fucking genius, that guy!"

That evening, another tribute took place at the local Holiday Inn. Unlike the small gathering of relatives and friends at La T's, this one was advertised and open to the public. A throng of Jaco fans from South Florida turned out to pay their respects to their hometown hero. Before engaging in a dynamic duet with Erskine, Metheny addressed the crowd: "I can tell you that today there are hundreds of thousands of people in the world who are really sad about Jaco not being around. But there's one thing I'm sure of. Jaco is checking us out, and he's really happy."

They were joined by Bernsen and other local musicians for versions of tunes that Jaco had loved to play: "Stella by Starlight," "All the Things You Are," "The Chicken," Herbie Hancock's "Cantaloupe Island," and, of course, "Fannie Mae." The 14-piece Peter

Graves Driftwood Orchestra offered faithful renditions of Jaco's "Liberty City," "Three Views of a Secret," and "Domingo" (one of Jaco's oldest compositions). And Jack Pastorius joined them on a rendition of "I've Got You Under My Skin" before picking up the drumsticks and showing off his one-handed roll in a rousing finale with Metheny and Bernsen.

The tribute concert lasted until the early-morning hours of September 26. As the musicians were packing their equipment, I stepped outside with James Cannings and noticed that it had begun to rain. James looked up at the sky and said, "Jaco is getting his first soaking." And then he remembered the last words Jaco had spoken to him: "Where I'm going, there's going to be plenty of water."

On December 2, 1987, Luc Havan was charged with second-degree murder in the death of John Francis Anthony Pastorius III, "The World's Greatest Bass Player." Havan maintained his innocence for a year before copping a guilty plea to the reduced charge of manslaughter. Since Havan had no prior convictions, he was sentenced to 22 months in jail and five years of probation. He was released from jail after four months, getting out early for good behavior.

EIGHT

Requiem

BACK IN NEW YORK, Ricky Sebastian and Alex Foster organized a two-night concert to benefit Jaco's children. It took place at the Lone Star Cafe on November 4 and 5, 1987. For that special event, Pat Metheny and Bob Moses played material from *Bright Size Life*, with Victor Bailey and Marcus Miller alternately filling in on bass for Jaco. Will Lee and Hiram Bullock joined with Delmar Brown, Kenwood Dennard, Don Alias, and Jerry González for a rousing version of "Teen Town," and then Will teamed with harmonica player William Gallison for a touching duet on "Blackbird." The 20-piece Word Of Mouth big band, with trumpeters Earl Gardner, Randy Brecker, Miles Evans, and Lew Soloff alongside saxophonists Alex Foster, Lou Marini, Lenny Pickett, and Paul McCandless, resurrected Jaco tunes like "Liberty City" and "Dania."

A giant blowup of the stunning Don Hunstein black and white portrait that appeared on the cover of Jaco's debut album hovered over the stage. Upstairs, the entire Pastorius clan danced to the joyful noise. (Both nights were filmed by Franco Schipanni for Italian distribution only.)

After the show, Ricky Sebastian commented, "I felt like I *had* to do this concert. There were a lot of people who were closer to Jaco than I was. I only knew him for the last four years of his life, but I felt as if I was chosen to be the instrument to pull off this whole thing."

©Jay Abend

Julius and Felix Pastorius playing at the tribute to Jaco, October 1993

Five years later, on October 7, 1993, Neil Weiss of Big World Music organized another tribute to Jaco. This one was held at the Grand, and the participants included trumpeters Lew Soloff, Miles Evans, Alan Rubin, Ryan Kisor, and Jeff Kievet; trombonists Dave Bargeron, Conrad Herwig, Tom "Bones" Malone, David Taylor, and Peter Graves; saxophonists Alex Foster, Butch Thomas, Lou Marini, and Ronnie Cuber; French-horn players Peter Gordon, John Clark, and Alex Brofski; percussionists Jerry González and Manolo Badrena; drummer Kenwood Dennard; guitarist Toninho Horta; keyboardist Gil Goldstein; and bassist Matthew Garrison, son of the long-time John Coltrane bassist, Jimmy Garrison.

The high point of this celebration was the appearance of the ten-year-old twins, Julius and Felix Pastorius, who took the stage with electric basses in hand to play their father's pieces "Continuum" and "Come On, Come Over." Their resemblance to Jaco was astonishing,

©Jay Abend

and their performance offered proof that the Pastorius legacy had been passed on to the next generation.

I still think of Jaco a lot. I can still picture him onstage in all his glory, charging around to the machine-gun pulse of "Teen Town" or swaying to the fervent swing of "Dania." I see him strutting around the psychiatric ward at Bellevue Hospital. I see him scuffling for a rebound on the basketball court, taking that ugly outside jump shot of his and occasionally hitting it. I remember him grinning that sly Jaco grin and saying "Who loves ya, babe?" the oft-repeated slogan he picked up from Telly Savalas as TV's Kojak. I remember his life-affirming presence, his sense of humor, his generosity of spirit.

I can still hear his late-night phone calls, full of outrageous Pastorius pronouncements and the insistence that I "Write it down!" The phone would ring, I'd pick it up, and a raspy voice at the other end would bark: "Joe Zawinul and Wayne Shorter are my biggest teachers to date ... *write it down!*" Or he might offer a gem like: "I'm doing a very bad imitation on the bass of Jerry Jemmott, Bernard Odum, Jimmy Fielder, Jimmy Blanton, Igor Stravinsky, Wayne Shorter, Féla Ransome Kuti ... *write it down!*" Once he called at 3 AM just to play a Ray Charles record over the phone. I sat and listened to the entire tune, and then Jaco came back on the phone and barked *"Write it down!"* before hanging up.

Charlie Brent will always remember Jaco as a steadfast pal. "You'd never want a more loyal friend," he says. "I mean, here is a guy who would take a bullet for you and say, 'Who loves ya, babe?' He was my buddy, my brother. Jaco was home team."

To Joni Mitchell he was "a great spirit with beautiful animal wisdom." To Ira Sullivan he was "like a meteor streaking across the Florida night sky." Carlos Santana believes Jaco "had his destiny cut out for him on this planet."

To Jimmy Haslip he was the Galileo of bass. To Marcus Miller he was the Willie Mays of bass. To Mark Egan he was the John McLaughlin of bass. Jeff Berlin calls him "our great emperor of bass," while to Stuart Hamm he was simply "God."

When he died, we all searched our record collections for our favorite Jaco tunes. Some found solace in "Fannie Mae" or "The Chicken" from *Invitation,* reveling in Jaco's jaunty, irrepressibly funky spirit. Some put on the aggressively macho "Teen Town" from *Heavy Weather,* or the eye-opening "Donna Lee" from his astounding debut album, or the explosive "Chromatic Fantasy" from *Word Of Mouth* to revel in his profound technical abilities on the bass. Some played "Liberty City" from *Word Of Mouth* or "Barbary Coast" from *Black Market* and instantly felt invigorated by the energy. Others chose darker, more turbulent expressions, like the wild free-jazz "Crisis" from *Word Of Mouth* or the angry "Reza" from *Invitation* or the volatile solo-bass showcase "Slang" from Weather Report's *8:30.* Others turned to the sublime lyricism of ballads like "A Remark You

Made" from *Heavy Weather* or "Portrait of Tracy" from *Jaco Pastorius* for emotional solace.

I didn't have to think twice about which Jaco song to put on. After getting the news of his death, I immediately cued up "Three Views of a Secret." To me, that's the one song that best captures the complexity of Jaco's character and the depth of his soul. In the course of six minutes, "Three Views of a Secret" reveals more about Jaco's character than any other piece he ever wrote. It's as if he had composed his own requiem.

Who Loves Ya, Jaco

JOE ZAWINUL
Former Miles Davis sideman and co-leader of Weather Report

We had a very competitive thing going off the bandstand, challenging each other to games of ping-pong and basketball or just throwing a Frisbee around. It was a fun thing to hang with Jaco. We did crazy stuff on tour, like diving from the rocks in France and playing baseball at midnight. We enjoyed each other's company, and we had that competitive spirit in common. But it was never a competition onstage. We all worked together—that was the secret of Weather Report. We all had mutual respect for one another. You wanted to play well for your compatriots in that band. That really kept us on our toes and helped to elevate the music to a very high level.

I loved Jaco. Every time I think of him, I smile. He was one of the nicest people I've ever known, and he did things that nobody ever knew about. When my parents had their Golden Wedding Anniversary in the tiny Austrian village outside of Vienna where I come from, he sent the biggest flower arrangement you've ever seen. And he always remembered my birthday, no matter where he was or what condition he was in. That was the kind of guy he was. Jaco was always making kind, thoughtful gestures for people he loved. He had a good soul and a good character.

Jaco had a tough life, but he was always a gentleman to me. I think he was a mischievous person in many ways, but never with bad intentions. He would do anything for a laugh or to get attention, no matter how outrageous it was. I just hope people remember him for what he was—a good, decent, very thoughtful human being.

PETER ERSKINE
Former drummer with Weather Report and Jaco's Word Of Mouth

When I saw that stunning black & white photograph on the cover of his first album [*Jaco Pastorius*], I got an impression of him as being very sophisticated. He had a Continental appearance—possibly French or maybe even Slavic. He looked like an impressive, regal character in that photo. So when I finally met him, I was very surprised: here was this skinny guy with stringy hair, wearing horn-rimmed glasses and a goofy Phillies baseball cap. He looked like some kind of hippie.

I was in Maynard Ferguson's band at the time, and we were playing a gig in Miami. One of the guys in the band [trumpeter Ron Tooley] was an old friend of Jaco's, so he introduced me to him. And although I was surprised by his bohemian appearance, I was impressed by how sweet and genuine he seemed.

We hung out that evening after our gig, and Jaco played the rough mixes of *Heavy Weather*. It was so exciting to hear that record for the first time. It sounded totally fresh. We stayed up all night, listening to the tape over and over again. When the band left Florida I gave Jaco a courtesy call, and he said to me, "You know, I'll be calling you for something one of these days." And a few months later I did get the call to join Weather Report.

JONI MITCHELL
Singer/songwriter who featured Jaco on four of her albums in the '70s

What can I say about Jaco? He was so accepting of everything going on around him at the same time that he was arrogant and challenging and always saying, "I'm the baddest!" He was so alert and so involved in the moment. When people are in that state, they're generally fun to be with. He was very alive. There was a time when Jaco and I first worked together when there was nobody I'd rather hang with than him. A lot of people couldn't take him. Maybe that's my peculiarity, but then, I also have a fondness for derelicts.

Jaco was a great spirit before his deterioration by these toxins. I thought he had wonderful eyes before drugs clouded them. Look at that portrait of him on his first album cover and see if he doesn't look like some Tibetan sage.

When his talent and inspiration began to be corroded by the clouding over of perception that accompanies overindulgence in drugs and alcohol, then he became a tragic figure on the scene. He started to become unruly. In the meantime I lost contact with him. It was more of a drifting apart than a breaking off. He went off with Weather Report and they played Japan and I heard tales of him jumping into fountains naked, going amok in the Orient. I just didn't see him that much after the Shadows and Light tour.

I think Jaco had a beautiful animal wisdom that I don't see as a madness at all. In Jaco, I saw some of those expressions as a celebration of life. Strange behavior, certainly, but I don't think it was demented. [As told to *Musician* magazine.]

CARLOS SANTANA
Guitarist and founder of the rock group Santana

I knew Jaco well enough to talk to him a couple of times and let him know that there was support for him. I told him one time about my father-in-law, who was a musician and used to back up Lester Young, Billie Holiday, and people like that. He told me he wished he could have done something to help Charlie Christian or Billie Holiday because they were living that life—a lot of drugs, partying and booze, not getting a lot of sleep. That kind of lifestyle is like burning the candle at both ends; it wears you out fast. And I told Jaco about that. I said, "You know, it's important to look at the other side. Look at the Duke Ellingtons and the Count Basies and the Eubie Blakes, people who went the long distance by pacing themselves." But Jaco wouldn't listen. He wasn't satisfied with certain things that normal people are satisfied with. He was like Jimi Hendrix. He had his destiny cut out for himself on this planet.

MIKE STERN

Guitarist formerly with Miles Davis and Jaco's Word Of Mouth, currently an Atlantic Jazz recording artist

Jaco was often a compassionate, caring person. But there was this other side to Jaco, an ugly side, where he would be insulting and confrontational. And he was very much on edge all the time. Sometimes he would be depressed to the point of crying on your shoulder, sometimes very manic and running around like a hyperactive kid.

I always thought Jaco's talent was a curse, in a way. Because no matter how fucked up he got on the bandstand, he could still play. The same thing happened with Bird. Their great talent enabled both of them to continue doing drugs and getting away with it, because they kept getting encouragement from people around them who told them how great they sounded. Jaco would play a great solo, and he'd be sitting on top of the world again, feeling invincible, with an attitude like, "There's nothing wrong with me." Jaco's talent was like a double-edged sword—it made it impossible for him to see how terrible things really were becoming.

I guess nobody was really shocked when they got the news [about Jaco's death], but I was devastated. I really cared about the guy. We were tight, close friends for a long time. I sure miss him—very deeply at times. It took me about three years to start thinking of him in the past tense.

JOHN SCOFIELD

Guitarist formerly with Miles Davis, currently a Blue Note recording artist

When Jaco came on the scene, I thought he was the greatest thing that ever happened. I wanted to get up my nerve to play with him, but by the time I was in a position to do that, he was so out of it that it was impossible. He asked me to come down to his gigs, but I wouldn't show up. You never knew if you were going to get paid, and I was really concerned at the time about getting my career together. I had a family to take care of, and I was trying to be more responsible and not hang out so much. I stopped doing cocaine and decided that I was going to get serious about music and my career, so I never accepted Jaco's offer to sit in on his gigs.

I was involved in some drunken jams with him at 55 Grand around 1982 or so, but at that point he was usually so fucked up that I don't count those jams as anything very musical. I used to play down there all the time with Mike Stern; we'd have our two guitars with Peter Warren on bass and Victor Lewis on drums. Jaco would come in and it would be like, "Oh shit, here he comes." He'd want to sing "Mustang Sally" and dance onstage and stuff. That whole scene was destructive for everybody involved, and Jaco was the worst offender. He was destroyed, man. I mean, he still had some great stuff on the bass, but by then he was just like a walking time bomb.

I have weird feelings about Jaco's music in New York. What he was doing really didn't make it for me. He was crazy and couldn't keep it together. I remember he would get up there at 55 Grand and start playing the themes to Weather Report tunes. But who wants to hear a drunken version of "Birdland"? It was just sad. I think Jaco played really great with Weather Report for a couple of years and then for whatever reason stopped listening to the other musicians he was playing with. He was still great, but he didn't have the kind of magic he had when he was a little more down to earth. I don't think anybody can be the greatest bass player who ever played if he doesn't listen to the musicians around him.

There's nobody—including Charlie Parker—who can continually come up with creative ideas when they're that high. You can't. If anything, you might be able to just get high enough so you can have fun playing the same old stuff. But you aren't going to come up with anything new when you have chemicals in your body, no matter who you are. And the saddest thing is, maybe Jaco realized this himself.

DELMAR BROWN
Keyboardist with Word Of Mouth septet

A lot of people say, "It was drugs that killed Jaco." It wasn't drugs that killed Jaco. And it wasn't alcohol. Jaco just gave up. He decided to split. It was obvious to me, but everybody likes to make these excuses to explain his behavior. His problem was inside. He gave up wanting to live—and that's what hurt me so deeply.

But what killed Jaco the most was family; his lack of control over that situation with his wives and kids really destroyed him. The love he had for his kids was beyond anything that anybody has talked about yet. People say, "Oh, Jaco left his babies and he left his family." And that was what was killing him—he got so depressed by his family situation. I guess it was partly guilt, but he started taking a lot out on himself. There was something tormenting the cat spiritually. He was very sensitive. He would have to be sensitive if he could reach out and touch people with his music the way he did. But that sensitivity worked against him in the end. It caused him to self-destruct. It got to a point where he was so self-destructive that I just couldn't pick him up off the streets anymore.

KENWOOD DENNARD
Drummer with Word Of Mouth and the PDB trio with Jaco and Hiram Bullock

We once did a show at the Berklee Performance Center in Boston where we walked onstage juggling oranges. I did the whole first song juggling these oranges with one hand and playing the drums with the other. That kind of silly inspiration came from Jaco.

I'll never forget one of the expressions that Jaco used all the time. He would always say, "Strap on in"—that was sort of like saying, "Buckle up your seat belts, there's danger ahead." He was definitely a daredevil. One thing about playing with Jaco: you never knew what was going to happen next. You really did have to "strap on in" to play with him.

Jaco had many qualities that are valuable on a deeper spiritual level. It's just a shame he took one part of his life out to the point where his body couldn't take it anymore. After he passed, I felt solid misery. Part of it was from knowing how violently he died, brutally beaten to death like that. Part of it was the frustration of living in a society that would allow something like that to happen to such a great artist.

DON ALIAS
Percussionist formerly with Miles Davis who played on Jaco's solo debut, toured with Jaco and Joni Mitchell, and later played in Jaco's Word Of Mouth band

Towards the end there were things he was doing that were "out" but still funny—sort of like Charlie Parker riding a fucking horse up Fifth Avenue. Everybody knows it's "out" behavior, but in retrospect that's a funny scene, man. I remember one time, on our way to Japan, when Jaco came on the plane in a dress and commandeered the microphone and started talking to the passengers. Maybe he was getting ready to go down mentally for doing something nuts like that, but I gotta give it to him anyway for even doing the shit. The cat was always funny. And I'm still waiting for the Grammy Awards to get hip and give this guy a tribute.

BRIAN MELVIN
Drummer who toured and recorded with Jaco and arranged for Jaco's release from Bellevue Hospital

Deep down, Jaco was a homeboy. He was the kind of cat who liked to wear baseball caps, watch TV, play sports, eat good food, and have a good time. He loved to laugh and he loved to tell jokes. And he loved the old school comedians like Johnny Carson, Don Rickles, Jack Benny, Bob Hope. He was just a very warm, very funny guy.

I think he was a spiritual cat, when you get right down to it. I always thought of him as a modern day shaman, like a high priest or witch doctor or something. The music was a vehicle for him, a tool to let people know what he was really into. Ultimately, he was coming from a higher place than just "I play the bass." Near the end of his life, he'd take his Fender bass and his Acoustic 360 amp and play this incredible feedback. Nobody understood it, but if you really listened you could hear what the real deal was. You could hear monsters coming out through his axe—the demons in his head and heart. It was complete and pure expression.

RASHIED ALI
Drummer formerly with John Coltrane

I met Jaco down at the 55 Grand in 1983 just after he got back from that tour where he fell off a balcony and broke his wrist. I had known about him and he had known about me, but we never really talked to each other until this one night at 55 Grand. I noticed some crazy guy up onstage playing bass with a cast on his arm, and I thought, "Who is this cat?"

Jaco and I got to be close friends, inseparable for a couple of years. We had a very special hookup rhythmically. To me, Jaco was a genius. He was a very intelligent person, plus he was a natural musician. I guess that's why I liked him a lot. He came into my life at a time when I was so down and depressed that I was thinking about giving up music completely. But he brought me back out of my depression and got me playing again. For that alone, I will never forget him.

ANITA EVANS
Widow of composer/arranger/bandleader Gil Evans

Even before he joined Weather Report, Jaco used to call up Gil and bug him for tips on arranging. Gil was pretty secretive about his tricks of the trade, but Jaco got more out of him than anybody else ever did. I don't think Gil would've shared that kind of information with him unless he saw that this young man could really do something with it. Later, Gil was delighted by the growth he saw in Jaco musically.

He had his rough times and we all tried to help. But one thing that always got him through was his sense of humor. He was such a funny guy and always made me laugh a lot. He used to call me at odd hours of the night, four or five in the morning, from all over the globe, just to tell me a joke or to talk. It's so strange that my phone doesn't ring in the middle of the night anymore. That's how I know he's gone. But he'll never really be gone. The relationship continues in my head. It's just that the phone has stopped ringing at four in the morning.

MILES EVANS
Trumpeter; son of Anita and Gil Evans

In 1978, he had more like a crazy-fun personality. Later, when he had gotten to the abusive point, he started to worry me. By 1984, he had stopped practicing and other bassists had started to catch up to him. And that was very upsetting to him.

He would stay over at our place a lot when he didn't have a place of his own. He would teach me tunes like "Punk Jazz" and talk to me about voicings on the piano. Sometimes I would try to talk to him about his health, but he wouldn't listen. His biggest problem was that he would never admit he had a problem. Whenever I would try to confront him on this issue, it would alienate him. We all came to realize that Jaco was going to have to do it on his own.

GIL GOLDSTEIN
Keyboardist and musical director of the Gil Evans Orchestra

Jaco's compositions are far and away above the music of any of his contemporaries. I think they are some of the best songs that have been written in the later jazz age, and I think they're going to have a history of being covered and re-covered. Of all the music that Jaco recorded, I think his classic pieces are "Teen Town" and "Three Views of a Secret."

I remember one time he said to Gil Evans, "Man, I stole everything I could from you without getting in trouble." Jaco owed a pretty heavy debt to Gil's writing. The voicings he used on "Dania," for instance, were just so … Gil.

I always had confidence that Jaco could take care of himself, because I had so much respect for him. But in the end, I thought he was experimenting with negativity. He used to tell me, "I'm just a daredevil." He was always being a daredevil, right up until the end.

JIMMY HASLIP
Bassist with the Yellowjackets

I took lessons with Jaco for about three weeks in Los Angeles, just after he joined Weather Report [in 1976]. It was really an illuminating experience. Basically, we hung out and played together, and he gave me a few pointers on right-hand techniques for picking. I also learned about playing with attitude from him.

When Jaco hipped me to all the diminished scales, it opened up a whole new world for me in terms of how I thought about soloing. I started seeing different possibilities on the bass. It was enlightening and exciting. And that began a long period of intensive woodshedding for me.

I kept in touch with Jaco over the years, and we remained friends up until the time he passed away. Although I must say that during the last couple of years he was around it was a little difficult to communicate with him. That really depressed me, because when I first met him he was like a live wire, full of spark. On first meeting the guy, you could tell he was extremely bright, articulate, very alert. But during the last couple of years all that changed.

I was in Florida the day he passed away, and I happened to be in Orlando on the day of his funeral. It was a sad day in my life. To have known such a great person and innovative cat, and to see him waste away like that—it was too sad.

I was truly inspired by Jaco, which is why I dedicated the tune "Galileo" [from the album *Politics* on MCA Records] to him. I actually conceived of that tune while I was in Florida. The idea came to me the day I found out that Jaco was in a coma. I started thinking about him and came up with this little melodic pattern, which is the basis for the song. And the reason I called the tune "Galileo" is because I thought that Jaco was like the Galileo of bass. The great astronomer Galileo was an innovator and ahead of his time; he was a genius who saw a new way of looking at the universe. And Jaco was certainly an innovator and ahead of his time—I consider him a genius who saw a new way of looking at the bass.

MUZZ SKILLINGS

Bassist formerly with Living Colour

My older brother Daryl used to put on Weather Report records and be blown away by Jaco. I would listen to these records and say, "Man, I can do that. What's the big deal?" And he said, "Yeah, but can you *come up* with something like that?" And that really struck me. It was the first time I thought about what it meant to be an innovator, which Jaco truly was. I could copy some of his lines, but I wasn't an innovator like he was. And that made me so depressed I actually stopped playing for a while, because I wasn't hearing anything innovative in my playing at all. I wasn't coming up with anything that was my own. That whole experience of addressing Jaco's contribution to the bass was a turning point for me. It made me rethink where I was at as a bass player.

MARK EGAN

Bassist formerly with the Pat Metheny Group and the Gil Evans Monday Night Orchestra, now co-leader of Elements

When I met Jaco down in Florida in 1973, he was a totally straight family man. He never did drugs, never drank. He played sports all the time and was very competitive. When he played baseball or basketball, he always wanted to win and got angry if he lost. In anything he did, he would challenge you to be the best. He had this kind of drive to win, and that's also what pushed him to do what he did on the bass.

In my lessons with Jaco we covered the technical points. He showed me right-hand techniques, and he made up a lot of exercises based on diatonic intervals in all the different modes. He had a lot of 12-tone exercises that he got from Slonimsky's *Thesaurus of Scales*, which is a book Coltrane also studied out of. Jaco taught me how to get all around the instrument. We would spend a couple of hours each lesson just playing together, and he was on such a high technical level that you couldn't help but learn just from being in the same room with him and watching him play.

We would also spend a lot of time listening to records, and Jaco always stressed the importance of playing grooves. After one of my lessons, he gave me a tape to take home and practice along with. It was Maceo Parker & All The King's Men—really funky James Brown-style R&B. Jaco had those heavy R&B roots, and he basically expanded on the tradition of bass playing that people like James Jamerson and Bernard Odum and Charles Sherrell developed.

Besides being amazed by Jaco's technique, I was inspired by his intensity. He used to tell me, "If you think you can walk through a wall, you can walk through a wall." And I believed him. He was always so intense and inspiring. Every time I left a lesson with him, I was buzzing with ideas and energy.

The groove was always important to Jaco. His attitude was, "You can take it as far out as you want as long as you don't lose the time and don't drift away from holding it down." Some of my bass students today have all this two-handed technique, but they can't lay down a groove. And to me, the definition of bass is the bottom. You have to have your feet firmly planted on the ground before you can take off. And once you have that foundation, there's infinite room for experimentation and creativity. Jaco taught me that.

STUART HAMM
Bassist formerly with Joe Satriani who has recorded with Steve Vai and as a leader for Relativity Records

When I enrolled at Berklee, I really wasn't aware of Weather Report. I'll never forget the first time I saw them, at the Orpheum Theatre in Boston. It was November 8, 1978—the night that changed my life. After that concert, I thought Jaco was God!

I was so impressed by the ease with which he played. The bass just seemed like putty in his hands—it was like an extension of his body. He totally communicated through his instrument. It went beyond the notes and rhythms to sheer emotional communication. He was really tapped into that while still playing the supportive role of bass. That whole idea of playing melodically while still holding down the groove really inspired me.

Jaco was responsible for getting me to experiment on my instrument. He got me into playing harmonics and chords on the bass. But more than that, he got me to play with abandon—to go totally crazy with the bass, like he did.

JACK BRUCE
Bassist/singer/songwriter inducted into the Rock & Roll Hall of Fame as a member of Cream

I met Jaco only once, around 1984. It was at a tiny little bar in SoHo called 55 Grand. I was doing a recording project, and I got a note in the rehearsal room that read: "I'm playing at this bar tonight. Would you please come by and say hello?" And it was signed "Jaco." So I went down there and we played a bit together. We talked, but he was kind of crazed at the time. He was going up to people in the bar and yelling, "Hey, here's the guy who wrote 'Sunshine of Your Love'" in a very strange way. He was in pretty bad shape, I must say. He seemed to be going in all directions at once. I felt very sorry for him.

At one point he told me there was going to be an after-hours jam at a recording studio and asked if I would come. I said, "Sorry, I can't. I've got something to do, but it's been really nice meeting you." He got really upset and ran off down the street. He turned the corner, and I never saw him again. It's such a shame. What a tragedy.

JEFF ANDREWS
Bassist who has worked with Steps Ahead, Tom Coster, and the Mike Stern trio

I remember the first time I heard Jaco on record: I was 15 years old and staying in a big house in Baltimore with a bunch of friends. I was sleeping in my room, and some guy was playing Weather Report's *Black Market* album so loud in the living room that it woke me up. It was the tune "Barbary Coast." I thought I was hearing a clavinet or something, so I went out to the living room to see what it was. The guy told me it was this new bassist named Jaco Pastorius.

I was amazed. It was so funky and he wasn't slapping at all. It was just his attack, his touch, his choice of notes, his whole rhythmic approach that made it sound so funky. I had never heard anything like it before. Musically, what Jaco was doing was way over my head at the time, but I could still feel the groove. That's the thing about Jaco. No matter how complex his music got, he always maintained that earthy quality. He always had that balance of emotion and intellect in his music, which is pretty rare. Most of the time it goes too far in one direction or the other. Jaco's music was brilliant, yet it still had that earthy feel to it, those R&B roots.

As a player, Jaco was a beacon for a lot of cats. He opened the door and we walked through. He taught us that the bass could be anything—a piano, a conga drum, a saxophone. He worked with it melodically, harmonically, and percussively. He played lyrically and he always played with attitude. He redefined the bass and raised the consciousness of a lot of players. He gave the electric bass credibility, because before Jaco came along a lot of jazz cats didn't accept it.

When Jaco was having a good night, when he was really *on*, there was no one—ever—who could touch him. It was frightening. He had the same effect on bass players that I imagine Charlie Parker had on alto sax players in his day.

JEFF BERLIN
Bassist formerly with Bruford and Kazumi Watanabe

I first heard Jaco when his debut album came out in '76, and I thought, "Unbelievable! Amazing!" He had such a personal voice and such a unique approach to the bass. I immediately went out and bought a fretless bass, but I stopped playing it after about three months because I didn't want to be imitative. I knew the guy was so original that anyone who played fretless would immediately be accused of trying to copy his thing, and I didn't want that. So I deliberately avoided listening to the Weather Report albums for years, because I knew that if I listened with a real focused attention to it, it would be nearly impossible for me not to copy him.

MARCUS MILLER
Bassist/producer formerly with the Miles Davis band

When I bought Jaco's first solo album in 1976, it pretty much didn't come off my turntable for about a year and a half. He's really the bass player who made me want to learn about music as opposed to just playing the bass. I got my basic chordal education from listening to his records. I can't even put into words how much the cat influenced me—me and a million other guys.

It's strange—right before he died I felt this urge to go out and buy *Heavy Weather*. I had worn out my third copy and needed to replace it. I don't know why, but for some reason I needed to hear it again. A few days later, I got the news that he had died.

Toward the end, Jaco would come up and sit in on my gigs and sometimes forget the changes in the middle of the song. That happened one night when we were playing "Maiden Voyage." It was kind of sad. And after the set, people would say, "Man, why did you let that dude take over the set?" And I would tell them, "You don't understand. That's Jaco!" It's like—imagine you're playing baseball in Central Park and Willie Mays walks over and wants to play. And some young cat says, "Man, why did you let that old dude play?" Because it's Willie Mays, that's why! What can I tell you? You gotta give respect. When Jaco was down and hurting and his playing was not so good, I still gave him respect.

BILL LASWELL
Bassist/producer; co-founder of Material and Last Exit

I recorded Jaco once. By that time [1984], however, he was already pretty far gone. It was for the *Deadline* album, a project for drummer Phillip Wilson. Phillip ran over to the Lone Star to get Paul Butterfield to play on one cut, and Jaco tagged along. We let him play for about three minutes at the end of one song, "Makossa Rock." Both he and Butterfield were in pretty bad shape then.

I saw him play live in his early days. He really had developed a unique voice. I didn't even think of it as bass; it was more this amazing vocal instrument in his hands. But then he got out there, got a taste of fame, and totally lost control.

The first time I met him, I was recording an Oliver Lake album; he walked into the studio and pretty much disrupted the session. He had a black eye, and at one point he pulled out these pictures of his daughter and started crying. He was totally out of it by then.

But what he did cannot be denied. His contribution was great. Nobody played like him. There were so many clones that came after Jaco, but none had his personality, his guts.

DR. JOHN
Pianist/singer/songwriter/producer, New Orleans legend

The first time I saw Jaco he was playing with Ira Sullivan's band down in Miami [around 1973] at a place called the Lion's Share. I was living in Miami at the time and producing sessions at Criteria Studios, so I had a chance to see Jaco a lot. I remember seeing him around the studio back then, and he struck me as just a sweet cat, someone who was very pleasant to be around. He wasn't into any of that wild behavior and show-off stuff that he got into later.

Then all of a sudden something happened. I saw him again in 1977, just after he had done that album with Joni Mitchell [*Hejira*], and I noticed right away that something had changed about him. He wasn't the same sweet guy I had known in Miami. He had started acting obnoxious, saying he was the greatest bass player in the universe, and that Charles Mingus wasn't shit and nobody was shit to him except him.

Around the early '80s, I started hearing so many horror stories about Jaco. Every time somebody would mention his name, it would be in connection with another weird story about something he did on the gig, back at the hotel, or in the street.

One night he came by the Lone Star when I was playing there. He was really acting crazy and wanted to sit in. I told him, "It ain't cool right now, you understand?" And he got all pissed off and jumped onstage and started banging on one end of my piano to get my attention. Then he took off his sweaty T-shirt and threw it in my face before storming out of the place. It was crazy. He was cool when he was sober and a complete wild man when he drank.

But I don't like to dwell on the bad times. I will always think of Jaco as that sweet cat I saw playing with Ira Sullivan down in Miami in the early '70s. That's the cat I like to remember.

IRA SULLIVAN
Saxophonist/trumpeter/composer

When I met Jaco, he was straight as an arrow and always full of kinetic energy. He had his family together, had his children together, and was taking care of business. He was playing wonderful music and revolutionizing his instrument.

Jaco was such a charismatic personality that people always wanted to be around him. Tracy would tell me stories about how he'd be out on the road and maybe two or three cats would come knocking on her door. These cats were from Germany, and they were making some kind of pilgrimage to Jaco's house. Tracy would tell them, "Jaco's not here," and they'd say, "Well, could we just come in and sit by his piano for a while," like he was some guru or something.

I loved playing with Jaco. He always came to play. And we frightened some cats with that band we had together. You have to wonder, though, had he lived—just like Bird—what things he would've expanded into because of that insatiable curiosity and love he had for music.

WILL LEE
Bassist in the house band on Late Show with David Letterman

It was after I came to New York that I first heard about Jaco—people were always talking about this bass player down in Florida. On one of my trips down to Miami to visit my father, who was dean of the jazz department at the University of Miami, I happened to hear Ira Sullivan play at the Lion's Share, and Jaco was on bass. I remember my first impression of him was, "Well, this guy sure is playing a lot of notes. But is he playing any bass?" I had my doubts at the time. The thing that was most interesting to me was that he was playing on a fretted bass that had no frets. The sound was awesome.

I only got to play with Jaco once. I sat in one night at Seventh Avenue South around 1982. The tune was "Fannie Mae," but I don't remember who else was in the band. I was so out of it from drugs myself in those days that I hardly remember anything for about a three-year period there. But I do remember being onstage next to Jaco and being really nervous. I was buzzed and totally self-conscious, but Jaco tried to make me feel relaxed. He was really sweet that way.

JOE FERRY
Producer of We Remember Pastorius *tribute album*

I was deeply, deeply influenced by Jaco. I think his writing ranks up there with anything Mozart composed. For me, Vincent Van Gogh and Jaco Pastorius are the two greatest artists in the history of the world. And they had a lot in common: But were tormented geniuses, both were very religious people, and both went out of control near the end of their lives. It just seems that in order to possess genius that deeply, you naturally operate on a different plane. We can't truly understand the way that they were because we're not like that. We're not geniuses.

The first time I met Jaco was when I almost accidentally hit him with my car. I was driving along in Greenwich Village one evening, and all of a sudden this figure darted out into traffic. I narrowly missed hitting him. I was very upset, so I stuck my head out of the window to yell at this guy—and I noticed it was Jaco. I was shocked. I had no idea he had sunk so low. That was the first time I had any indication that he was hanging out on the streets and begging for money. It was a sad sight.

The next time I met him was at Sweet Basil. He walked into the club with his bass—no case, no shoes. Just Jaco with a shirt, some pants, and his bass. He sat in with the band and sounded great. And that's the first time I actually got to talk to him. He was pretty coherent that night, and after the set we sat around while he told stories of Weather Report.

One of the last times I saw Jaco, I was in a restaurant in the Village having dinner with a friend and he walked in. He recognized me and came over and started talking. He was kind of incoherent, and at some point he turned to my friend and told her he was God. Then he stood up, gave me a hug, and left. And of course my friend didn't understand him. She said, "That guy is pretty fucked up, isn't he?" And I said, "Man, he's not fucked up. We're the ones who are fucked up." I mean, I understood what he was saying; he was not saying that he could walk on water or that he was some kind of higher being. What I believed him to be saying was that there is a higher spirituality—call it God—in all of us. And to me, that's a profound statement, not a crazy statement. There aren't too many people walking around on this planet who are as deeply in touch with their soul and their spirit as Jaco was.

For me, Jaco's spirit is still here with us. His body has moved through the doorway to the next plane of existence, but his spirit is here.

OTHELLO MOLINEAUX
Steel pans player with Word Of Mouth band

I played with Jaco on his first album, and I also played on a steel-drums album he produced for Warner Bros. in 1982 that was never released [*Holiday for Pans*]. They apparently didn't think much of this album, so it was just put on the shelf and forgotten. And I think that really hurt him deeply. It was after that point that he started running around New York and acting crazy. He was hurt spiritually by that rejection, and he was drowning his hurt in drugs and alcohol, it seemed.

I moved up to New York in the summer of 1985 to be close to Jaco. By that time, he was hanging out in Washington Square Park and getting in trouble all the time. I went through a really emotional period with him, and I tried to help him in any way I could. But he was raging out of control, and you just got this helpless feeling that there was nothing you could do. His sense of doom was just so strong.

I kept in touch with Jaco, feeling that there was something I could do to turn him around. I was living with that hope, but seeing him in the last months of his life you could just sense that the spirit was gone. He was like an empty shell. I felt he really wanted to go. He sort of said as much to me at times. That spirit in him, that's what protected him all those years when he was sleeping on the basketball courts and wandering around for days without sleeping. That spirit got him through from day to day. And near the end, you could feel that spirit was gone. That spirit was what made us smile; that life-force was what made him Jaco. That was what gave us hope for years that he would balance out his life again. But after a while he finally let go of that life-force.

JERRY JEMMOTT
Legendary session bassist with Atlantic Records in the '60s

What made Jaco special was his musicianship, his ability to express and interpret the music as he felt it. And, of course, the facility he had on the instrument was incredible. There are a lot of Jaco clones out there, but they don't have the music. They might have the technique, but they don't have his soul. That's something you just can't copy.

VICTOR BAILEY
Bassist formerly with Weather Report, Weather Update, and Steps Ahead; more recently with Madonna

I remember first hearing Jaco when I was in 11th grade. A teacher came in with *Black Market* and the *Jaco Pastorius* album. I was completely blown away by them. I had just started playing bass about a year before that. I was playing fretless and doing what I thought was melodic bass and harmonics, but after hearing Jaco I was just mesmerized. He had everything I thought I was doing, but he did it a thousand times better.

The first time I met Jaco was six months after I started playing in Weather Report. He was really open and always said positive things to me. And he gave me a couple of tips that helped my bass playing considerably.

Jaco used to tell me, "You gotta play your thing and make Joe think it's what he wants to hear." Because Joe Zawinul is a super-sensitive cat, and if you're feeling at all insecure, he'll pick up on that. For the first tour with Weather Report, I was always kind of looking at Joe out of the corner of my eye, like, "I wonder if he likes this?" But then Jaco told me, "Man, you can play! Just go ahead and do what you do, and do it!" So the second time out with Weather Report my attitude really changed. From that point on, I was walking right up to the keyboard, looking right in Joe's face, and saying, "Here, motherfucker, play with this!" And that totally changed our relationship. Then Joe, I think, really respected me, so I could relax and do what I do best.

STANLEY CLARKE
Legendary bassist/producer and solo artist

A lot of people used to think we were enemies because, supposedly, we were the two premier electric bass players. But we got to be good friends. Jaco and I got close in the last five years of his life. A short while before he died, he gave my son the old baseball glove he had used as a kid. That was a side to Jaco that few people ever saw. He could be very giving, very compassionate.

I have some great memories of Jaco. About a year before he died, I was touring with my band and Jaco came by and sat in. He was sober, and he really sounded good. We jammed on "School Days" and "Birdland." I will never forget that.

To me, Jaco was like the Sid Vicious of jazz. They were both wild, rebellious figures who were self-destructive and died tragically young. But he will definitely go down in history as one of *the* cats.

BRANFORD MARSALIS
Saxophonist and former leader of the Tonight Show *band*

I bumped into Jaco all the time when I first got to New York in 1984. He sure was in bad shape, man. It was really disappointing to see him in that condition. That was really a letdown, because I had loved his solo record so much.

The first time I met him he wanted to play some basketball, but he really was not a good player. He was knocking me all over the court—very clumsy. It was on West Fourth Street, which had become kind of like his home. The last time I saw him semi-sane was in Japan. We were at the airport, and he pulled out this big wad of blow [cocaine] in the baggage-claim area. He was saying, "I got some good blow, man. You want some?" And I said, "Even if I did, don't you think you should not be doing that in baggage claim with cops around?" And he said, "Fuck that, man, they can't do nothin' to me." And he kept saying, "Come on, man. Hit it with me! Hit it with me!" It was a crazy scene. Jaco was hard to be around when he was high. But he was a great cat whenever he was straight.

JAMES CANNINGS
Guitarist; Jaco's roommate in 1985

Jaco's spirit was broken because he couldn't get a gig, he couldn't get a record deal, and he would constantly be hearing other bassists copying his style. That really angered him. But I think he intentionally sabotaged his own attempts to get back into the music industry. Just when something would be within his grasp, like a record deal or an endorsement deal with some instrument company, he would find a way to blow it. He would show up for a meeting drunk and out of control, or just disappear and miss the meeting altogether. He would go just so far toward getting his career back together, and then he would pull back.

In the end, Jaco really believed he had nothing more to live for. He said he had given the world everything he had to give and he had nothing more to offer. He made his statement and then decided it was time to go. I tried to tell him there was more room, that there were more things left for him to do musically. But he would say, "I don't have the spirit to do it."

PAUL BLEY
Free jazz pioneer who worked with Jaco in the mid '70s

I would speculate that Jaco had the same problem that Vivian Leigh had, in that he was hyper and never slept. I remember he used to come by my pad at four in the morning and knock on my door, requesting that we go to a jam session. He was always super hyper. When we were rehearsing, he'd keep playing with the amp off between tunes. His fingers never left the fretboard. And when he stopped playing, he'd run across the street and play ball in the park.

The tragedy of Jaco can't be explained by saying he got famous too fast. It was that he was super hyper and got frustrated because life wasn't high enough. He felt that if he wasn't playing all the time, he wasn't living up to his promise.

AIRTO MOREIRA
Percussionist formerly with Miles Davis and Weather Report

There was a spiritual side to Jaco that was very strong, and not many people ever knew about that. I remember calling him to do a recording with me on one of my albums, *I'm Fine, How Are You*. We did a beautiful duet together. We needed seven minutes of music to finish the album, so we decided to play free stuff in the studio. We both finished playing simultaneously, and when we went in the control room to check the time, it was exactly seven minutes—sort of a magical hookup. Jaco ended up naming the piece "Nativity," because he said the music was born there in the studio.

I always felt there was mutual respect between us. But I think his music got bigger than himself. He couldn't really play everything he wanted to play. The guy was way out there, man. And I respect that. His creative spirit was beautiful.

BOB MOSES
Drummer who played in a trio with Jaco and Pat Metheny

Long before I met Jaco, the psychedelic thing was happening, and I was pretty deeply into it. With psychedelics, there's a kind of heightened perception of reality, where every sound can be huge and every visual image larger than life. Jaco was there all the time. For some people, that's a special place where they would go occasionally—and others would never go there in a whole lifetime—but Jaco was able to sustain that naturally, somehow, just by being who he was. It was almost as if he was on an acid trip all the time, in the sense of being in that heightened state and having that kind of insight into his emotions. He was there all the time.

It's the kind of thing people attribute to gurus, but in reality there are probably very few gurus who are there at all. A lot of them are just playing at being there, so they can get the spoils. Jaco never set himself up to be a guru, yet he was always in that heightened state of consciousness.

GREGORY PASTORIUS
Jaco's younger brother

Jaco never slowed down. He was always on the manic edge, always pushing fun to the limit. He took me to the beach during the worst hurricanes, just to feel the power. It was a totally natural reaction to his environment. So many things came easily to him—music, sports, school—but it was music that came most naturally. That's why he did it. He said he heard music in everything—a baby crying, a car passing by, the wind in the palm trees. All of a sudden, he'd say, "Shhh!" and he'd listen. I didn't hear a thing.

Discography

CONTEMPORARY RECORDINGS

Jaco did his most important work as a leader and as a member of Weather Report and a sideman with Joni Mitchell. Therefore, those recordings are listed first. Other recordings follow, listed roughly in chronological order.

As A Leader

Jaco Pastorius, Epic 33949
   1976; with Herbie Hancock, Wayne Shorter, Don Alias, David Sanborn, Michael Brecker, Randy Brecker, Peter Graves, Howard Johnson, Narada Michael Walden, Bobby Economou, Michael Gibbs, Hubert Laws, Sam & Dave, Lenny White, Alex Darqui, Othello Molineaux, Leroy Williams, and Ron Tooley.

Word Of Mouth, Warner Bros. BSK 3535
   1981; with Herbie Hancock, Wayne Shorter, Michael Brecker, Toots Thielemans, Peter Erskine, Jack DeJohnette, Don Alias, Bobby Thomas Jr., Othello Molineaux, Leroy Williams, Dave Bargeron, John Clark, Jim Pugh, Bill Reichenbach, David Taylor, Snooky Young, Howard Johnson, Tom Scott, James Walker, and George Young.

Twins I & II, Warner Bros. 23876 (Japanese import)

1983 live recording from Word Of Mouth big band tour of Japan with Randy Brecker, Elmer Brown, Forrest Buchrel, Jon Faddis, Ron Tooley, Wayne Andre, Peter Graves, Bill Reichenbach, Dave Bargeron, Mario Cruz, Alex Foster, Bob Mintzer, Paul McCandless, Peter Gordon, Brad Warnaar, Toots Thielemans, Peter Erskine, Othello Molineaux, and Don Alias.

Invitation, Warner Bros. 237876-1

1983; U.S. compilation of *Twins I & II*; same lineup.

With Weather Report

Black Market, Columbia PC 24099

1976; with Wayne Shorter, Joe Zawinul, Alphonso Johnson, Chester Thompson, Narada Michael Walden, Alejandro Acuña, and Don Alias.

Heavy Weather, Columbia PC 24418

1977; with Wayne Shorter, Joe Zawinul, Alex Acuña, and Manolo Badrena.

Mr. Gone, Columbia JC 35358

1978; with Wayne Shorter, Joe Zawinul, Peter Erskine, Steve Gadd, and Tony Williams.

8:30, Columbia PC2 35358

1979 live recording with Wayne Shorter, Joe Zawinul, and Peter Erskine.

Night Passage, Columbia JC 36793

1980; with Wayne Shorter, Joe Zawinul, Peter Erskine, and Robert Thomas Jr.

Weather Report, Columbia PC 37616

1982; with Wayne Shorter, Joe Zawinul, Peter Erskine, and Robert Thomas Jr.

Havana Jam I, Columbia PC2 36053

1979 concert in Havana, Cuba, with Weather Report; also featuring the Trio Of Doom with John McLaughlin and Tony Williams.

Havana Jam II, Columbia PC2 36180

More material from the 1979 concert in Havana.

With Joni Mitchell

Hejira, Asylum 7E 1087

1976; with Larry Carlton and Bobbye Hall.

Don Juan's Reckless Daughter, Asylum BB-701

1977; with Don Alias, Manolo Badrena, Airto, Wayne Shorter, Alex Acuña, and John Guerin.

Mingus, Asylum 5E 505

1979; with Wayne Shorter, Herbie Hancock, Peter Erskine, Don Alias, and Emil Richards.

Shadows and Light, Asylum 704

1979 live recording with Pat Metheny, Lyle Mays, Michael Brecker, Don Alias, and the Persuasions.

With Little Beaver

Party Down, Cat 2604

1974; featuring Jaco (listed as Nelson "Jacko" Padron) with Willie "Little Beaver" Hale, Timmy Thomas, George Perry, and Robert Ferguson.

With Paul Bley

Jaco, Improvising Artists IAI-373846

1974; with Bley, Bruce Ditmas, and Pat Metheny.

With Pat Metheny

Bright Size Life, ECM 1073

1975; with Metheny and Bob Moses.

With Ira Sullivan

Ira Sullivan, A&M/Horizon SP-706

1975; featuring Jaco on one track, "Portrait of Sal La Rosa," with Steve Bagby, Joe Diorio, and Don Alias.

With Albert Mangelsdorff

Trilogue-Live!, Pausa PR-7055
> 1976 recording at the Berlin Jazz Festival featuring the trio of Jaco, Mangelsdorff, and Alphonse Mouzon. Reissued on CD in 1994 by Verve/MPS as part of a two-disc Mangelsdorff retrospective.

With Al Di Meola

Land of the Midnight Sun, Columbia PC 34074
> 1976; featuring Jaco on one track, "Suite: Golden Dawn," with Di Meola, Alphonse Mouzon, and Barry Miles.

With Airto

I'm Fine, How Are You, Warner Bros. BS 3084
> 1977; featuring Jaco on one track, "Nativity," a duet with Airto.

With Herbie Hancock

Sunlight, Columbia JC 34907
> 1978; featuring Jaco on one track, "Good Question," with Hancock, Tony Williams, Bill Summers, and Raul Rekow.

Mr. Hands, Columbia JC 36578
> 1980; featuring Jaco on one track, "4 A.M.," with Hancock, Harvey Mason, and Bill Summers.

With Ian Hunter

All-American Alien Boy, Columbia FC 34142
> 1976; featuring Jaco on the entire album, including guitar on the final track, "God (Take One)."

With Tom Scott

Intimate Strangers, Columbia JC 35557
> 1978; featuring Jaco on the track "Lost Inside the Love of You."

With Flora Purim

Everyday Everynight, Warner Bros. BSK 3168
> 1978; featuring Jaco on four tracks, "The Hope," "Five Four," "Blues Ballad," and his own composition "Las Olas."

With Cockrell & Santos

New Beginnings, A&M SP-4712
  1978; featuring Jaco on one track, "I Tried It All."

With Michel Colombier

Michel Colombier, Chrysalis CHR 1212
  1979; with Herbie Hancock, Michael Brecker, Tom Scott, Larry
  Carlton, Ray Parker Jr., Lee Ritenour, Peter Erskine, Steve Gadd,
  Airto, Michael Boddicker, and the London Symphony Orchestra.

With Bob Mintzer

Source, Agharta C25Y-0035
  1982; featuring Jaco on two tracks, "I Don't Know" and "Spiral,"
  with Mintzer, Randy Brecker, Lew Soloff, Alan Ruben, Tom Malone, Bill Washer, Don Grolnick, and Peter Erskine.

With Randy Bernsen

Music For Planets, People & Washing Machines, Zebra 5756
  1984; featuring Jaco on two tracks, "Olde Hats" and "Windsong,"
  with Bernsen, Peter Erskine, Taras Kovayl, Paul Horn-Muller,
  Othello Molineaux, Robert Thomas Jr., Herbie Hancock, Michael
  Urbaniak, Urszula Dudziak, Melton Mustafa, and Rich Frank.
Mo' Wasabi, Zebra ZEB 5857
  1986; featuring Jaco on two tracks, "Swing Thing" and "Cali-
  foric," with Bernsen, Peter Erskine, Toots Thielemans, Taras
  Kovayl, Herbie Hancock, Bobby Economou, Robert Thomas Jr.,
  and Ray Lyon.
Paradise Citizens, Zebra ZEB 42132
  1988; featuring Jaco on one track, the title cut, with Bernsen,
  Alex Darqui, and Mark Griffith. Includes a version of Jaco's
  "Continuum."

With Deadline

Down by Law, Celluloid 6122
  1985; featuring Jaco on one track, "Makossa Soul," with Jonas

Hellborg, Paul Butterfield, Bill Laswell, Phillip Wilson, and Manu Dibango.

With Brian Melvin

Night Food, Timeless SJP 214
1985; with Melvin, Rick Smith, Jon Davis, and Paul Mousavi.
Jazz Street, Timeless SJP 258
1986; with Melvin, Rick Smith, Jon Davis, and Paul Mousavi. Released posthumously in 1989.
Nightfood, Global Pacific GPD 333
1986; with Melvin, Bob Weir, Jon Davis, Rick Smith, Paul Mousavi, Merl Saunders, and Andy Narell. Released posthumously in 1988.
Standards Zone, Global Pacific R2 79335
1986; with Melvin and Jon Davis. Released posthumously in 1990.

With Jimmy Cliff

Cliff Hanger, Columbia CK 40002
1985; featuring Jaco on one track, "Brown Eyes."

With Mike Stern

Upside Downside, Atlantic 81656-1
1986; featuring Jaco on one track, "Mood Swings," with Stern, Steve Jordan, and Bob Berg.

With Bireli Lagrene

Stuttgart Aria, Jazzpoint JP 1019
1986 studio recording with Lagrene, Peter Lubke, Vladislaw Sendecki, and Serge Bringolf.
Live in Italy, Jimco JIM-0068
1986 live recording with Lagrene and Thomas Borocz. Released posthumously in 1990.

POSTHUMOUS RELEASES

It is a sad irony that the number of posthumous Jaco releases exceeds his recorded output during the years when he was alive. And like the material that has been rushed onto the market after other great artists have died, the posthumous Jaco releases vary greatly in quality, ranging from poorly recorded impromptu jam sessions to some fairly decent documents of his later years.

In addition to the recordings listed below, there are a number of other projects in the works. Warner Bros. is reportedly preparing a boxed set of previously unissued Jaco material, including performances from Jaco's 30th birthday party jam. And Bob Bobbing, Jaco's friend from the early days in South Florida, has formed Holiday Park Records in order to release *Portrait of Jaco: The Evolution of a Genius,* a two-CD anthology of early recordings by Jaco, culled from Bobbing's personal archive of gig tapes from 1968 to 1975.

Regarding the recordings listed here, it's important to note that many of them have been marketed without any concern for, or benefit to, Jaco's family. One exception is the recordings issued by Neil Weiss of Big World Records, who appears to be working in good faith with the Pastorius estate. An avid Jaco fan, Weiss attended many of Jaco's gigs in New York City in 1985–86 and recorded virtually everything with a Sony Pro Walkman. "I made no secret about the fact that I was recording," says Weiss. "I never sat in the back of the room and hid the tape recorder under the table. I always sat up front and had the microphone in clear view."

Unfortunately, Weiss's cassettes of Jaco's gigs do not rival professional live recordings, and it's a matter of debate whether or not these tapes should have been released. It is the contention of Jaco's brothers, Rory and Greg, as well as Jaco's father and his first wife, Tracy, that Weiss is doing a disservice to Jaco's legacy. "My children wept when they heard these CDs," says Tracy. "They're terrible. I personally don't need 19 minutes of 'Teen Town,' and I don't think the rest of the world does either." Nevertheless, Weiss is contributing $1.00 per CD sold toward a fund set up to provide for Jaco's four children. In addition, he is paying royalties to all of the musicians who appear on the discs.

Most of the other posthumous recordings are bootlegs, which means they do not benefit anyone other than the company that issued them. And most are of exceedingly poor quality. While they may hold some value for scholars (and fanatics), it's impossible to recommend them on either musical or ethical grounds. Perhaps the most controversial of all is the notorious *Holiday for Pans,* which was released in 1991 on the Japanese Sound Hills label. Originally recorded by Jaco in 1982 as a showcase for steel-pans virtuoso Othello Molineaux, it was rejected by Warner Bros. as lacking in commercial potential. The tapes eventually fell into the hands of engineer and would-be entrepreneur Kenny Jackel (see Chapter 7), who tried to sell them to various U.S. labels before finding a buyer in Japan. The Pastorius estate has sued to prevent distribution of *Holiday for Pans,* but it is still widely available throughout Europe, Canada, and Asia.

Live in New York City, Vol. 1: Punk Jazz, Big World 1001
    1985 recordings with Hiram Bullock, Kenwood Dennard, Alex
    Foster, Butch Thomas, Delmar Brown, Michael Gerber, and Jerry
    Gonzalez; released in 1990.
Live in New York City, Vol. 2: Trio, Big World 1002
    1985 recordings with Hiram Bullock and Kenwood Dennard;
    released in 1991.
Live in New York City, Vol. 3: Promise Land, Big World 1003
    1985 recordings with same lineup as Vol. 1; released in 1991.
Live in New York City, Vol. 4: Trio 2, Big World 1004
    1984–85 recordings with Hiram Bullock, Kenwood Dennard, Victor Lewis, and Steve Ferrone; released in 1992.
Honestly, Jimco JIM-0069
    Live solo performance from March, 1986, in Italy; released in 1990.

Live in Italy, Jimco JIM-0068

   1986 performance with Bireli Lagrene and Thomas Borocz; released in 1990.

Blackbird, Timeless ALCR-123

   1984 live duet performance with Rashied Ali; released in 1991.

PDB, DIW-827

   1986 live recording with Hiram Bullock and Kenwood Dennard; released in 1989.

Natural, DIW-331

   1985 jam in the studio with Yaco Grau, Francisco Mondragon Rio, and Hugh Peterson; released in 1988.

Essence, DIW-831

   1984 recording with Delmar Brown, Michael Gerber, Yaco Grau, and Carlos Cervantes; released in 1988.

Holiday for Pans, Sound Hills 8001

   Stolen master tapes of sessions from 1982, notorious for fradulent use of Jaco clones filling in missing basslines on the unfinished master tapes. Released in Japan in 1993, it has been legally banned from any Stateside distribution following an exhaustive legal case mounted by the Pastorius estate.

The Birthday Concert, Warner Bros. 45290-2

   Jaco in fine form fronting a 23-piece Word Of Mouth big band featuring such superb soloists as tenor saxophonists Michael Brecker and Bob Mintzer, trumpeter Randy Brecker and steel pans ace Othello Molineaux. Recorded live to 24-track remote at Mr. Pip's nightclub in Fort Lauderdale, Florida on the occcasion of Jaco's 30th birthday in 1981; released in 1995.

Stone Free: A Tribute To Jimi Hendrix, Reprise 45438-2

   On Pat Metheny's raucous interpretation of "Third Stone From The Sun," a sample of a Jaco signature bass groove is used to hold down the funk while bassist Matthew Garrison plays the melody on top in real time; released in 1993.

TRIBUTES

Jaco's friends and colleagues have remembered him by playing his compositions, recording compositions inspired by or dedicated to him, and even putting together entire albums in his memory. Three of the notable tribute albums are:

Bob Mintzer, *I Remember Jaco*, RCA/Novus (1992)
> An album of original impressions of Jaco, including a version of Jaco's "Three Views of a Secret"; players include Mintzer, Michael Formanek, Jeff Andrews, Peter Erskine, Joey Calderazzo, and Frank Malabe.

Joe Ferry, *We Remember Pastorius*, Toshiba/Japan (1991)
> More original impressions, including versions of Jaco's "Teen Town" and "Portrait of Tracy"; players include Will Lee, Dr. John, Adam Nussbaum, George Mraz, Eddie Gomez, Randy Brecker, Alex Foster, Kenwood Dennard, Hiram Bullock, Joey Calderazzo, Dave Weckl, Glenn Alexander, Charles Blenzig, and Rob Aries.

Basstorius: Music Inspired by the Genius of Jaco Pastorius, Hot Wire Records/Germany (1993)
> Compiled by Bert Gerecht, this tribute features bassists from around the world, including England's Laurence Cottle and Mo Foster, Germany's Ben Hullenkremer and Kai Eckhardt, Spain's Carlos Benavent, Scotland's Alan Thomson, Italy's Carlo Mombelli, and Americans Dave LaRue and Matt Garrison.

Individual tracks that honor Jaco can be found on many albums, including:

Marc Beacco, *The Crocodile Smile*, Nova (1991)
> Includes track titled "A Dirty Dance with Jaco."

Michel Camilo, *Suntan*, ProJazz (1987)
> Includes Jaco's "(Used to Be a) Cha-Cha" and "Las Olas."

Michel Camilo, *On the Other Hand*, Epic (1990)
> Includes Jaco's "City of Angels."

Stanley Clarke, *If This Bass Could Only Talk*, Portrait (1990)
> Includes "Goodbye Pork Pie Hat" (dedicated to Jaco & Gil Evans).

Miles Davis, *Amandla,* Warner Bros. (1989)
    Includes the Marcus Miller composition, "Mr. Pastorius."
Miles Davis, *Live Around The World,* Warner Bros. (1996)
    Includes a live version of "Mr. Pastorius."
Kenwood Dennard, *Just Advance,* Big World (1992)
    Includes Jaco's "Teen Town."
Elements, *Spirit River,* RCA/ Novus (1990)
    Includes "Carnavaloco" (dedicated to Jaco).
Eliane Elias, *So Far So Close,* Blue Note (1989)
    Includes track titled "Straight Across (To Jaco)."
Mo Foster, *Bel Assis,* Relativity (1991)
    Includes track titled "Jaco."
Roberto Gatto, *Ask,* Gala (1988)
    Includes "Tango's Time (To Jaco Pastorius)."
Michael Gerber, *This Is Michael Gerber,* Big World (1994)
    Includes Jaco's "Las Olas" and "Continuum."
Gil Goldstein, *City of Dreams,* Blue Note (1990)
    Includes Jaco's "Three Views of a Secret" and "Balloon Song."
Jonas Hellborg, *Bass,* Day Eight Music (1987)
    Includes track titled "Jaco."
Bireli Lagrene, *Acoustic Moments,* Blue Note (1991)
    Includes Jaco's "Three Views of a Secret."
Pat Metheny Group, ECM (1978)
    Includes Pat Metheny's "Jaco."
Marcus Miller, *The Sun Don't Lie,* PRA (1993)
    Includes Jaco's "Teen Town."
Othello Molineaux, *It's About Time,* Big World (1993)
    Includes Jaco's "Havona."
Bob Moses, *Time Stood Still,* Gramavision (1994)
    Includes track titled "Jaco."
Perri, *Celebrate!,* Zebra/MCA (1986)
    Includes Pat Metheny's "Jaco."
Wallace Roney, *Misterios,* Warner Bros. (1994)
    Includes Jaco's "71+."
Dave Samuels, *Three Degrees North,* MCA (1989)
    Includes track titled "Para Pastorius."
Leni Stern, *Secrets,* Enja (1989)
    Includes "Who Loves You" (dedicated to Jaco).
Turtle Island String Quartet, *Metropolis,* Windham Hill (1989)
    Includes Pat Metheny's "Jaco."
UZEB, *World Tour '90,* Disque Avant-Garde/France (1991)
    Includes "Donna Lee" (in memory of Jaco).
Lenny White, *The Manhattan Project,* Blue Note (1990)
    Includes Jaco's "Dania."
Yellowjackets, *Politics,* MCA (1988)
    Includes "Galileo" (dedicated to Jaco).

Index

BIRD. TRANE. JIMI. JACO.

The Great Ones
Always Gave Us
Reason To Celebrate

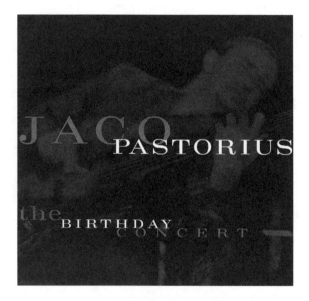

JACO
THE BIRTHDAY CONCERT

Recorded December, 1981
featuring the Word Of Mouth Orchestra
with Michael Brecker, Bob Mintzer,
Peter Erskine, Don Alias, et al.

Available on WB Records